East
of the Sun

HARCOURT BRACE JOVANOVICH, PUBLISHERS
Orlando   San Diego   Chicago   Dallas

East of the Sun

ODYSSEY **An HBJ Literature Program**
Second Edition

Sam Leaton Sebesta

Consultants

Elaine M. Aoki

Willard E. Bill

Sylvia Engdahl

Myra Cohn Livingston

Daphne P. Muse

Sandra McCandless Simons

Margaret D. Simpson

Barre Toelken

Acknowledgments

For permission to reprint copyrighted material, grateful acknowledgment is made to the following sources:

The Ashland Poetry Press: "Today Song" from *A Poetry Ritual for Grammar Schools* by Robert McGovern. The Ashland Poetry Press, 1974.

Atheneum Publishers, Inc.: Adaptation of "Hieroglyphics" from *The Egypt Game* by Zilpha Keatley Snyder. Copyright © 1967 by Zilpha Keatley Snyder. "Metaphor" from *It Doesn't Always Have to Rhyme* by Eve Merriam. Copyright © 1964 by Eve Merriam. "Wailed a ghost in a graveyard at Kew" from *A Lollygag of Limericks* by Myra Cohn Livingston (A Margaret K. McElderry Book). Copyright © 1978 by Myra Cohn Livingston. First verse from "Hickenthrift and Hickenloop" in THE PHANTOM ICE CREAM MAN *More Nonsense Verse* by X. J. Kennedy (A Margaret K. McElderry Book). Copyright © 1979 by X. J. Kennedy.

The Bobbs-Merrill Company, Inc. and Faber and Faber Limited: "My Uncle Dan" and "My Aunt Dora" from *Meet My Folks* by Ted Hughes. Copyright © 1961, 1973 by Ted Hughes. From *Steal Away Home* by Jane Kristof. Copyright © 1969 by Jane Kristof.

Brandt & Brandt Literary Agents, Inc.: "Wilbur Wright and Orville Wright" from *A Book of Americans* by Stephen Vincent Benet. Copyright 1933 by Rosemary and Stephen Vincent Benet; renewed copyright © 1961 by Rosemary Carr Benet. Published by Holt, Rinehart and Winston, Inc.

Don Congdon Associates, Inc.: "The Homecoming" from *The Homecoming and Other Plays* by Earl Hamner, Jr. Copyright © 1973 by Earl Hamner, Jr.

Coward, McCann & Geoghegan, Inc.: Adapted from *Where Was Patrick Henry on the 29th of May?* by Jean Fritz. Text copyright © 1975 by Jean Fritz.

The Dial Press: "I Never Asked for No Allergy" from *Philip Hall Likes Me. I Reckon Maybe* (Retitled: "An Allergy Is a Bothersome Thing") by Bette Greene. Copyright © 1974 by Bette Greene.

Dodd, Mead & Company: "There was an Old Lady of Chertsey" and "There Was a Young Girl of Majorca" from *The Complete Nonsense Book* by Edward Lear.

Doubleday & Company, Inc.: From *Call Me Ruth* (Titled: "Our First Thanksgiving") by Marilyn Sachs. Copyright © 1982 by Marilyn Sachs. "Direction" by Alonzo Lopez from *The Whispering Wind,* edited by Terry Allen. Copyright © 1972 by the Institute of American Indian Arts. "Dinky" from *The Collected Poems of Theodore Roethke* by Theodore Roethke. Copyright 1953 by Theodore Roethke. Text and melody from "John Henry" by Bascom Lamar Lunsford.

E. P. Dutton: From *My Side of the Mountain* (Retitled: "Bando") by Jean George. Copyright © 1959 by Jean George. "Wind is a ghost" from *Whirlwind Is a Ghost Dancing* by Natalia Belting. Text copyright © 1974 by Natalia Belting.

Environmental Action: "This Earth Is Sacred" (Titled: "All Things Are Connected") by Chief Sealth from page 7 in *Environmental Action,* November 11, 1972.

Farrar, Straus and Giroux, Inc.: From *KneeKnock Rise* (Retitled: "The Megrimum") by Natalie Babbitt. Copyright © 1970 by Natalie Babbitt. From *The Cricket in Times Square* (Retitled: "A Very Talented Cricket") by George Selden. Illustrated by Garth Williams. Copyright © 1960 by George Selden Thompson and Garth Williams.

Four Winds Press, a division of Scholastic Magazines, Inc.; "Riddle me, riddle me . . ." and "Why is hot bread . . ." from *The Nonsense Book,* collected by Duncan Emrich. Text copyright © 1970 by Duncan Emrich. From *The Hodgepodge Book,* collected by Duncan Emrich. Text copyright © 1972 by Duncan Emrich.

Grosset & Dunlap, Inc.: "Riddle" from *The Sparrow Bush* by Elizabeth Coatsworth. Copyright © 1966 by Grosset & Dunlap, Inc.

Harcourt Brace Jovanovich, Inc.: "I called to the wind" by Kyorai from *More Cricket Songs: Japanese Haiku,* translated by Harry Behn. Copyright © 1971 by Harry Behn. "Laughing Gas," slightly adapted from *Mary Poppins* by

P. L. Travers. Copyright 1934, 1962 by P. L. Travers. Abridged and adapted from *Half Magic* (Retitled: "The Tournament") by Edward Eager. Copyright 1954 by Harcourt Brace Jovanovich, Inc.

Harcourt Brace Jovanovich, Inc., M. T. Parsons and The Hogarth Press: Slight abridgment and adaptation of "Two of Everything" by Li Po from *The Treasure of Li-Po* by Alice Ritchie. Copyright 1949 by Harcourt Brace Jovanovich, Inc.; renewed 1977 by M. T. Ritchie.

Harper & Row, Publishers, Inc.: "Stories from Kansas" (Retitled: "Which") in *Allegiances* by William Stafford. Copyright © 1968 by William Stafford. "Running away . . ." from NEAR THE WINDOW TREE: *Poems and Notes* by Karla Kuskin. Copyright © 1975 by Karla Kuskin. Adapted text from "The Worst Morning" in *. . . and now Miguel* by Joseph Krumgold (Thomas Y. Crowell Co.). Copyright 1953 by Joseph Krumgold. "When first I appear . . .," "A nickel and a dime . . .," and "Why did the lobster . . ." from *The American Riddle Book* by Carl Withers and Dr. Sula Benet (Abelard-Schuman Co.). Copyright 1954 by Carl Withers and Dr. Sula Benet. Five lines from "A Tooter Who Tooted a Flute . . .," 24 lines from "Betty Botter," and 13 lines from "A tree toad . . ." in *A Twister of Twists, a Tangler of Tongues* by Alvin Schwartz (J. B. Lippincott). Copyright © 1972 by Alvin Schwartz.

Holt, Rinehart and Winston, Publishers: "The Secret Sits" from *The Poetry of Robert Frost,* edited by Edward Connery Lathem. Copyright 1942 by Robert Frost. Copyright © 1969 by Holt, Rinehart and Winston. Copyright © 1970 by Lesley Frost Ballantine.

Houghton Mifflin Company: From *Island of the Blue Dolphins* (Titled: "Dangerous Voyage") by Scott O'Dell. Copyright © 1960 by Scott O'Dell.

Alfred A. Knopf, Inc.: "Sea Calm" from *Selected Poems of Langston Hughes* by Langston Hughes. Copyright 1926 by Alfred A. Knopf, Inc.; renewed 1954 by Langston Hughes.

Little, Brown and Company: "I Want That Dog" from *Mine For Keeps* by Jean Little. Copyright © 1962 by Jean Little.

Little, Brown and Company in association with the Atlantic Monthly Press: "Saved by a Whisker" from *By the Great Horn Spoon!* by Sid Fleischman. Copyright © 1963 by Albert A. Fleischman.

Lothrop, Lee & Shepard Co., a division of William Morrow & Company: Adapted from pages 66–92 in *Thank You, Jackie Robinson* (Retitled: "Something for Davy") by Barbara Cohen. Copyright 1974 by Barbara Cohen.

Macmillan Publishing Company: "Ambassador to the Enemy," adapted from Chapter XII of *Caddie Woodlawn* by Carol Ryrie Brink. Copyright 1935 by Macmillan Publishing Company; renewed 1963 by Carol Ryrie Brink. Adapted from *The House of Dies Drear* by Virginia Hamilton. Copyright © 1968 by Virginia Hamilton.

Macmillan Publishing Co., Inc. and Collins Publishers: From *The Lion, The Witch and The Wardrobe* (Retitled: "Lucy's Adventure") by C. S. Lewis. Copyright 1950 by Macmillan Publishing Co., Inc.; copyright renewed 1978 by Arthur Owen Barfield.

McGraw-Hill Book Company: "Old Ben" from *Dawn of Remembered Spring* by Jesse Stuart. Copyright © 1972 by Jesse Stuart.

David McKay Co., Inc. and Mrs. Helen Thurber: from Plays and How To Put Them On by Moyne Rice Smith. © 1961 by Moyne Rice Smith. Published by Henry Z. Walck, Inc. Based on the book *The Great Quillow* by James Thurber. Copyright © 1944 by James Thurber. Copyright © 1972 by Helen W. Thurber. Published by Harcourt Brace Jovanovich, Inc.

Eve Merriam: "Elizabeth Blackwell" from *Independent Voices* by Eve Merriam. Copyright © 1968 by Eve Merriam.

William Morrow & Co.: "I brought to the New World the gift of devotion" from *North Star Shining* by Hildegard Hoyt Swift. Copyright 1947 by Hildegard Hoyt Swift and Lynd Ward.

Clarkson N. Potter, Inc., a division of Crown Publishers, Inc.: "The Walrus and the Carpenter" from *The Annotated Alice* by Lewis Carroll. Introduction and notes by Martin Gardner. Copyright © 1960 by Martin Gardner.

Rand McNally & Co.: Two riddles from *Would You Put Money In a Sand Bank?* by Harold Longman. Copyright 1968 by Harold Longman. Published by Rand McNally & Co.

Marian Reiner, agent for the author: "The Fourth" by Myra Cohn Livingston. Copyright © 1976, 1986 by Myra Cohn Livingston. This poem, under the title "Fourth of July, 1976," appeared in a slightly different version in *Cricket,* July, 1976.

The Heirs of Knud Rasmussen: "And I think over again . . ." (Retitled: "Song") from *Intellectual Culture of the Copper Eskimos,* translated by Knud Rasmussen.

Rothco Cartoons, Inc.: "There Was a Young Lady of Bright" by A. H. Reginald Buller from *Punch Magazine.* © Punch/Rothco.

Charles Scribner's Sons: From *Farmer in the Sky* (Retitled: "Emergency in Space") by Robert A. Heinlein. Copyright 1950 by Robert A. Heinlein.

Ian Serraillier: Slight abridgment from *The Way of Danger* (Retitled: "A Hero's Promise") by Ian Serraillier. Published by Henry Z. Walck, Inc. Copyright © 1962 by Ian Serraillier; © 1965 by Heinemann Educational Books, London.

United Educators, Inc.: "East O' the Sun and West O' the Moon" from *The Magic Garden of My Book House* (Vol. 7) in *My Book House,* edited by Olive Beaupre Miller. © The United Educators, Inc.

Viking Penguin Inc.: "The Incredible Shrinking Machine" from *Einstein Anderson Science Sleuth* by Seymour Simon. Copyright © 1980 by Seymour Simon.

Art Acknowledgments

Chuck Bowden: 213, 277, 315, 393, 451 (adapted from photographs from the following sources: 315, courtesy Farrar Straus & Giroux; 393, courtesy of Houghton Mifflin Company; 451, courtesy Little, Brown & Co.); Sharon Harker: 84–85 top, 87, 100–103 top, 153, 214–217 top, 239, 335, 413, 432–439 top, 467; Jean Little: 231 (adapted from photograph courtesy Little, Brown & Co.); Jerry Smath: 84–85 bottom, 100–103 bottom, 214–217 bottom, 432–439 bottom.

Cover: Tom Leonard.

Maps: Joanna Adamska Koperska.

Unit Openers: Jane Teiko Oka, 1–6.
Robert Masheris, 7.

Photo Acknowledgments

RESEARCH CREDITS: Waldemar H. Lehn, University of Manitoba: 82; FRANKLIN INSTITUTE: 96; The Bettmann Archive: 234; Horsehead Nebula (source unknown): 264; © Stock Imagery, Sally Brown: 370; DPI, © Leverett Bradley: 371 bottom; Gamma-Liaison, © Chip Hires: 371 top; Shostal: 372, 373; Frederick Lewis, Inc.: 374; The Granger Collection: 461.

Contents

3 Never Give Up *155*

1 It Must Be a Trick

A Tricky Twisty Trio

Traditional tongue twisters collected by Alvin Schwartz

Betty Botter
　　bought some butter,
But, she said,
　　the butter's bitter.
If I put it
　　in my batter,
It will make
　　my batter bitter.
But a bit
　　of better butter—
That would make
　　my batter better.
So she bought
　　a bit of butter,
Better than
　　her bitter butter.
And she put it
　　in her batter,
And the batter
　　was not bitter.
So 'twas better
　　Betty Botter
Bought a bit
　　of better butter.

A tree toad loved a she-toad
    That lived up in a tree.
She was a three-toed tree toad,
    But a two-toed toad was he.
The two-toed toad tried to win
    The she-toad's friendly nod,
For the two-toed toad loved the ground
    On which the three-toed toad trod.
But no matter how the two-toed tree toad tried,
    He could not please her whim.
In her tree-toad bower,
    With her three-toed power,
The she-toad vetoed him.

A tooter who tooted a flute
    Tried to tutor two tutors to toot.
Said the two to the tutor,
    "Is it harder to toot or
To tutor two tutors to toot?"

Illustrated by Marie-Louise Gay

The Incredible Shrinking Machine

A story by Seymour Simon

Illustrated by Keith Neely

No case is ever too tough for Einstein Anderson, Science Sleuth, and his sidekick Margaret Michaels. Armed only with a talent for scientific reasoning, Einstein and Margaret solve riddles and puzzles many people cannot figure out.

Once in a while, however, Einstein and Margaret try to trick each other to see who is the better science detective. So far, Einstein has always figured out Margaret's puzzles. This time, however, Margaret may have come up with a puzzle that even Einstein cannot solve!

Margaret Michaels was Einstein's good friend and arch rival. Science was their favorite subject. Einstein and Margaret were always talking about important things like atoms, planets, and who was the best science student.

Margaret had left to visit her aunt for a week as soon as school was let out for the summer. Einstein knew that Margaret was back and wondered why she hadn't called him. Finally he decided to call and find out.

"Hello, Margaret, what's happening? How is your aunt? How come you didn't call?"

"Einstein," Margaret said, "I was just about to call you. Aunt Bess drove me home two days ago and stayed to visit my parents. She's going to drive back tomorrow, and she said it would be O.K. if I invited a friend to her house for the weekend. She's a biology professor at State University and has all kinds of science stuff at her house that you might like to see. How would you like to go?"

Einstein was about to refuse because his family was going to the beach on Sunday, when Margaret continued.

"Also, I have a science puzzle to show you at Aunt Bess's that even the great Einstein Anderson can't solve."

Well, that changed everything. Einstein couldn't turn down a science challenge from Margaret, so he agreed to go. He spent the rest of the day playing baseball with some classmates and wondering about the puzzle that Margaret had mentioned.

Einstein and Margaret were driven by Aunt Bess early in the morning on Saturday. They arrived at Remsen, a town near the State University, just after 8:00 A.M. Aunt Bess's house was in a sort of clearing surrounded by trees. Instead of first going inside,

Margaret led Einstein behind the house and down a twisting path in the woods.

Hidden from the house at the end of the path was a small shack with a bright yellow door. The early-morning sun shone directly on the yellow door and made it look almost like gold.

Margaret unlocked the yellow door and motioned Einstein inside. Einstein noticed that the single room they entered had no other doors and only one small window. The only objects in the room were a large stone table and a small black box sitting on the table.

"Einstein, look over the stone table closely," Margaret said. "It was put together right in this room. You can see that it is too big to pass through the door or the window. You would have to break it into little pieces to get it out of the room."

18

Einstein checked the table carefully. He could see that what Margaret said was true. You would need a bulldozer to break up that old stone table.

"I'm now going to switch on my incredible shrinking machine," said Margaret. She flipped a switch on the side of the little black box. Nothing much happened except that the black box sort of burbled once and then was quiet.

Margaret motioned Einstein to follow her out. "We'll have to leave the room so as not to shrink ourselves," she said. "But when we come back in a few hours, the table will be gone without a trace. The incredible shrinking machine will have reduced it down to the size of an atom."

Margaret led Einstein back to Aunt Bess's house. For the rest of the day Einstein and Margaret experimented with chemical indicators such as litmus and brom thymol blue. They used a microscope to look at the protozoa in a drop of pond water. They fed food pellets to Aunt Bess's laboratory white mice. Lunch for Einstein and Margaret was peanut butter and jelly sandwiches.

Aunt Bess started an outdoor barbecue going late in the afternoon. They had grilled hamburgers, newly picked corn, a fresh tomato salad, and watermelon for dessert. It was all delicious and they didn't finish washing and straightening up till eight o'clock.

It was twilight when Margaret led Einstein back by a different path to the shack. They arrived just as the setting sun shone directly on the yellow door, turning it golden, just as it had done in the morning.

Margaret unlocked the door and they went inside. The room looked almost the same: one door, one small window, and one small black box. But the big stone table was gone. Nothing, not even a chip of stone, remained on the floor.

At first Einstein couldn't believe his eyes. Margaret might really stump him this time. How could that big stone table just disappear? Had Margaret really invented a shrinking machine?

Margaret smiled at the look on Einstein's face. "Well," she asked, "what do you think of my incredible shrinking machine?"

Einstein was quiet for a few minutes. Then his face changed and he began to laugh. He pushed back his glasses, which had slipped down. "You almost had me there for a minute, Margaret," he said. "I think I know what happened to the table. And if I'm correct, there is no such thing as an incredible shrinking machine."

Can you solve the puzzle: What do you think happened to the table?

"The key to the puzzle," Einstein began his explanation, "is the sun."

"The sun!" Margaret exclaimed. "What does the sun have to do with the shrinking machine?"

"You know that the sun rises in the east in the morning and sets in the west in the evening," Einstein explained. "Yet both the rising sun and the setting sun shone directly on the yellow door. That's impossible."

"So what's the answer?" Margaret asked.

"Simple," Einstein said. "There must be two doors and two rooms in the shack, one in back and one in front. The sun shone on one door in the morning and on the other door in the afternoon. You must have taken me into one room in the morning but into the other room in the afternoon. The first room contained the stone table. The other room didn't have anything in it."

"You're right," said Margaret.

They left the shack and started back to the house. "I see that I made one mistake," Margaret said, shaking her head.

"What's that?" Einstein asked.

"I should have shown you my incredible shrinking machine on a cloudy day."

"Right," said Einstein. "Your machine had me in the dark for a while. But it was the sun that let me see the light."

Questions

1. Do you think Margaret, or Aunt Bess, or both, planned the trick on Einstein? Explain.

2. Each clue below could be used to solve Margaret's puzzle. Which clue did Einstein use? Explain how it helped him.
   a. Two paths led to the shack. (pages 18 and 20)
   b. The sunlight shone on the door both in the morning and the evening. (pages 18 and 20)

3. If the story had happened on a cloudy day, how could Einstein have solved the puzzle?

4. Which word in parentheses means the same as each underlined word from the story?
   a. It was an <u>incredible</u> (unbelievable, huge) shrinking machine.
   b. The table disappeared without a <u>trace</u> (drawing, sign).
   c. Margaret almost <u>stumped</u> (tricked, surprised) Einstein.

Activity   Draw and Explain a Diagram

Margaret drew a careful *diagram,* or plan, of the small shack, its rooms, and the surrounding paths. She used the diagram to work out her puzzle for Einstein. Here is part of Margaret's diagram. Redraw the diagram on a piece of paper. Then finish it and label each part. Use details from the story to help you. Be ready to use the diagram to show exactly how Margaret's plan worked.

Margaret's Diagram

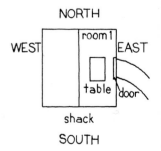

23

The Tournament

From the novel *Half Magic* by Edward Eager

Illustrated by Jerry Smath

The old coin that Jane found looked almost like a nickel, but it bore strange signs and worked a strange magic—it granted half the wishes its owners made. Soon Jane, her brother Mark, and her sisters Katharine and Martha were all wishing on the magic charm.

Katharine remembered to double her wishes when her turn came. "I wish," she said, "that we may go back twice as far as to the days of King Arthur, and see two tournaments, and go on two quests, and do two good deeds." With the charm's "half magic," the four children found themselves in the England of King Arthur's time. The quest that followed led them to Sir Launcelot, the greatest knight of the Round Table, who was locked in a dungeon by his enemy, Morgan le Fay. With the charm's help, Katharine rescued Sir Launcelot. But was he grateful? Not a bit. He preferred to escape without the help of magic. So an angry Katharine undid her good deed and wished herself and the others to a tournament at Camelot. When they arrive, Katharine still has half of two good deeds to do.

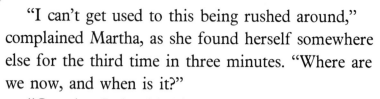

"I can't get used to this being rushed around," complained Martha, as she found herself somewhere else for the third time in three minutes. "Where are we now, and when is it?"

"Camelot, I should think," said Katharine, "in tournament time! Look!"

Jane and Mark and Martha looked. Camelot and the field of tournament looked exactly as you would expect them to look, from the descriptions in *The Boy's King Arthur* and the wonderful books of Mr. T. H. White. Trumpets were blowing clarion calls, and pennons fluttered on the blue air, and armor flashed in the bright light. Gallant knights and trusty squires and faithful pages and ladies fair were crowding into the stands in hundreds to watch the chivalrous sport.

The four children had front-row grandstand seats, for Katharine had made that a part of her wish. They looked around them, taking in the sights.

King Arthur sat enthroned on a high platform at one end of the field. The children could see him clearly, with his kind, simple, understanding face like the warm sun come to shine on merry England. Queen Guinevere was seated at his right, and Merlin, the magician, thin and wise and gray-bearded, at his left.

And now the trumpets blew an extra long fanfare, and the tournament began.

Sir Launcelot was among the first to ride out on the field. The children recognized him by his armor.

"I told you he'd come out all right," said Katharine, a bit bitterly.

But when Sir Launcelot got going in that tournament, even Katharine had to admire him.

He smote down five knights with his first spear, and four knights with his second spear, and unhorsed three more with his sword, until all the people sitting round on the benches began crying out, "Oh, Gramercy, what marvelous deeds that knight doth do in that field!"

Jane sighed a satisfied sigh. "Kind of glorious, isn't it?" she murmured.

"It's the most wonderful age in human history," said Mark solemnly. "If only it didn't have to end!"

"Why did it?" asked Martha, who hadn't read *The Boy's King Arthur* yet.

"Partly 'cause some of the other knights got tired of being knocked down all the time and having Launcelot always win," Mark told her.

"Yes," said Katharine, in rather a peculiar voice, "it would really be a good deed, in a way, if somebody knocked *him* down for a change, wouldn't it?"

Mark gave her a sharp look, but just then Sir Launcelot started knocking down more knights, and he had to watch the field. When he looked again, Katharine wasn't there.

Mark nudged Jane hard, as a horrible thought came into his mind.

Jane turned and saw the empty spot where Katharine had been, and Mark could tell that she was having the same thought, too.

Just then there was an interruption in the tournament. A strange knight rode out on the field of combat and straight up to King Arthur's platform.

"I crave your Majesty's permission to challenge Sir Launcelot to single combat!" cried the strange knight in a voice loud enough for the children to hear clearly from where they sat.

The hearts of Jane and Mark sank.

Even Martha now guessed the horrid truth. "How dare she?" she whispered.

"I don't know," said Mark. "She's been getting too full of herself ever since we started this wish!"

"Wait till I get her home!" said Jane grimly.

"How call they you, strange sir?" King Arthur was saying, meanwhile, "and whence do you hail?"

"They call me Sir Kath," said the strange knight, "and I hail from Toledo, Ohio."

"I know not this Toledo," said King Arthur, "but fight if you will. Let the combat begin."

The trumpets sounded another clarion call, the strange knight faced Sir Launcelot, and there began the strangest combat, it is safe to say, ever witnessed by the knights of the Round, or any other, Table.

The intrepid Katharine thought herself very clever at this moment. She had wished she were wearing two suits of armor and riding two horses, and she had wished she were two and a half times as tall and strong as Sir Launcelot, and she had wished that she would defeat him twice. And immediately here she was, wearing one suit of armor and riding one horse, and she was one and a quarter times as tall and strong, and she couldn't wait to defeat him once.

But in her cleverness she had forgotten one thing. She had forgotten to wish that she knew the rules of jousting. And here she was, facing the greatest knight in the world, and she didn't know how to start. She knew she'd win in the end, because she'd wished it that way, but what was she to do in the beginning and middle?

Before she could work out another wish to take care of this, Sir Launcelot rode at her, struck her with his lance, and knocked her back onto her horse's tail. Then he rode at her from the opposite direction and knocked her forward onto her horse's neck.

The crowd roared with laughter.

The feelings of Jane, Mark and Martha may well be imagined.

As for the feelings of Katharine, they knew no bounds. She still held the magic charm clutched in one hot hand, and she wasn't bothering about correct arithmetic now.

"I wish I could fight ten times as well as you, you bully! Yah!" were the words that the valiant Sir Kath spoke upon the field. It was a cry of pure temper.

And immediately she could fight five times as well as Sir Launcelot, and everyone knows how good *he* was.

What followed would have to be seen to be believed. Katharine came down like several wolves on the fold. She seemed to spring from all sides at once. Her sword flashed like a living thunderbolt. Her lance whipped about, now here, now there, like a snake gone mad.

"Zounds!" cried the people, and "Lackaday" and "Wurra wurra!"

Jane, Mark and Martha watched with clasped hands.

If Sir Launcelot had not been the greatest knight in the world, he would never have lived to tell the tale. Even as it was, the end was swift. In something less than a trice he was unseated from his horse, fell to the ground with a crash, and did not rise again.

Katharine galloped round and round the field, bowing graciously to the applause of the crowd.

But she soon noticed that the crowd wasn't applauding very loudly. And it was only the traitorous knights like Sir Mordred and Sir Agravaine, the ones who were jealous of Launcelot, who were applauding at all.

The rest of the crowd was strangely silent. For Launcelot, the flower of knighthood, the darling of the people's hearts, the greatest champion of the Round Table, had been defeated!

Queen Guinevere looked furious. King Arthur looked sad. The attendant knights, except for the traitorous ones, looked absolutely wretched. Merlin looked as if he didn't believe it.

Jane and Mark and Martha looked as though they believed it, but didn't want to.

And it was then that the full knowledge of what she had done swept over Katharine.

She had succeeded and she had failed. She had defeated the greatest knight in history. But she had pretended to herself that she was doing it for a good deed. Really it had been just because she was annoyed with Launcelot for not appreciating her help enough, back in Morgan le Fay's castle.

Her cheeks flamed and she felt miserable. It was hot inside her helmet suddenly, and she dragged it off. Then she remembered too late that she'd forgotten something else when she made her wish. She had wished to be in armor, and to be on horseback, and to be tall and strong, and to win. But she had forgotten to say anything about not being Katharine any longer.

Now, as the helmet came away, her long brown hair streamed down onto her shoulders, and her nine-year-old face blinked at the astonished crowd.

Those sitting nearest the ringside saw. Sir Mordred tittered. Sir Agravaine sneered. The mean knights who were jealous of Sir Launcelot began to laugh, and mingled with the laughter were the cruel words, "Beaten by a girl!"

Sir Launcelot came to and sat up. He heard the laughter. He looked at Katharine. Katharine looked away, but not before he had recognized her. He got to his feet. There was silence all round the field; even the mean knights stopped laughing.

Sir Launcelot came over to Katharine. "Why have you done this to me?" he said.

"I didn't mean to," said Katharine.

With flushed cheeks, but with head held high, Sir Launcelot strode to King Arthur's platform and knelt in the dust before it. In a low voice he asked leave to go on a far quest, a year's journey away at least, that he might hide his shame till by a hundred deeds of valor he would win back his lost honor.

King Arthur did not trust himself to speak. He nodded his consent.

Queen Guinevere did not even look at Sir Launcelot as he walked away from the field of tournament.

Merlin spoke a word in King Arthur's ear. King Arthur nodded. He rose, offered an arm to Guinevere, and led her from the stand. Merlin spoke another word, this time to the attendant knights. They began clearing the people from the field.

Most of the people went quietly, but three children in the front row of the grandstand put up quite a fuss, saying that they had to find their sister Katharine, who'd done something terrible. But a sister was a sister and they'd stick up for her, anyway. The knights cleared them away with the rest.

Presently, after what seemed like at least a year, Katharine found herself alone before Merlin. She was crying.

Merlin looked at her sternly.

"Fie on your weeping," he said. "I wot well that ye be a false enchantress, come here in this guise to defeat our champion and discredit our Table Round!"

"I'm not! I didn't!" said Katharine.

"Ye be, too!" said Merlin, "and you certainly have! After today our name is mud in Camelot!"

"Oh, oh," wept Katharine.

"Silence, sorceress," said Merlin. He waved his wand at her. "I command that you appear before me in your true form!"

Immediately Katharine wasn't tall or strong or in armor any more, but just Katharine.

Merlin looked surprised.

"These fiends begin early!" he said. "However, doubtless ye be but the instrument of a greater power." He waved his wand again. "I command that your allies, cohorts, aids, accomplices and companions be brought hither to stand at your side!"

Jane and Mark and Martha appeared beside Katharine, looking nearly as unhappy and uncomfortable as she.

Merlin looked really quite startled. Then he shook his head sadly.

"So young," he said, "and yet so wicked!"

"We're not!" said Martha, making a rude face.

The behavior of the others was more seemly.

"You see, sir," began Mark.

"We didn't mean to," began Jane.

"Let me," said Katharine. "I started it."

And in a rush of words and tears she told Merlin everything, beginning with the charm, and her wish to travel back in time, and going on to what she had hoped to do, and what she'd done and where she'd gone wrong.

"I wanted to do a good deed," she said, "and I *did* one when I rescued Launcelot from that old dungeon. But then he wasn't properly grateful at all and made me undo it so he could rescue himself, all for the sake of his old honor! And that made me cross! And just now I pretended I was defeating him so the other knights wouldn't be so jealous of him, but really I was just trying to get back at him for being so stuck-up! And I always wanted to fight in a real tournament, anyway!"

"Well, now you have," said Merlin, "and what good did you do by it? Just made everybody thoroughly unhappy!"

"I know," said Katharine.

"That's what comes of meddling," said Merlin. "There is a pattern to history, and when you try to change that pattern, no good may follow."

Katharine hung her head.

"However," went on Merlin, and to the surprise of the four children, he was smiling now, "all is not lost. I have a few magic tricks of my own, you know. Let me see, how shall I handle this? I *could* turn time back, I suppose, and make it as though this day had never happened, but it would take a lot out of me."

"Really?" said Katharine in surprise. "It would be a mere nothing to *us!*"

Merlin looked at her a bit grimly.

"Oh, it would, would it?" he said.

"Oh, yes," went on Katharine happily. "I could wish Launcelot were twice as near as here again, and then I could wish that he'd defeat me twice, and then I could wish that the people would honor him twice as much as they ever did, and then I could wish . . ."

"Hold!" cried Merlin, in alarm. "A truce to your wishes, before you get us in worse trouble! I think I had best see this wonderful charm of yours." He made a pass at Katharine with his wand. "If there be any magic among you, let it appear now or forever hold its peace."

Katharine's hot hand, which for so long had clutched the charm, opened in spite of itself, and the charm lay in plain sight on her palm.

Merlin looked at it. His eyes widened. He swept his tall hat from his head and bowed low before the charm, three times. Then he turned to the children.

"This is a very old and powerful magic," he said. "Older and more powerful than my own. It is, in fact, too powerful and too dangerous for four children, no matter how well they may intend, to have in their keeping. I am afraid I must ask you to surrender it."

He made another pass with his wand. The charm leaped gracefully from Katharine's hand to his own.

Mark spoke.

"But it came to us in our own time," he said, "and that's a part of history, too, just as much as this is. Maybe we were *meant* to find it. Maybe there's some good thing we're supposed to do with it. There is a pattern to history, and when you try to change that pattern, no good may follow."

Merlin looked at him.

"You are a wise child," he said.

"Just average," said Mark modestly.

"Dear me," said Merlin. "If that be so, if all children be as sensible as you in this far future time you dwell in . . ." He broke off. "What century did you say you come from?"

"We didn't," said Mark, "but it's the twentieth."

"The twentieth century," mused Merlin. "What a happy age it must be—truly the Golden Age that we are told is to come."

He stood thinking a moment. Then he smiled.

"Very well. Go back to your twentieth century," he said, "and take your magic with you, and do your best with it. But first, I have something to say."

He held the charm at arm's length, rather as though he feared it might bite him, and addressed it with great respect.

"I wish," he said, "that in six minutes it may be as though these children had never appeared here. Except that they—and I—will remember. And I further wish that our tournament may begin all over again and proceed as originally planned by history. Only twice as much so," he added, to be on the safe side.

"Now may I have it back, please?" Katharine asked, when he had done.

"In a minute,'" said Merlin. "By the way, have you been making a lot of wishes lately? It feels rather worn out to me. It won't last forever, you know."

"Oh dear, we were afraid of that," said Jane. "How many more do we get?"

"That would be telling," said Merlin. "But you'd best not waste too many. It might be later than you think."

"Oh!" cried Martha. "Maybe we'll never get home!"

"Don't worry," said Merlin, smiling at her. "There are still a few wishes left for you. And one more for me." Again he held the charm out before him.

"And I thirdly wish," he said, "for the future protection of the world from the terrible good intentions of these children and for their protection against their own folly. May this charm, for twice the length of time that it shall be in their hands, grant no further wishes carrying said children out of their own century and country, but may they find whatsoever boon the magic may have in store for them in their own time and place." He put the charm into Katharine's hands. "And now you'd best be going. Because in less than a minute by my wish, it will be as though you'd never appeared here. And if you aren't home when that happens, goodness knows where you *will* be!"

"But what about the good deed I wished?" said Katharine. "None of the ones I tried worked out!"

"My child," said Merlin, and his smile was very kind now, "you have done your good deed. You have brought me word that for as far into time as the twentieth century, the memory of Arthur and of the Round Table, which I helped him to create, will be living yet. And that in that far age people will still care for the ideal I began, enough to come back through time and space to try to be of service to it. You have brought me that word, and now I can finish my work in peace and know that I have done well. And if that's not a good deed, I should like to know what is. Now good-bye. Wish quickly. You have exactly seventeen seconds."

Katharine wished.

And because their mother had been worried yesterday by their being so long away, Katharine put in that when they got home, they should only have been gone two minutes, by real time.

This was really quite thoughtful of Katharine. Perhaps she, too, like Mark the day before, had learned something during her day of adventure.

The next thing the four children knew, they were sitting together in Katharine and Martha's room, and it was still that morning, and they had only been away from home a minute. Yet that minute was packed with memories.

"Did we dream it?" Katharine asked.

"I don't think so, or we wouldn't all remember it," said Mark.

"And we all do, don't we?" said Jane.

And they all did.

Questions

1. What good deed did Katharine *intend* to do? According to Merlin, what good deed did she *really* do?

2. A *theme* is the main idea expressed in a piece of writing. In this story, Merlin states the theme when he says, "There is a pattern to history, and when you try to change that pattern, no good may follow." Who tried to change history? How?

3. How might Launcelot's defeat have changed the history of Camelot?

4. What do you think Katharine learned from her day of adventure? How might this knowledge change what she does on the next adventure?

5. Choose the word that means the same as each underlined word from the story.
      fearless   resounding   courage
   a. "Trumpets were blowing <u>clarion</u> calls."
   b. Launcelot planned "a hundred deeds of <u>valor</u>."
   c. "The <u>intrepid</u> Katharine" fought boldly.

Activity   Write Expressions

"Grammercy! Zounds! Lackaday!" and "Wurra wurra!" are expressions of excitement, disappointment, or surprise from the English tournament in the story. Such expressions change with time. Think of a tournament or game that people watch today. List that game and four expressions that might be used by the people watching it. For each expression, list an event that could make people act that way.

The Walrus and the Carpenter

A poem by Lewis Carroll

Illustrations by Robert Van Nutt

based on the drawings of Sir John Tenniel

The sun was shining on the sea,
    Shining with all his might:
He did his very best to make
    The billows smooth and bright—
And this was odd, because it was
    The middle of the night.

The moon was shining sulkily,
    Because she thought the sun
Had got no business to be there
    After the day was done—
"It's very rude of him," she said,
    "To come and spoil the fun!"

The sea was wet as wet could be,
    The sands were dry as dry.
You could not see a cloud, because
    No cloud was in the sky:
No birds were flying overhead—
    There were no birds to fly.

The Walrus and the Carpenter
   Were walking close at hand:
They wept like anything to see
   Such quantities of sand:
"If this were only cleared away,"
   They said, "it would be grand!"

"If seven maids with seven mops
   Swept it for half a year,
Do you suppose," the Walrus said,
   "That they could get it clear?"
"I doubt it," said the Carpenter,
   And shed a bitter tear.

"O Oysters, come and walk with us!"
   The Walrus did beseech.
"A pleasant walk, a pleasant talk,
   Along the briny beach:
We cannot do with more than four,
   To give a hand to each."

43

The eldest Oyster looked at him,
  But never a word he said:
The eldest Oyster winked his eye,
  And shook his heavy head—
Meaning to say he did not choose
  To leave the oyster-bed.

But four young Oysters hurried up,
  All eager for the treat:
Their coats were brushed, their faces washed,
  Their shoes were clean and neat—
And this was odd, because, you know,
  They hadn't any feet.

Four other Oysters followed them,
  And yet another four;
And thick and fast they came at last,
  And more, and more, and more—
All hopping through the frothy waves,
  And scrambling to the shore.

The Walrus and the Carpenter
    Walked on a mile or so,
And then they rested on a rock
    Conveniently low:
And all the little Oysters stood
    And waited in a row.

"The time has come," the Walrus said,
    "To talk of many things:
Of shoes—and ships—and sealing wax—
    Of cabbages—and kings—
And why the sea is boiling hot—
    And whether pigs have wings."

"But wait a bit," the Oysters cried,
    "Before we have our chat;
For some of us are out of breath,
    And all of us are fat!"
"No hurry!" said the Carpenter.
    They thanked him much for that.

"A loaf of bread," the Walrus said,
    "Is what we chiefly need:
Pepper and vinegar besides
    Are very good indeed—
Now, if you're ready, Oysters dear,
    We can begin to feed."

"But not on us!" the Oysters cried,
    Turning a little blue.
"After such kindness, that would be
    A dismal thing to do!"
"The night is fine," the Walrus said.
    "Do you admire the view?

"It was so kind of you to come!
    And you are very nice!"
The Carpenter said nothing but
    "Cut us another slice.
I wish you were not quite so deaf—
    I've had to ask you twice!"

"It seems a shame," the Walrus said,
 "To play them such a trick.
After we've brought them out so far,
 And made them trot so quick!"
The Carpenter said nothing but
 "The butter's spread too thick!"

"I weep for you," the Walrus said:
 "I deeply sympathize."
With sobs and tears he sorted out
 Those of the largest size,
Holding his pocket-handkerchief
 Before his streaming eyes.

"O Oysters," said the Carpenter,
 "You've had a pleasant run!
Shall we be trotting home again?"
 But answer came there none—
And this was scarcely odd, because
 They'd eaten every one.

TWO OF EVERYTHING

A Chinese tale told by Li Po
Illustrated by Jane Teiko Oka

Mr. and Mrs. Hak-Tak were rather old and rather poor. They had a small house in a village among the mountains and a tiny patch of green land on the mountain side. Here they grew the vegetables which were all they had to live on. When it was a good season and they did not need to eat up everything as soon as it was grown, Mr. Hak-Tak took what vegetables they could spare in a basket to the next village. There, he sold them for as much as he could get and bought some oil for their lamp, and fresh seeds. Every now and then, but not often, he bought a piece of cotton stuff to make new coats and trousers for himself and his wife. You can imagine they did not often get the chance to eat meat.

Now, one day it happened that when Mr. Hak-Tak was digging in his precious patch, he unearthed a big brass pot. He thought it strange that it should have been there for so long without his having come across it before, and he was disappointed to find that it was empty. Still, he thought they would find some use for the pot, so when he was ready to go back to the house in the evening he decided to take it with him.

It was very big and heavy, and in his struggles to get his arms round it and raise it to a good position for carrying, his purse, which he always took with him in his belt, fell to the ground. So, to be quite sure he had the purse safe, he put it inside the pot and staggered home with his load.

As soon as he got into the house Mrs. Hak-Tak hurried from the inner room to meet him.

"My dear husband," she said, "whatever have you got there?"

"For a cooking pot it is too big; for a bath a little too small," said Mr. Hak-Tak. "I found it buried in our vegetable patch and so far it has been useful in carrying my purse home for me."

"Alas," said Mrs. Hak-Tak. "Something smaller would have done as well to hold any money we have or are likely to have," and she stooped over the pot and looked into its dark inside.

As she stooped, her hairpin—for poor Mrs. Hak-Tak had only one hairpin for all her hair and it was made of carved bone—fell into the pot. She put in her hand to get it out again, and then she gave a loud cry which brought her husband running to her side.

"What is it?" he asked. "Is there a viper in the pot?"

"Oh, my dear husband," she cried. "What can be the meaning of this? I put my hand into the pot to fetch out my hairpin and your purse, and look, I have brought out two hairpins and two purses, both exactly alike."

"Open the purse. Open both purses," said Mr. Hak-Tak. "One of them will certainly be empty."

But not a bit of it. The new purse contained exactly the same number of coins as the old one—for that matter, no one could have said which was the new and which the old—and it meant, of course, that the Hak-Taks had exactly twice as much money in the evening as they had had in the morning.

"And two hairpins instead of one!" cried Mrs. Hak-Tak, forgetting in her excitement to do up her hair which was streaming over her shoulders. "There is something quite unusual about this pot."

"Let us put in the sack of lentils and see what happens," said Mr. Hak-Tak, also becoming excited.

They heaved in the bag of lentils and when they pulled it out again—it was so big it almost filled the pot—they saw another bag of exactly the same size waiting to be pulled out in its turn. So now they had two bags of lentils instead of one.

"Put in the blanket," said Mr. Hak-Tak. "We need another blanket for the cold weather." And, sure enough, when the blanket came out, there lay another behind it.

"Put my wadded coat in," said Mr. Hak-Tak, "and then when the cold weather comes there will be one for you as well as for me. Let us put in everything we have in turn. What a pity we have no meat, for it seems that the pot cannot make anything without a pattern."

Then Mrs. Hak-Tak, who was a woman of great intelligence, said, "My dear husband, let us put the purse in again and again and again. If we take two purses out each time we put one in, we shall have enough money by tomorrow evening to buy everything we lack."

"I am afraid we may lose it this time," said Mr. Hak-Tak, but in the end he agreed, and they dropped in the purse and pulled out two, then they added the new money to the old and dropped it in again and pulled out the larger amount twice over. After a while the floor was covered with old leather purses and they decided to throw the money in by itself. It worked quite as well and saved trouble. Every time, twice as much money came out as went in, and every time they added the new coins to the old and threw them all in together. It took them some hours to tire of this game, but at last Mrs. Hak-Tak said, "My dear husband, there is no need for us to work so hard. We shall see to it that the pot does not run away, and we can always make more money as we want it. Let us tie up what we have."

It made a huge bundle in the extra blanket and the Hak-Taks lay and looked at it for a long time before they slept, and talked of all the things they would buy and the improvements they would make in the cottage.

The next morning they rose early and Mr. Hak-Tak filled a wallet with money from the bundle and set off for the big village to buy more things in one morning than he had bought in a whole fifty years.

Mrs. Hak-Tak saw him off and then she tidied up the cottage and put the rice on to boil and had another look at the bundle of money, and made herself a whole set of new hairpins from the pot, and about twenty candles instead of the one which was all they had possessed up to now. After that she slept for a while, having been up so late the night before, but just before the time when her husband should be back, she awoke and went over to the pot. She dropped in a cabbage leaf to make sure it was still working properly, and when she took two leaves out she sat down on the floor and put her arms around it.

"I do not know how you came to us, my dear pot," she said, "but you are the best friend we ever had."

Then she knelt up to look inside it, and at that moment her husband came to the door, and, turning quickly to see all the wonderful things he had bought, she lost her balance and fell into the pot.

Mr. Hak-Tak put down his bundles and ran across and caught her by the ankles and pulled her out. But, oh, mercy, no sooner had he set her carefully on the floor than he saw the kicking legs of another Mrs. Hak-Tak in the pot! What was he to do? Well, he could not leave her there, so he caught her ankles and pulled, and another Mrs. Hak-Tak so exactly like the first that no one would have told one from the other, stood beside them.

"Here's an extraordinary thing," said Mr. Hak-Tak, looking helplessly from one to the other.

"I will not have a second Mrs. Hak-Tak in the house!" screamed the first Mrs. Hak-Tak.

All was confusion. The first Mrs. Hak-Tak shouted and wrung her hands and wept, Mr. Hak-Tak was scarcely calmer, and the second Mrs. Hak-Tak sat down on the floor as if she knew no more than they did what was to happen next.

"One wife is all *I* want," said Mr. Hak-Tak, "but how could I have left her in the pot?"

"Put her back in it again!" cried Mrs. Hak-Tak.

"What? And draw out two more?" said her husband. "If two wives are too many for me, what should I do with three? No! No!" He stepped back quickly as if he was stepping away from the three wives and, missing his footing, lo and behold, he fell into the pot!

Both Mrs. Hak-Taks ran and each caught an ankle and pulled him out and set him on the floor, and there, oh, mercy, was another pair of kicking legs in the pot! Again each caught hold of an ankle and pulled, and soon another Mr. Hak-Tak, so exactly like the first that no one could have told one from the other, stood beside them.

Now the first Mr. Hak-Tak liked the idea of his double no more than Mrs. Hak-Tak had liked the idea of hers. He stormed and raged and scolded his wife for pulling him out of the pot, while the second Mr. Hak-Tak sat down on the floor beside the second Mrs. Hak-Tak and looked as if, like her, he did not know what was going to happen next.

Then the first Mrs. Hak-Tak had a very good idea. "Listen, my dear husband," she said. "Now, do stop scolding and listen, for it is really a good thing that there is a new one of you as well as a new one of me. It means that you and I can go on in our usual way, and these new people, who are ourselves and yet not ourselves, can set up house together next door to us."

And that is what they did. The first Hak-Taks built themselves a fine new house with money from the pot. Then they built one just like it next door for the new couple, and they lived together in the greatest friendliness, because, as Mrs. Hak-Tak said, "The new Mrs. Hak-Tak is really more than a sister to me, and the new Mr. Hak-Tak is really more than a brother to you.''

The neighbors were very much surprised, both at the sudden wealth of the Hak-Taks and at the new couple who resembled them so strongly that they must, they thought, be very close relations of whom they had never heard before. The neighbors said: ''It looks as though the Hak-Taks, when they so unexpectedly became rich, decided to have two of everything, even of themselves, in order to enjoy their money more.''

The Great Quillow

A play by Moyne Rice Smith
based on the story by James Thurber
Illustrated by Sal Murdocca

Characters

Lamplighter	Baker
Town Crier	Candlemaker
Town Clerk	Cobbler
Blacksmith	Carpenter
Tailor	Locksmith
Butcher	Quillow, the Toymaker
Candymaker	Hunder, the Giant

Setting: Village square.
Time: Many years ago.

The village clock strikes seven. Lamplighter enters with his long staff and lights the street lamp.

Town Crier *(Ringing his bell and chanting)*: Town meeting tonight. Town meeting tonight. Town meeting tonight. . . .

Lamplighter: What good is a town meeting when the Giant Hunder sits above our village and curses it. What can we do? He has plundered the villages of the far countryside. And today the earth shook when he strode onto our hillside. He pulled up four trees to make room to sit down!

Town Crier: The Town Clerk has gone to hear Hunder's will. We meet now to hear his demands. *(He continues chanting, ringing his bell softly.)* Town meeting tonight. Town meeting tonight. Town meeting tonight. . . .

(The Lamplighter *is joined now by the* Villagers, *who follow the* Town Clerk *onto the stage.)*

Town Clerk *(As he enters, carrying scroll and quill, and takes his place)***:** There are ninety-nine other men in the town, but it's the Town Clerk this, and the Town Clerk that, and the Town Clerk everything!

(The Villagers, *who are the* Town Councilors, *mutter and whisper to each other.* Quillow *has followed them in.)*

Town Clerk: Town meeting will come to order! Town meeting will come to order! *(They quiet down.)* I will now call the roll.

Blacksmith: We're all here. You can see that!

Town Clerk *(As each name is called, the* Councilors *answer impatiently.)***:** Tailor, Butcher, Candymaker, Blacksmith, Baker, Candlemaker, Lamplighter,

Cobbler, Carpenter, Locksmith, Town Crier. *(He looks over his spectacles at* Quillow.*)* We have a visitor tonight, as usual. *(All turn and look amusedly at* Quillow.*)* Quillow, the Toymaker. I will make the proper entry in the minutes.

Blacksmith: Never mind the minutes. Read us the demands of Hunder the Giant. *(Cries of* Hear! Hear!*)*

Town Clerk *(Writing with a flourish)***:** Quillow, the Toymaker. Now, I will read the minutes of the last meeting.

Candymaker: Let's dispense with the minutes of the last meeting. *(Cries of* Hear! Hear!*)*

Town Clerk: It must be properly moved and duly seconded.

Tailor *(Quickly)***:** I do so properly move.

Butcher: And I duly second.

Blacksmith: Now read the demands of Hunder the Giant! *(Cries of* Hear! Hear!*)*

Town Clerk *(Unrolling scroll)***:** We come now to the business of the day. I have here the demands of Hunder the Giant. The document is most irregular.

It does not contain a single "greeting" or "whereas" or "be it known by these presents." *(Reads)* "I, Hunder, must have three sheep every morning."

Villagers *(Together)*: Three sheep!

Butcher *(Aghast)*: Why that would use up all the sheep in the valley in a week and a fortnight,[1] and there would be no mutton for our own people!

Town Clerk: "I, Hunder, must have a chocolate a day as high and as wide as a spinning wheel."

Candymaker: Why, that would exhaust all the chocolate in my storeroom in three days!

Town Clerk: "I, Hunder, must have a new jerkin[2] made for me in a week and a fortnight."

Tailor *(Gasps)*: Why, I would have to work night and day to make a jerkin in a week and a fortnight for so large a Giant, and it would use up all the cloth on my shelves and in my basement.

Town Clerk: "I, Hunder, must

have a new pair of boots within a week and a fortnight."

Cobbler *(Moans)*: Why, I would have to work night and day to make a pair of boots for so large a Giant in a week and a fortnight. And it would use up all the leather in my workshop and in my back room.

---

1. fortnight: a period of two weeks or fourteen days.
2. jerkin: a close-fitting jacket or vest with no sleeves, popular several hundred years ago.

Town Clerk: "I, Hunder, must have an apple pie each morning made of a thousand apples."

Baker: Why, that would use up all the apples and flour and shortening in town in a week and a fortnight. It would take me night and day to make such a pie, so that I could bake no more pies or cakes or cookies, or blueberry muffins or cinnamon buns or cherry boats or strawberry tarts or plum puddings for the people of the town.

Town Clerk: "I, Hunder, must have a house to live in by the time a week and a fortnight have passed."

Carpenter (*Sobs*): Why, I would have to work night and day to build a house for so large a Giant in a week and a fortnight. And all my nephews and uncles and cousins would have to help me, and it would use up all the wood and pegs and hinges and glass in my shop and in the countryside.

Locksmith: I will have to work night and day to make a brass key large enough to fit the keyhole in the front door of the house of so large a Giant. It will use up all the brass in my shop and in the community.

Candlemaker: And I will have to make a candle for his bedside so large it will use up all the wick and tallow in my shop and the world!

Town Clerk: This is the final item. "I, Hunder, must be told a tale each day to keep me amused."

Quillow (*Who has sat all this time with his arms folded and his eyes shut, now opens his eyes and raises his hand*): I will be the teller of tales. I will keep the Giant amused.

Candymaker: Does anyone have any idea of how to destroy the Giant?

(*The* Councilors *think, and then in turn are inspired with a great idea.*)

Lamplighter: I could creep up on him in the dark and set fire to him with my lighter.

Quillow: The fire of your lighter would not harm him any more

62

than a spark struck by a colt-shoe in a meadow.

Blacksmith: Quillow is right. But I could build secretly at night an enormous catapult which would cast a gigantic stone and crush Hunder.

Quillow: He would catch the stone as a child catches a ball, and he would cast it back at the town and squash all our houses.

Tailor: I could put needles in his suit.

Cobbler: I could put nails in his boots.

Candlemaker: I could put gunpowder in his candles.

Candymaker: I could put oil in his chocolates.

Butcher: I could put stones in his mutton.

Baker: I could put tacks in his pies.

Locksmith: I could make the handle of his brass key as sharp as a sword.

Carpenter: I could build the roof of his house insecurely so that it would fall on him.

Quillow: The plans you suggest would merely annoy Hunder as the gadfly annoys the horse and the flea annoys the dog.

Blacksmith: Perhaps the Great Quillow has a plan of his own. *(All laugh.)*

Candymaker: Has the Great Quillow a plan? *(He does not answer.)*

(The Councilors *go out slowly and sadly, muttering about their heavy tasks of the night. Quillow sits alone thinking. Suddenly his face lightens. He pantomimes the suggestion of the doll he is going to make. He skips off gleefully as the lights dim to off. The town clock strikes five and the Lamplighter enters and puts out the street light.)*

Town Crier *(Enters on tiptoe)*: Sh! Don't wake the Giant.

Lamplighter: Sh! His food may not be ready.

Town Crier (*Softly*)**:** Five o'clock, and all's well!

(*The* Villagers *tiptoe on, wearily carrying their foodstuffs. They line up facing the hill with the sleeping* Giant.)

Baker: The pie is baked.

Candymaker: The chocolate is made.

Butcher: The sheep are dressed.

Locksmith: I worked all night on the great brass key.

Blacksmith: I helped him with my hammer and anvil.

Candlemaker: I have scarcely begun the enormous candle.

Carpenter: I am weary of sawing and planing.

Tailor: My fingers are already stiff, and I have just started the Giant's jerkin.

Cobbler: My eyes are tired, and I have hardly begun to make his boots.

Town Crier: Where is Quillow? Where is that foolish little fellow?

Lamplighter: He was in his shop at midnight, making toys.

Villagers (*Together*)**:** Toys!

Locksmith: He could have helped with the key.

Baker: The pie.

Butcher: The sheep.

Cobbler: The shoes.

(Quillow *appears smiling and bowing.*)

Blacksmith: Well!

Quillow: Good morning.

Blacksmith: I worked all night with my hammer and anvil helping the locksmith with the great brass key. The Lamplighter tells us YOU spent the night making toys!

Quillow (*Cheerily*): Making toys, and thinking up a tale to amuse the Giant Hunder.

Blacksmith: And a hard night you must have spent hammering out your tale.

Locksmith: And twisting it.

Carpenter: And leveling it.

Baker: And rolling it out.

Tailor: And stitching it up.

Cobbler: And fitting it together.

Candlemaker: And building it around a central thread.

Butcher: And dressing it up.

Candymaker: And making it not too bitter and not too sweet.

Hunder (*Awakening, his head and shoulders appear above the hillside.*): HO! HO! (*He claps his hands and the* Villagers *fall backwards. He roars with laughter.*) Bring me my sheep, my pie, my chocolate! (*The* Villagers *lug their foodstuffs across the stage, climb on the bench and heave them up to the* Giant.) Tell me your silly names, and what you do. (Hunder *gnaws greedily at his food as the* Villagers *quickly tell their trades, each bowing as he speaks.*)

Hunder: You! You with the white hair, who are you?

Quillow: I am Quillow, the teller of tales.

Hunder: Bow!

Quillow: Wow! (*The others are aghast at his impudence.*)

Hunder (*Scowls with fury, then suddenly laughs*): You are a fairly droll fellow. Perhaps your tales will amuse me. If they do not, I will put you in the palm of my hand and blow you so far it will take men five days to find you. Now, the rest of you, be off to your work. (*The* Villagers *sneak off in terror, as* Hunder *continues to eat.*) Now, you, tell me a tale.

Quillow (*Sits cross-legged*): Once upon a time, a Giant came to our town from a thousand leagues away, stepping over the hills and rivers. He was so mighty a Giant that he could

stamp upon the ground with his foot and cause the cows in the fields to turn flip-flops in the air and land on their feet again.

Hunder: Garf! I can stamp upon the ground with my foot and empty a lake of its water.

Quillow: I have no doubt of that, O Hunder. But the Giant who came over the hills and rivers many and many a year ago was a lesser Giant than Hunder. He was weak. He fell ill of a curious malady.[3]

Hunder: Rowf! That Giant was a goose, that Giant was a grasshopper. Hunder is never sick. *(He smites his chest.)*

Quillow: This other Giant had no ailment of the chest or the stomach or the mouth or the ears or the eyes or the arms or the legs.

Hunder: Where else can a Giant have an ailment?

Quillow *(Dreamily)*: In the mind, for the mind is a strange and intricate thing. In lesser men than Hunder it is subject to mysterious maladies.

Hunder: Wumf! Hunder's mind is strong like the rock! *(He smites his forehead.)*

---

3. **malady** (MAL•uh•dee): an illness, usually one lasting a long time.

Quillow: No one to this day knows what brought on this dreadful disease in the mind of the other Giant. He suffered no pain. His symptoms were marvelous and dismaying. First he heard the word. For fifteen minutes one morning, beginning at a quarter of six, he heard the word.

Hunder: Harumph! What was the word the Giant heard for fifteen minutes one day?

Quillow: The word was "woddly." All words were one word to him. All words were "woddly."

Hunder: All words are different to Hunder. And do you call this a tale you have told me? A blithering goose of a Giant hears a word and you call that a tale to amuse Hunder? I hear all words. This is a good chocolate; otherwise I should put you in the palm of my hand and blow you over the housetops.

Quillow (*As the town clock strikes six*)**:** I shall bring you a better tale tomorrow. No one knows to this day what caused the weird illness in the mind of the other Giant. (*Hunder growls,*

yawns, and sinks his great head onto his arms and goes to sleep. Quillow *smiles.*)

Quillow (*Calling softly*)**:** Town Crier! Town Crier! (*The* Town Crier *tiptoes on.*) Call the people. Tell them Quillow has a plan to destroy the Giant Hunder. Call them quietly.

Town Crier (*Chanting softly*)**:** Town meeting in the village square. Town meeting in . . .

(*As the lights dim into dusk, the* Villagers *enter quietly and form a group around* Quillow.)

Blacksmith: What is this clown's whim that brings us here like sheep?

(Quillow *whispers to the group. They nod and whisper to each other conspiratorially.*)

Lamplighter: It will never work.
Candymaker: It is worth trying.
Town Crier: I have a better plan. Let all the women and all the children stand in the streets and gaze sorrowfully at the Giant, and perhaps he will go away.

Candymaker: Let us try Quillow's plan. He has a magic, the little man.

(The lights dim to off. The Villagers *quietly move to either side of the stage and sit. As the lights rise for morning, the* Villagers *are discovered in their places, with* Quillow *sitting cross-legged on the bench below the hillside.)*

Hunder *(Awakening with great noises)*: Tell me a tale, smallest of men, and see to it that I do not nod, or I shall put you in the palm of my hand and blow you through yonder cloud.

Quillow: Once upon a time, there was a King named Anderblusdaferafan, and he had three sons named Ufabrodoborobe, Quamdelrodolanderay and Tristolcomofarasee.

Hunder: Why did this King and his sons have such long and difficult names?

Quillow: Ah, it was because of the King's mother, whose name was Isoldasadelofandaloo. One day as the King and his sons were riding through the magical forest, they came upon a woddly. Woddly woddly woddly woddly. Woddly, woddly, woddly. . . .

WODDLY, WODDLY, WODDLY...

Hunder *(Bellows)*: Say it with words! You say naught but woddly!!

Quillow: Woddly woddly woddly woddly. . . .

Hunder *(Roars)*: Can this be the malady come upon me? Or do you seek to frighten Hunder?

Quillow: Woddly woddly woddly. Woddly woddly woddly.

Hunder *(In terror, shouts at the* Villagers*)*: You, Blacksmith, tell me your name? *(To another)* What is the time of day? . . . Where are you going? . . . How are you feeling? . . . All talk! All talk! Say words!

(The Villagers *carry on conversations with each other using only the word* Woddly.*)*

Hunder *(Silencing them with his roaring)*: It is the malady! I have heard the word! It is the malady! What am I to do to cure the malady? *(The town clock strikes six.)*

Quillow: I was telling you how the King and his three sons rode through the magical forest. . . .

Hunder: I heard the word. All men said the word.

Quillow: What word?

Hunder: Woddly.

Quillow: That is but the first symptom, and it has passed. Look at the chimneys of the town. Are they not red?

Hunder: Yes, the chimneys are red. Why do you ask if the chimneys are red?

Quillow: So long as the chimneys are red, you have no need to worry, for when the second symptom is upon you, the chimneys of the town turn black.

Hunder: I see only red chimneys, but what could have caused Hunder to hear the word?

Quillow *(As the lights dim)*: Rest well. I will tell you another tale tomorrow. *(As* Hunder *goes to sleep,* Quillow *signals to the* Villagers. *They quietly move to the chimneys which they pretend to paint. They remove the red cutouts and when they have finished and have returned to their places, the lights come up again for morning.)*

Hunder *(Stirs, rubs eyes, yawns,*

70

stretches, and then stares): The chimneys! The chimneys are black! The malady is upon me again. Teller of tales, tell me what I must do. The chimneys are black! Look, teller of tales, name me fairly the color of yonder chimneys.

Quillow: The chimneys are red, O Hunder. The chimneys are red. See how they outdo the red rays of the sun.

Hunder: The rays of the sun are red, but the chimneys of the town are black.

Quillow: You tremble, and your tongue hangs out, and these are indeed the signs of the second symptom. But still there is no real danger, for you do not see the blue men. Or do you see the blue men, O Hunder?

Hunder: I see the men of the town staring at me. But their faces are white and they wear clothes of many colors. Why do you ask me if I see blue men?

Quillow: When you see the blue men, it is the third and last symptom of the malady. If that should happen, you must rush to the sea and bathe in the waters or your strength will become the strength of a kitten. Perhaps if you fast for a day and a night, the peril will pass.

Hunder: I will do as you say, teller of tales, for you are wise beyond the manner of men. Bring me no food today, tell me no tale. (*He moans and covers his eyes and sleeps.*)

(*The light dims and the* Villagers *softly steal behind the screens so that when the morning light rises there is no one visible except* Quillow, *the sleeping* Giant, *and the* Town Crier.)

Quillow (*As the town clock strikes five*)**:** Cry the hour. Cry all's well.

Town Crier: Five o'clock! Five o'clock and all's well!

Hunder (*Awakens and looks cautiously at the village*)**:** The chimneys are still black, but I see no blue men. (*He grins, smites his chest and roars.*) HO, Councilors! Bring me my sheep and my pie and my chocolate, for I have a vast hunger. Behold I am still a whole man! I have heard the word and I have seen the chimneys, but I have not beheld the blue men.

Quillow: That is well, for he who beholds the blue men must bathe in the yellow waters in the middle of the sea, or else he will dwindle first to the height of the pussy willow, then to the height of the daffodil, then to the height of the violet, until finally he becomes a small voice in the grass, lost in the thundering of the crickets.

Hunder: But I shall remain stronger than the rock and taller than the oak.

Quillow: If you are stronger than the rock and taller than the oak, then stamp on the ground and make yonder cow in the field turn a flip-flop.

Hunder (*Gleefully*)**:** Behold, I will make the cow turn twice in the air. (*He stamps heavily.*)
(*The blue men slide over the village walls and dance up and down in the air.*)

Hunder (*Cries in anguish*)**:** The blue men! The blue men have come! The world is filled with little blue men!

Quillow: I see no blue men, but you have begun to shrink like the brook in dry weather, and that is the sign of the third symptom.

Hunder *(Shaking with terror)*: The sea! The sea! Point me to the sea!

Quillow: It is many leagues to the east. Run quickly toward the rising sun and bathe in the yellow waters in the middle of the sea.

(Bellowing with anguish, Hunder *disappears behind his hillside. As his roaring diminishes, the* Villagers *enter.)*

Villagers *(Lifting* Quillow *to their shoulders)*: The Great Quillow!

Questions

1. The mysterious *malady,* or illness, that Quillow described had three stages. What were they?

2. What did the villagers think of Quillow at the beginning of the story? at the end of the story?

3. Actors in a play must understand the *stage directions,* the instructions for how to move and speak. If actors in this play are *aghast at Quillow's impudence,* how should they act?
   a. pleased at Quillow's importance
   b. upset at Quillow's lack of wisdom
   c. shocked at Quillow's boldness

4. If actors in this play *whisper conspiratorially,* what are they doing?
   a. secretly plotting
   b. quietly arguing
   c. silently meeting

Activity   Design a Poster or Newspaper Ad

Giant Hunder's big sister has come to the village. She is as kind as Hunder was mean. Next week she will appear in the play *The Great Quillow and Hunder's Sister.* Design a poster or newspaper ad to advertise the play. Make sure your poster shows the characters in the play and hints at some exciting event or problem. Include the time and place for the play, too.

Performing the Play

The Great Quillow play was written to be acted on a stage, but it can be performed in other ways, too. You can perform it as *Readers Theatre,* a group reading in which the actors read aloud from *scripts*—the written text of the play.

In Readers Theatre, each performer, or reader, may wear a sign that tells what part he or she is reading. Performers may stand or sit as they read their parts, looking straight at the audience as much as possible. The readers use their voices to show the characters' different feelings—anger, fear, excitement, or joy. The people in the audience use their imaginations to picture the characters and the action.

You can give a Readers Theatre performance of *The Great Quillow* with only readers and their scripts. You can also add scenery, costumes, and *props,* the movable objects used by actors in a play. *Scenery,* or backgrounds used to show places, might include a town clock, a street light, and the chimneys that turn from red to black. A colorful hat, scarf, or belt could become a simple costume to help each character look the part. Props could include a paper scroll with the list of Hunder's demands, and paper cutouts of Hunder's food and the blue men. These props, scenery, and costumes can be added little by little, after the readers know their parts well.

When the readers are ready, invite an audience to share the fun.

CONNECTIONS

Can You Believe Your Eyes?

a.

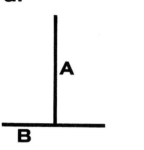

Is line A longer than line B?

b.

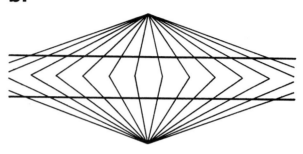

Are the two horizontal lines straight or curved?

c.

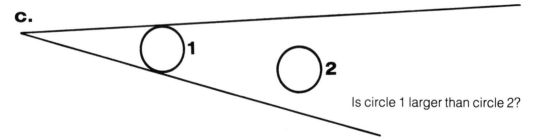

Is circle 1 larger than circle 2?

People say, "Seeing is believing," but this saying is not always true. Your eyes and your brain can be fooled.

The drawings on this page can fool your eyes and your brain. Did they fool you? The lines in *a* are the same length. The long lines in *b* are straight. The circles in *c* are the same size.

Each of these drawings is an *optical illusion*. An *optical illusion* happens when your eyes and your brain see something that is not really what it appears to be.

Illustrated by Jack Wallen and John S. Walter

How Optical Illusions Happen

Your eyes and your brain work together to help you see. Light carries a picture, or *image,* of an object into each of your eyes. As light enters your eyes, the image of the object is turned upside-down. You receive two upside-down images of the object—one in each eye.

Messages about these upside-down images travel along your *optic nerves* to your brain. Sight centers in your brain turn the images right side up. The centers also combine the two images into one. Your brain then figures out what you are looking at and you "see" the object.

Then your brain must make sense of what you see. To do this, your brain compares what you are seeing to what you have seen in the past. Sometimes your brain does not do a very good job. It puts in curves that are not really there. It makes objects seem smaller or bigger than they really are. Your brain fools you and an optical illusion happens.

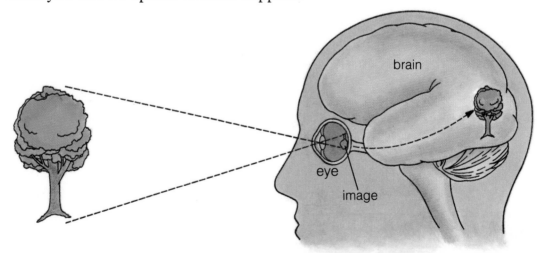

Sometimes an optical illusion picture makes your brain see the picture in two different ways. When you look at the picture, you see one thing. When you look again, you see something else.

Look at the drawing in *a*. As you look at it, the picture will seem to change. Sometimes you will see a vase. Sometimes you will see two faces. Your brain sees the picture in two different ways.

Look at the drawing in *b*. As you look at it, you may see a young woman at one time and an old woman at another. Your brain changes what it sees each time.

A.

Do you see a vase or two faces?

B.

Do you see a young woman or an old woman?

In pictures *a* and *b*, there really are two different images. Your brain can see and understand both of them. So your brain flips back and forth between the two.

Sometimes your brain sees colors that are not there. Look at the picture of the blue-green star for a minute. Then look at the white space next to it.

The red star you see on the white paper is an optical illusion called an *afterimage*. An afterimage repeats the same image that your brain saw, but changes its colors.

Afterimages happen because of the way the back wall, or *retina*, of your eye works. The retina has a group of cells that pick up colors from the light and images that come through your eyes. Some of these cells pick up blue. Some cells pick up green. Some cells pick up red. Cells work together to pick up other colors like yellow and purple.

When you looked at the blue-green star, the cells that pick up blue and green got tired and stopped working. Only the cells that pick up red kept working. So when you looked at the white paper, your eyes saw a red star.

Optical Illusions on Stage

Some optical illusions are caused by things that happen *outside* the eye. The brain is working fine and so is the retina. The light coming to the eye brings an image of something that is not really there.

Pepper's Ghost

All stage lights off.

Actor on stage demonstrating that the ghost is real. The actor can be seen through the ghost.

Sheet of plate glass

Audience

Actor in ghost costume

Light   Stage

The ghost appears to the audience here.

Black-lined pit

Reflector

A hundred years ago, a magician named John Pepper made audiences see something that was not there—a "ghost." Here is how he did it.

The stage was nearly dark when the ghost appeared. A big, slanted sheet of plate glass was propped between the audience and the stage. But the audience could not see it. An actor dressed as a ghost was hidden in a black-lined pit in front of and below the stage. When a light was shined on the actor, his likeness, or *reflection,* appeared on the glass. The reflection seemed to be a "ghost" on the stage. The ghost could "walk" through a chair. Other actors could put their hands through him. When the stage lights went on, Pepper's "ghost" would vanish.

Nature's Optical Illusions

Optical illusions happen in nature, too. Nature bends light rays and makes you see things that are not there. One of nature's most familiar optical illusions is a trick of light called the *mirage* (mih·RAHZH). A mirage happens when an object that is far away appears to be quite close. A mirage can make you think a pool of water is on the road ahead. A mirage can change the shape of an object and make it look like something entirely different from what the object really is.

A mirage is caused by the bending of light through layers of air of different temperatures. A road's hot surface heats the air just above it. The hot air layer acts like a mirror. Light from the sky is reflected back toward someone coming down the road. What looks like a puddle of water across the road is really an image of the sky.

A road puddle mirage

In the Arctic, there is another kind of mirage. This mirage forms when cold ground or water makes the air nearby colder than the air above. When the light bends, images are seen out of place. Faraway objects may seem closer and higher than they really are. It is even possible to see an image of a distant city or boat that is far from actual view!

Arctic mirages may have changed the course of history. A thousand years ago people called the Vikings sailed the North Atlantic. The Vikings lived in Europe but found their way to Iceland and Greenland. They also reached Canada.

Some scientists think the Arctic mirage may have helped the Vikings reach new shores. These scientists

An Arctic mirage

believe that Viking sailors saw Arctic mirages of faraway coasts. By chasing the mirage, the Vikings reached real land.

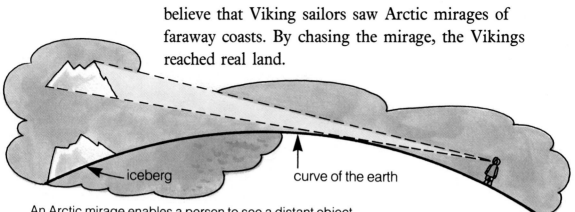

iceberg

curve of the earth

An Arctic mirage enables a person to see a distant object, such as an iceberg, that is actually hidden beyond the curve of the earth.

The Arctic mirage may also explain stories of sea monsters. A mirage can change the shape of something in the water. A floating log can look long and thin. The log can also look short and thick. A mirage can change the shape of a whale so that sailors would not recognize it for what it was.

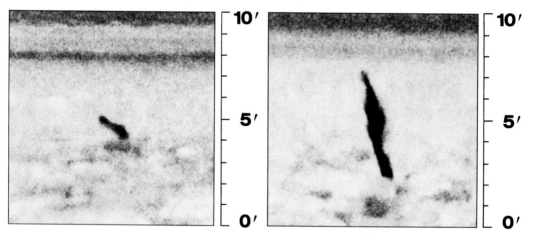

A mirage makes the stick in the water look shorter and wider.

A mirage makes the stick look longer and thinner.

Like those long-ago sailors, you may not always see what you think you see. Optical illusions can fool you. Seeing is not always believing!

Questions

1. How do your eyes and brain work together to help you see?

2. What is the difference between an afterimage and a mirage?

3. Suppose you lived in John Pepper's time, and you wanted to prove his "ghost" was fake. How could you do it without leaving your front-row seat?

Activities

1. **Draw an Optical Illusion**

   Make a drawing in which two squares are the same size, but one looks bigger. Make another drawing in which two lines are the same length, but one looks longer. Try your drawings out on a friend.

2. **Design an Afterimage**

   Make a colored picture for which the afterimage looks like a blue-green star. Make another picture with a red circle as the afterimage. Make a third picture that causes the afterimage to be a purple square inside a yellow circle.

3. **Follow the Vikings' Route**

   Use a globe to follow the route the Vikings probably took from Greenland or Iceland to the North American continent. As you are making your journey, notice how the curve of the Earth hides the land the Vikings were really looking for.

What's So Punny?

> RIDDLE ME,
> RIDDLE ME,
> WHAT IS THAT,
> OVER THE HEAD
> AND UNDER
> THE HAT?
>
> ·HAIR.

When first I appear I seem mysterious,
But when I'm explained I'm nothing serious.
—*A riddle.*

Riddles are among the world's favorite guessing games. For centuries, people everywhere have had fun trying to catch each other with riddles such as the one at the left.

Of all the different kinds of riddles people ask, the trickiest to answer is the *trick question:*

> Why is your nose in the middle of your face?
> *Because it's a scenter.*

In many trick questions, like the one above, the answers contain what we call *puns*. A pun is the humorous use of two words that sound alike but have different meanings. In the answer to the riddle about your nose, the word *scenter* sounds like *center*, even though the spellings and meanings of the two words are different. When you read the answer aloud, it means both ''nose'' (scenter) and ''middle'' (center).

Here are two more trick questions:

> A nickel and a dime were crossing a bridge and the nickel fell off. Why didn't the dime fall too?
> *It had more sense (cents) than the nickel.*

> Why did the lobster blush?
> *Because it saw the salad dressing.*

In the riddle about the nickel and the dime, the pun again is made on two words—*cents* and *sense*—that sound alike but have different meanings and spellings. In the riddle about the lobster, the pun is made on two meanings of a word—*dressing*—whose spelling doesn't change.

In each of the following trick questions, the under-lined word gives a sensible answer but spoils the pun. Change the word to make a pun. The picture next to each trick question offers a clue to the answer. (Answers are given at the bottom of the page.)

1. What did the kindling wood say to the fireplace?
Good-bye! I've met my fire.

2. Why did the rooster refuse to fight?
Because it was afraid.

3. What did the steak say to the plate?
Pleased to see you.

4. What is the tallest building in town?
The library. It has the most floors.

For fun, write down five of your favorite trick questions. Remember that the answers should be puns. Ask your friends these trick questions to see if they can identify and explain the puns in the answers.

(Answers: 1. match; 2. chicken; 3. meat; 4. stories.)

Food for Thought

Trick questions collected by Duncan Emrich

THAT BEET'S ALL!

What is worse than raining cats and dogs?

(Hailing buses and taxis.)

Why is the end of a dog's tail like the heart of a tree?

(Because it is farthest from the bark.)

Why should people never suffer from hunger in the Sahara desert?

(Because of the sand which is there.)

How many hard-boiled eggs could the giant Goliath eat on an empty stomach?

(One. After that his stomach would not be empty.)

Why is the letter K like flour?

(You can't make cake without it.)

Which is correct?
    The yolk of an egg *is* white?
    The yolk of an egg *are* white?

(Neither; the yolk of an egg is yellow.)

If you were invited out to dinner and on sitting down at the table saw nothing but a beet, what would you say?

(That beet's all!)

BOOKSHELF

The Great Ringtail Garbage Caper by Timothy Foote. Houghton Mifflin, 1980. A group of daring raccoons organize a scheme to hijack a sanitation truck when their food supply is threatened by overly enthusiastic garbage collectors.

Honestly Myron by Dean Hughes. Atheneum, 1982. Myron decides to become totally honest after his teacher talks about telling the truth in class.

How to Eat Fried Worms by Thomas Rockwell. Franklin Watts, 1973. When Billy bets fifty dollars that he can eat fifteen worms, his family and friends help him invent different ways to cook them.

The Mouse and the Motorcycle by Beverly Cleary. William Morrow, 1965. After a young mouse named Ralph learns to ride a toy motorcycle, he and the boy who taught him share a series of exciting adventures. Ralph's adventures are continued in **Runaway Ralph** and **Ralph S. Mouse.**

Summer Switch by Mary Rodgers. Harper & Row, 1982. Benjamin Andrews has a secret desire to be like his father. Suddenly it happens. Benjamin becomes his father on his way to a movie conference, and his father becomes Benjamin on his way to summer camp.

The Mariah Delaney Lending Library Disaster by Sheila Greenwald. Houghton Mifflin, 1977. Mariah Delaney's parents can't understand her delight in thinking of money-making schemes. Mariah's latest venture would shock them—a lending library of books from the Delaney's collection.

2 Truly Amazing Talents

My Aunt Dora

A poem by Ted Hughes

You've heard how a green thumb
Makes flowers come
Quite without toil
Out of any old soil.

Well, my aunt's thumbs were green.
At a touch, she had blooms
Of prize chrysanthemums—
The grandest ever seen.

People from miles around
Came to see those flowers
And were truly astounded
By her unusual powers.

One day a little weed
Pushed up to drink and feed
Among the pampered flowers
At her water-can showers.

Day by day it grew
With ragged leaves and bristles
Till it was tall as me or you—
It was a king of thistles.

"Prizes for flowers are easy,"
My aunt said in her pride.
"But was there ever such a weed
The whole world wide?"

She watered it, she tended it,
It grew alarmingly.
As if I had offended it,
It bristled over me.

"Oh, Aunt!" I cried. "Beware of that!
I saw it eat a bird."
She went on polishing its points
As if she hadn't heard.

"Oh, Aunt!" I cried. "It has a flower
Like a lion's beard—"
Too late! It was devouring her
Just as I had feared!

Her feet were waving in the air—
But I shall not proceed.
Here ends the story of my aunt
And her ungrateful weed.

My Uncle Dan

A poem by Ted Hughes

My Uncle Dan's an inventor. You may think that's very fine.
You may wish he were your uncle instead of being mine—
If he wanted he could make a watch that bounces when it drops,
He could make a helicopter out of string and bottle tops
Or any really useful thing you can't get in the shops.
But Uncle Dan has other ideas:
The bottomless glass for ginger beers,
The toothless saw that's safe for the tree,
A special word for a spelling bee
(Like Lionocerangoutangadder),
Or the roll-uppable rubber ladder,
The mystery pie that bites when it's bit—
My Uncle Dan invented it.
My Uncle Dan sits in his den inventing night and day.
His eyes peer from his hair and beard like mice from a load of hay.
And does he make the shoes that will go for walks without your feet?
A shrinker to shrink instantly the elephants you meet?
A carver that just from the air carves steaks cooked and ready to eat?
No, no, he has other intentions—
Only perfectly useless inventions:
Glassless windows (they never break),
A medicine to cure the earthquake,
The unspillable screwed-down cup,
The stairs that go neither down nor up
The door you simply paint on a wall—
Uncle Dan invented them all.

Illustrated by Mila Lazarevich

93

The Amazing Ben Franklin

Ask, "Who was Benjamin Franklin?" and most people will answer that he was a statesman who helped form the first American government in 1776. Some people might also talk about Ben's role in the Revolutionary War. Ben traveled to France to get help for George Washington's troops. Other people think of Ben Franklin as a writer. They know his saying, "Early to bed and early to rise/Makes a man healthy, wealthy, and wise."

But most people do not know that Ben Franklin was also an "idea man." Many of his ideas—and the inventions that came from some of them—are still used today.

Benjamin Franklin was born in Boston on January 17, 1706. He died on April 17, 1790, in Philadelphia.

One of Ben's ideas had to do with books. Books were costly in Ben's time. People did not have much money to buy many of them. So Ben started a "subscription book service." People put their money together and bought books to share. Today most towns and cities have *libraries,* where people can go to borrow books.

Ben also was the first to think of the idea of *matching funds.* The city of Philadelphia needed a hospital. At Ben's suggestion, the colonial government agreed to match any money Ben could collect. Ben and his friends then raised enough money to start the hospital, with the government's help. Matching funds is still a popular way to raise money.

Ben also suggested *daylight-saving time.* His idea was that people could work by daylight instead of lamplight for more hours during the summer than during the rest of the year. Daylight-saving time is in use today.

Another of Ben's inventions was the *lightning rod.* He noticed that lightning always struck the highest part of a building. His experiments showed that electricity flows most quickly into pointed objects. It also flows most easily through metals.

Ben's idea was to put a sharp metal rod on the roof of a building. The rod went down the side of the building. It was buried in the ground at the bottom. If lightning struck, it would hit the rod. The electrical charge flowed down into the ground without causing harm.

Today lightning rods protect many tall buildings and those that are out in the open.

generator

Ben invented two more devices that used what he knew about electricity. One invention was a machine that made, or *generated*, electricity. The other was a battery that stored electricity. Of course, these devices were not useful until machines run by electricity were invented. The batteries and generators of today are different from Ben's, but the idea behind them is the same.

In Ben Franklin's time, houses were cold and difficult to heat. Huge fires roared in people's fireplaces, yet the warm air went straight up the chimney. Cold air was pulled in through leaky doors and windows to replace the warm air. Someone standing near the fire could be, as Ben said, "scorcht before and froze behind." At the same time, smoke from the fire was often sucked down into the room.

Ben took care of these problems with a new invention, a stove. Ben's stove was one metal box inside another. A false back blocked off part of the fireplace. Cool room air was taken in. It was heated in the inside box by the fire in the outside box. The heated metal walls of the outside box also heated the room air. The outside box was enclosed, so smoke could not get into the room.

Franklin stove

In many places, the *Franklin stove* is still used. People burn wood or coal and save money on their heating bills.

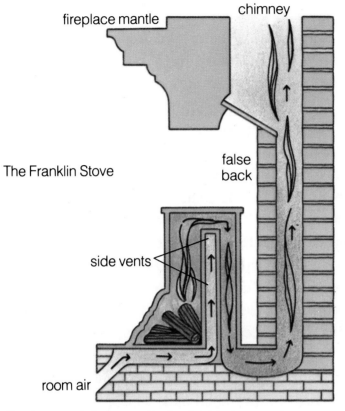

The Franklin Stove

1. Cool room air is heated in the inside box and comes out vents in the side.
2. Cool room air is heated when it touches the hot metal or the outside box.
3. The stove top can be used to keep pots and kettles hot.
4. Smoke is forced up the chimney.

As Ben grew older, he needed glasses for close-up work like reading. He already wore glasses for seeing objects far away. It was a bother to have to carry two pairs of glasses. So Ben invented a pair of glasses that helped him see both close up and far away.

bifocals

odometer

armonica

The curved glass, or *lenses,* in the top halves of the glasses were for seeing things far away. The lenses in the bottom halves were for seeing things close up. Ben looked down if he wanted to see something close up. He looked up if he wanted to see something in the distance. Ben's special glasses, known as *bifocals,* are worn by many people today.

Another of Ben's inventions was the *odometer* (oh·DOM·uh·tuhr). It was attached to a carriage to show how far the carriage had traveled. Cars, trucks, and buses today still use the odometer to measure the distance traveled.

In Europe, Ben Franklin saw a musician play tunes on glasses filled with water. Sweet, bell-like sounds were made by rubbing a finger around the rim of a glass. Different amounts of water in the glasses made different tones.

Ben had an idea for a musical instrument based on this idea. He called it the *armonica.* It used 37 glass bowls of different sizes, each with a hole in the center. The bowls were placed on a metal spindle that passed through the holes. The spindle and bowls lay in an open wooden case that had legs like a piano. A wheel at the side, turned by a foot pedal, made the spindle rotate, turning the bowls. The player sat in front of the armonica and turned the spindle. The player touched different bowls as they moved around.

Ben Franklin invented things he needed, like the stove, bifocals, and lightning rod. He also invented things for pleasure, like the armonica. His inventions came from the goals he had in life: "the graceful and easy, as well as the Useful."

Questions

1. What information did Ben Franklin have to get before he could decide on a good design for a lightning rod?

2. How was playing the glass armonica different from playing groups of glasses with water in them?

Activities

1. **Make an Inventions Chart**

   Make a chart of Ben Franklin's inventions. Next to each invention, describe the needs it filled. The beginning of the chart might look like this:

Invention	Needs Filled
daylight savings time	work longer hours, save energy
subscription book service	have more books to read

2. **Design Your Own Invention**

   Design an invention of your own. It can be useful, like one of Ben Franklin's inventions. It can also be a silly invention, such as a machine that uses many parts to turn the pages of a book. Begin by thinking about the need your invention will fill. Write a description of what your invention looks like and how it works. You might also want to draw a picture of it.

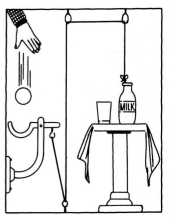

Writing Quatrains by Myra Cohn Livingston

Think of some of the old songs, verses, and rhymes that you remember best. Why do you remember them so well? There may be several reasons—perhaps they are fun and easy to say, and maybe they are written in a four-line pattern called a *quatrain.* You may wish to know that the word quatrain comes from the Latin word *quattor* (KWAH·tor) meaning "four." *Cuatro* (KWAH·troh) in Spanish also means four.

The quatrain is often a complete verse by itself, like the rhyming quatrain below.

As I was standing in the street,	A
As quiet as could be,	B
A great big ugly man came up	C
And tied his horse to me.	B

There is a rhyming pattern in this quatrain. To find it, look at the last word in each line and at the letter beside it. We use letters to label the sounds of these end-words so that we can describe and talk about the rhyming pattern. In line 1 the word *street* has a sound you can call A. In line 2 the word *be* has a different sound than *street* so it is labeled B. Line 3 ends with *up*, a still different sound, so it is called C. But the *me* in line 4 rhymes with *be* in line 2, so it is called B also. The pattern for this rhyming quatrain is A–B–C–B.

100

Although A–B–C–B is the rhyming pattern poets use most often in writing a quatrain, there are many others. Notice the pattern that X. J. Kennedy uses in this first verse from his poem, "Hickenthrift and Hickenloop."

Hickenthrift and Hickenloop	A
Stood fourteen mountains high.	B
They'd wade the wind, they'd have to stoop	A
To let the full moon by.	B

In lines 1 and 3, the last words rhyme (*Hickenloop* and *stoop*), so they are both called A, just as *high* in line 2 and *by* in line 4 rhyme and are called B. This pattern is called A–B–A–B and is a little harder to write than the A–B–C–B pattern.

There are a number of rhyming patterns you can use in a quatrain. The following three quatrains use patterns that are different from the two patterns you've learned about. Can you tell the rhyme pattern for each one? (The answers are upside down on the next page.)

1. I went to the animal fair.
   The birds and the beasts were there.
   The big baboon, by the light of the moon,
   Was combing his auburn hair.

2. I had a little pig, his name was Ben,
   He learned how to count from one to ten.
   I dressed him up to look like a clerk
   With a collar and a suit and sent him to work.

3. O what's the weather in a Beard?
   It's windy there, and rather weird,
   And when you think the sky has cleared
   —Why, there is Dirty Dinky.

The third quatrain above, which has a more unusual
pattern, is from Theodore Roethke's poem ''Dinky'' on

(Answers: 1. A–A–B–A; 2. A–A–B–B; 3. A–A–A–B.)

page 242. In each quatrain in that poem, the first three lines (A) all rhyme, and the last line (B) is repeated throughout the poem.

It is possible also to write a quatrain with no rhyming words, like this part of the poem "Which" by William Stafford.

> Which of the horses
> we passed yesterday whinnied
> all night in my dreams?
> I want that one.

Quatrains offer many possibilities for your own writing. Quatrains can be funny or serious. If you like to write riddles, the quatrain is a good pattern to use for these. If you want to write poetry, just one quatrain can make a whole poem, or you can put together two, three, or many quatrains into a much longer poem. You can even use quatrains to tell a story, as Ted Hughes does in his poem "My Aunt Dora" on page 90. Because they can be used alone or in many combinations, quatrains are the "building blocks" of poetry.

When you *do* write your own quatrain, keep in mind that, whether or not you use rhyme, you will always need *rhythm*. To keep a good rhythm, try to use about the same number of syllables in all of the lines and say your verse aloud. You'll be able to hear if a line seems too short or too long for all the others.

Laughing Gas

From the novel *Mary Poppins* by P.L. Travers

Illustrated by Bert Dodson

Jane and Michael Banks were glad that the woman who had been taking care of them had gone, for they had never liked her. Anything, they thought, would be better than Katie Nanna—if not much better.

But they weren't expecting a nanny[1] quite like Mary Poppins, who blew into their house, slid up the bannister to the second floor, and unpacked a roomful of items from an empty suitcase! True, she seemed to be a rather severe nanny, with her sharp words, frowns, and lack of patience. But Michael and Jane quickly came to be very fond of Mary Poppins and her magical ability to bring impossible events into their lives.

Mary Poppins, Jane, and Michael turned the corner and pulled the bell of Number Three, Robertson Road. Jane and Michael could hear it faintly echoing from a long way away and they knew that in one minute, or two at the most, they would be having tea with Mary Poppins's uncle, Mr. Wigg, for the first time ever.

"If he's in, of course," Jane said to Michael in a whisper.

---

1. **nanny:** in England, a child's nurse.

At that moment the door flew open and a thin, watery-looking lady appeared.

"Is he in?" said Michael quickly.

"I'll thank you," said Mary Poppins, giving him a terrible glance, "to let *me* do the talking."

"How do you do, Mrs. Wigg," said Jane politely.

"Mrs. Wigg!" said the thin lady, in a voice even thinner than herself. "How dare you call me Mrs. Wigg? No, thank you! I'm plain Miss Persimmon *and* proud of it. Mrs. Wigg indeed!" She seemed to be quite upset, and they thought Mr. Wigg must be a very odd person if Miss Persimmon was so glad not to be Mrs. Wigg.

"Straight up and first door on the landing," said Miss Persimmon, and she went hurrying away down the passage saying: "Mrs. Wigg indeed!" to herself in a high, thin, outraged voice.

Jane and Michael followed Mary Poppins upstairs. Mary Poppins knocked at the door.

"Come in! Come in! And welcome!" called a loud, cheery voice from inside. Jane's heart was pitter-pattering with excitement.

"He *is* in!" she signalled to Michael with a look.

Mary Poppins opened the door and pushed them in front of her. A large cheerful room lay before them. At one end of it a fire was burning brightly and in the center stood an enormous table laid for tea—four cups and saucers, piles of bread and butter, crumpets, coconut cakes, and a large plum cake with pink icing.

"Well, this is indeed a Pleasure," a huge voice greeted them, and Jane and Michael looked round for

its owner. He was nowhere to be seen. The room
appeared to be quite empty. Then they heard Mary
Poppins saying crossly:

"Oh, Uncle Albert—not *again?* It's not your birthday, is it?"

And as she spoke she looked up at the ceiling.
Jane and Michael looked up too and to their surprise
saw a round, fat, bald man who was hanging in the
air without holding on to anything. Indeed, he appeared to be *sitting* on the air, for his legs were
crossed and he had just put down the newspaper
which he had been reading when they came in.

"My dear," said Mr. Wigg, smiling down at the children, and looking apologetically at Mary Poppins, "I'm very sorry, but I'm afraid it *is* my birthday."

"Tch, tch, tch!" said Mary Poppins.

"I only remembered last night and there was no time then to send you a postcard asking you to come another day. Very distressing, isn't it?" he said, looking down at Jane and Michael.

"I can see you're rather surprised," said Mr. Wigg. And, indeed, their mouths were so wide open with astonishment that Mr. Wigg, if he had been a little smaller, might almost have fallen into one of them.

"I'd better explain, I think," Mr. Wigg went on calmly. "You see, it's this way. I'm a cheerful sort of man and very disposed to laughter. You wouldn't believe, either of you, the number of things that strike me as being funny. I can laugh at pretty nearly everything, I can."

And with that Mr. Wigg began to bob up and down, shaking with laughter at the thought of his own cheerfulness.

"Uncle Albert!" said Mary Poppins, and Mr. Wigg stopped laughing with a jerk.

"Oh, beg pardon, my dear. Where was I? Oh, yes. Well, the funny thing about me is—all right, Mary, I won't laugh if I can help it!—that whenever my birthday falls on a Friday, well, it's all up with me. Absolutely U.P.," said Mr. Wigg.

"But why——?" began Jane.

"But how——?" began Michael.

"Well, you see, if I laugh on that particular day I become so filled with Laughing Gas that I simply can't keep on the ground. Even if I smile it happens. The first funny thought, and I'm up like a balloon. And until I can think of something serious I can't get down again." Mr. Wigg began to chuckle at that, but he caught sight of Mary Poppins's face and stopped the chuckle, and continued:

"It's awkward, of course, but not unpleasant. Never happens to either of you, I suppose?"

Jane and Michael shook their heads.

"No, I thought not. It seems to be my own special habit. Once, after I'd been to the Circus the night before, I laughed so much that—would you believe it?—I was up here for a whole twelve hours, and couldn't get down till the last stroke of midnight. Then, of course, I came down with a flop because it was Saturday and not my birthday any more. It's rather odd, isn't it? Not to say funny?

"And now here it is Friday again and my birthday, and you two and Mary P. to visit me. Oh, don't make me laugh, I beg of you—" But although Jane and Michael had done nothing very amusing, except to stare at him in astonishment, Mr. Wigg began to laugh again loudly, and as he laughed he went bouncing and bobbing about in the air, with the newspaper rattling in his hand and his spectacles half on and half off his nose.

He looked so comic, floundering in the air like a great human bubble, clutching at the ceiling sometimes and sometimes at the gas bracket as he passed it, that Jane and Michael, though they were trying hard to be polite, just couldn't help doing what they did. They laughed. *And* they laughed. They shut their mouths tight to prevent the laughter escaping, but that didn't do any good. And presently they were rolling over and over on the floor, squealing and shrieking with laughter.

"Really!" said Mary Poppins. "Really, *such* behavior!"

"I can't help it, I can't help it!" shrieked Michael as he rolled into the fender. "It's so terribly funny. Oh, Jane, *isn't* it funny?"

Jane did not reply, for a curious thing was happening to her. As she laughed she felt herself growing lighter and lighter, just as though she were being pumped full of air. It was a curious and delicious feeling and it made her want to laugh all the more. And then suddenly, with a bouncing bound, she felt herself jumping through the air. Michael, to his astonishment, saw her go soaring up through the room. With a little bump her head touched the ceiling and then she went bouncing along it till she reached Mr. Wigg.

"Well!" said Mr. Wigg, looking very surprised indeed. "Don't tell me it's *your* birthday, too?" Jane shook her head.

"It's not? Then this Laughing Gas must be catching! Hi—whoa there, look out for the mantelpiece!" This was to Michael, who had suddenly risen from the floor and was swooping through the air, roaring with laughter, and just grazing the china ornaments on the mantelpiece as he passed. He landed with a bounce right on Mr. Wigg's knee.

"How do you do," said Mr. Wigg, heartily shaking Michael by the hand. "I call this really friendly of you—bless my soul, I do! To come up to me since I couldn't come down to you—eh?" And then he and Michael looked at each other and flung back their heads and simply howled with laughter.

"I say," said Mr. Wigg to Jane, as he wiped his eyes. "You'll be thinking I have the worst manners

in the world. You're standing and you ought to be
sitting—a nice young lady like you. I'm afraid I can't
offer you a chair up here, but I think you'll find the
air quite comfortable to sit on. I do."

Jane tried it and found she could sit down quite
comfortably on the air. She took off her hat and
laid it down beside her and it hung there in space
without any support at all.

"That's right," said Mr. Wigg. Then he turned
and looked down at Mary Poppins.

"Well, Mary, we're fixed. And now I can inquire
about *you*, my dear. I must say, I am very glad to
welcome you and my two young friends here today—
why, Mary, you're frowning. I'm afraid you don't
approve of—er—all this."

He waved his hand at Jane and Michael, and said hurriedly:

"I apologize, Mary, my dear. But you know how it is with me. Still, I must say I never thought my two young friends here would catch it, really I didn't, Mary! I suppose I should have asked them for another day or tried to think of something sad or something—"

"Well, I must say," said Mary Poppins primly, "that I have never in my life seen such a sight. And at your age, Uncle—"

"Mary Poppins, Mary Poppins, do come up!" interrupted Michael. "Think of something funny and you'll find it's quite easy."

"Ah, now do, Mary!" said Mr. Wigg persuasively.

"We're lonely up here without you!" said Jane, and held out her arms towards Mary Poppins. "*Do* think of something funny!"

"Ah, *she* doesn't need to," said Mr. Wigg sighing. "She can come up if she wants to, even without laughing—and she knows it." And he looked mysteriously and secretly at Mary Poppins as she stood down there on the hearthrug.

"Well," said Mary Poppins, "it's all very silly and undignified, but, since you're all up there and don't seem able to get down, I suppose I'd better come up, too."

With that, to the surprise of Jane and Michael, she put her hands down at her sides and without a laugh, without even the faintest glimmer of a smile, she shot up through the air and sat down beside Jane.

"How many times, I should like to know," she said snappily, "have I told you to take off your coat when you come into a hot room?" And she unbuttoned Jane's coat and laid it neatly on the air beside the hat.

"That's right, Mary, that's right," said Mr. Wigg contentedly, as he leaned down and put his spectacles on the mantelpiece. "Now we're all comfortable—"

"There's comfort *and* comfort," sniffed Mary Poppins.

"And we can have tea," Mr. Wigg went on, apparently not noticing her remark. And then a startled look came over his face.

"My goodness!" he said. "How dreadful! I've just realized—that table's down there and we're up here. What *are* we going to do? We're here and it's there. It's an awful tragedy—awful! But oh, it's terribly comic!" And he hid his face in his handkerchief and laughed loudly into it. Jane and Michael, though they did not want to miss the crumpets and the cakes, couldn't help laughing too, because Mr. Wigg's mirth was so infectious.

Mr. Wigg dried his eyes.

"There's only one thing for it," he said. "We must think of something serious. Something sad, very sad. And then we shall be able to get down. Now— one, two, three! Something *very* sad, mind you!"

They thought and thought, with their chins on their hands.

Michael thought of school, and that one day he would have to go there. But even that seemed funny today and he had to laugh.

Jane thought: "I shall be grown up in another fourteen years!" But that didn't sound sad at all, but quite nice and rather funny. She could not help smiling at the thought of herself grown up, with long skirts and a handbag.

"There was my poor old Aunt Emily," thought Mr. Wigg out loud. "She was run over by an omnibus. Sad. Very sad. Unbearably sad. Poor Aunt Emily. But they saved her umbrella. That was funny, wasn't it?" And before he knew where he was, he was heaving and trembling and bursting with laughter at the thought of Aunt Emily's umbrella.

"It's no good," he said, blowing his nose. "I give it up. And my young friends here seem to be no better at sadness than I am. Mary, can't *you* do something? We want our tea."

To this day Jane and Michael cannot be sure of what happened then. All they know for certain is that, as soon as Mr. Wigg had appealed to Mary Poppins, the table below began to wriggle on its legs. Presently it was swaying dangerously, and then with a rattle of china and with cakes lurching off their plates on to the cloth, the table came soaring through the room, gave one graceful turn, and landed beside them so that Mr. Wigg was at its head.

"Good girl!" said Mr. Wigg, smiling proudly upon her. "I knew you'd fix something. Now, will you take the foot of the table and pour out, Mary? And the guests on either side of me. That's the idea," he said, as Michael ran bobbing through the air and sat down on Mr. Wigg's right. Jane was at his left hand. There they were, all together, up in the air and

the table between them. Not a single piece of bread-
and-butter or a lump of sugar had been left behind.

Mr. Wigg smiled contentedly.

"It is usual, I think, to begin with bread-and-
butter," he said to Jane and Michael, "but as it's my
birthday we will begin the wrong way—which I
always think is the *right* way—with the Cake!"

And he cut a large slice for everybody.

"More tea?" he said to Jane. But before she had time to reply there was a quick, sharp knock at the door.

"Come in!" called Mr. Wigg.

The door opened, and there stood Miss Persimmon with a jug of hot water on a tray.

"I thought, Mr. Wigg," she began, looking searchingly round the room, "you'd be wanting some more hot— Well, I never! I simply *never!*" she said, as she caught sight of them all seated on the air round the table. "Such goings on I never did see. In all my born days I never saw such. I'm sure, Mr. Wigg, I always knew *you* were a bit odd. But I've closed my eyes to it—being as how you paid your rent regular. But such behavior as this—having tea in the air with your guests—Mr. Wigg, sir, I'm astonished at you! It's that undignified, and for a gentleman of your age—I never did—"

"But perhaps you will, Miss Persimmon!" said Michael.

"Will what?" said Miss Persimmon haughtily.

"Catch the Laughing Gas, as we did," said Michael.

Miss Persimmon flung back her head scornfully.

"I hope, young man," she retorted, "I have more respect for myself than to go bouncing about in the air like a rubber ball on the end of a bat. I'll stay on my own feet, thank you, or my name's not Amy Persimmon, and—oh dear, oh *dear*, my goodness, oh *DEAR*—what *is* the matter? I can't walk, I'm going, I—oh, help, *HELP!*"

For Miss Persimmon, quite against her will, was off the ground and was stumbling through the air, rolling from side to side like a very thin barrel, balancing the tray in her hand. She was almost weeping with distress as she arrived at the table and put down her jug of hot water.

"Thank you," said Mary Poppins in a calm, very polite voice.

Then Miss Persimmon turned and went wafting down again, murmuring as she went: "So undignified—and me a well-behaved, steady-going woman. I must see a doctor—"

When she touched the floor she ran hurriedly out of the room, wringing her hands, and not giving a single glance backwards.

"So undignified!" they heard her moaning as she shut the door behind her.

"Her name can't be Amy Persimmon, because she *didn't* stay on her own feet!" whispered Jane to Michael.

But Mr. Wigg was looking at Mary Poppins—a curious look, half-amused, half-accusing.

"Mary, Mary, you shouldn't—bless my soul, you shouldn't, Mary. The poor old body will never get over it. But, oh, my Goodness, didn't she look funny waddling through the air—my Gracious Goodness, but didn't she?"

And he and Jane and Michael were off again, rolling about the air, clutching their sides and gasping with laughter at the thought of how funny Miss Persimmon had looked.

"Oh dear!" said Michael. "Don't make me laugh any more. I can't stand it! I shall break!"

"Oh, oh, oh!" cried Jane, as she gasped for breath, with her hand over her heart. "Oh, my Gracious, Glorious, Galumphing Goodness!" roared Mr. Wigg, dabbing his eyes with the tail of his coat because he couldn't find his handkerchief.

"IT IS TIME TO GO HOME." Mary Poppins's voice sounded above the roars of laughter like a trumpet.

And suddenly, with a rush, Jane and Michael and Mr. Wigg came down. They landed on the floor with a huge bump, all together. The thought that they would have to go home was the first sad thought of the afternoon, and the moment it was in their minds the Laughing Gas went out of them.

Jane and Michael sighed as they watched Mary Poppins come slowly down the air, carrying Jane's coat and hat.

Mr. Wigg sighed, too. A great, long, heavy sigh.

"Well, isn't that a pity?" he said soberly. "It's very sad that you've got to go home. I never enjoyed an afternoon so much—did you?"

"Never," said Michael sadly, feeling how dull it was to be down on the earth again with no Laughing Gas inside him.

"Never, never," said Jane, as she stood on tiptoe and kissed Mr. Wigg's withered-apple cheeks. "Never, never, never, never. . . !"

Questions

1. How did Jane and Michael get up to the ceiling? How did Mary Poppins get there? How did Miss Persimmon get there?

2. Reread pages 114 and 119. What tells you that Mr. Wigg probably knew about Mary Poppins's magical powers?

3. Why is it fitting that, in a story of magic, laughter would make people rise in the air?

4. Match each word with what a person might say if he or she were feeling apologetic, persuasive, or scornful.

   apologetic   a. "How dare you speak to me!"
   persuasive   b. "I'm sorry."
   scornful   c. "Please change your mind."

Activity   Create and Describe a Fantasy Device

The story "Laughing Gas" is a kind of highly imaginative story called a *fantasy.* In the story, the laughing gas that makes people float is used as a *fantasy device*—something the author created to make the story more fanciful. Use your imagination to create a new fantasy device for another Mary Poppins adventure. First draw a picture of the device and list words that describe it. Then write a description of how the device works and also what makes it stop.

Fast on Their Feet

Three limericks

There was a young lady of Bright,
Whose speed was far faster than light.
    She set out one day
    In a relative way,
And returned home the previous night.

        —A. H. Reginald Buller

There was an Old Lady of Chertsey,
Who made a remarkable curtsy;
    She twirled round and round,
    Till she sank underground,
Which distressed all the people of Chertsey.

        —Edward Lear

There was a Young Girl of Majorca,
Whose Aunt was a very fast walker;
   She walked seventy miles,
   And leaped fifteen stiles,
Which astonished that Girl of Majorca.

              —Edward Lear

Illustrated by Marie-Louise Gay

A Very Talented Cricket

From the novel *The Cricket in Times Square* by George Selden

Illustrated by Garth Williams

Trapped under the roast beef sandwiches in a picnic basket, Chester the country cricket arrives at the Times Square subway station in New York City. Wriggling free, Chester is found by Mario Bellini, a lonely boy who helps his parents run a tiny newsstand. Soon, Chester has a home in a matchbox on the newsstand counter and two new friends—a talkative mouse named Tucker and Tucker's thoughtful friend, Harry the Cat.

Chester, Tucker, and Harry all live happily at the newsstand until one night when their carelessness causes a fire that just about puts the Bellini newsstand out of business. Convinced that the cricket has brought the family bad luck, Mama Bellini says Chester must go. Then Chester begins to chirp a mournful and lovely tune he learned from the radio. Tears come to Mama's eyes—it is her favorite song—and the Bellinis learn of Chester's unique musical talent. So begins the most remarkable week in Chester Cricket's life.

The next morning, which was the last Sunday in August, all three Bellinis came to open the newsstand. They could hardly believe what had happened yesterday and were anxious to see if Chester would continue to sing familiar songs. Mario gave the cricket his usual breakfast of mulberry leaves and water, which Chester took his time eating. He could see that everyone was very nervous and he sort of enjoyed making them wait. When breakfast was over, he had a good stretch and limbered his wings.

Since it was Sunday, Chester thought it would be nice to start with a hymn, so he chose to open his concert with "Rock of Ages." At the sound of the first notes, the faces of Mama and Papa and Mario broke into smiles. They looked at each other and their eyes told how happy they were, but they didn't dare to speak a word.

During the pause after Chester had finished "Rock of Ages," Mr. Smedley came up to the newsstand to buy his monthly copy of *Musical America.* His umbrella, neatly folded, was hanging over his arm as usual.

"Hey, Mr. Smedley—my cricket plays hymns!" Mario blurted out even before the music teacher had a chance to say good morning.

"And opera!" said Papa.

"And Italian songs!" said Mama.

"Well, well, well," said Mr. Smedley, who didn't believe a word, of course. "I see we've all become very fond of our cricket. But aren't we letting our imagination run away with us a bit?"

"Oh, no," said Mario. "Just listen. He'll do it again."

Chester took a sip of water and was ready to play some more. This time, however, instead of "Rock of Ages," he launched into a stirring performance of "Onward Christian Soldiers."

Mr. Smedley's eyes popped. His mouth hung open
and the color drained from his face.

"Do you want to sit down, Mr. Smedley?" asked
Papa. "You look a little pale."

"I think perhaps I'd better," said Mr. Smedley,
wiping his forehead with a silk handkerchief. "It's
rather a shock, you know." He came inside the newsstand and sat on the stool so that his face was just

a few inches away from the cricket cage. Chester chirped the second verse of "Onward Christian Soldiers," and finished with a soaring "Amen."

"Why the organist played that in church this morning," exclaimed the music teacher breathlessly, "and it didn't sound *half* as good! Of course the cricket isn't as loud as an organ—but what he lacks in volume, he makes up for in sweetness."

"That was nothing," said Papa Bellini proudly. "You should hear him play *Aïda.*"

"May I try an experiment?" asked Mr. Smedley.

All the Bellinis said yes at once. The music teacher whistled the scale—do, re, mi, fa, sol, la, te, do. Chester flexed his legs, and as quickly as you could run your fingers up the strings of a harp, he had played the whole scale.

Mr. Smedley took off his glasses. His eyes were moist. "He has absolute pitch," he said in a shaky voice. "I have met only one other person who did. She was a soprano named Arabella Hefflefinger."

Chester started to play again. He went through the two other hymns he'd learned—"The Rosary" and "A Mighty Fortress Is Our God"—and then did the violin concerto. Naturally, he couldn't play it just as it was written without a whole orchestra to back him up, but he was magnificent, all things considered.

Once Mr. Smedley got used to the idea that he was listening to a concert given by a cricket, he enjoyed the performance very much. He had special praise for Chester's "phrasing," by which he meant the neat way the cricket played all the notes of a passage without letting them slide together. And sometimes, when he had been deeply moved by a section, the music teacher would touch his chest over his heart and say, "That cricket has it *here!*"

As Chester chirped his way through the program, a crowd collected around the newsstand. After each new piece, the people applauded and congratulated the Bellinis on their remarkable cricket. Mama and Papa were fit to burst with pride. Mario was very happy too, but of course he had thought all summer that Chester was a very unusual person.

When the playing was over, Mr. Smedley stood up and shook hands with Papa, Mama, and Mario. "I want to thank you for the most delightful hour I have ever spent," he said. "The whole world should know of this cricket." A light suddenly spread over his face. "Why I believe I shall write a letter to the music editor of the New York *Times*," he said. "They'd certainly be interested."

And this is the letter Mr. Smedley wrote:

To the Music Editor of the New York Times *and to the People of New York—*

Rejoice, oh New Yorkers—for a musical miracle has come to pass in our city! This very day, Sunday, August 28th, surely a day which will go down in musical history, it was my pleasure and privilege to be present at the most beautiful recital ever heard in a lifetime devoted to the sublime art. (Music, that is.) Being a musicologist myself, and having graduated—with honors—from a well-known local school of music, I feel I am qualified to judge such matters, and I say, without hesitation, that never have such strains been heard in New York before!

"But who was the artist?" the eager music lover will
ask. *"Was it perchance some new singer, just lately arrived
from a triumphant tour of the capitals of Europe?"*

No, music lovers, it was not!

*"Then was it some violinist, who pressed his cheek with
love against his darling violin as he played?"*

Wrong again, music lovers.

*"Could it have been a pianist—with sensitive, long
fingers that drew magic sounds from the shining ivory keys?"*

*Ah—music lovers, you will never guess. It was a
cricket! A simple cricket, no longer than half my little
finger—which is rather long because I play the piano—but
a cricket that is able to chirp operatic, symphonic, and
popular music. Am I wrong then in describing such an
event as a miracle?*

*And where is this extraordinary performer? Not in
Carnegie Hall, music lovers—nor in the Metropolitan
Opera House. You will find him in the newsstand run by
the Bellini family in the subway station at Times Square.
I urge—I implore!—every man, woman, and child who
has music in his soul not to miss one of his illustrious—
nay, his glorious—concerts!*

> *enchantedly yours,*
> *Horatio P. Smedley*

P.S. I also give piano lessons. For information write to:
> *H. P. Smedley*
> *1578 West 63rd Street*
> *New York, N. Y.*

The music editor of the New York *Times* was
quite surprised to get Mr. Smedley's letter, but he
believed in the freedom of the press and had it

printed on the theatrical and musical page of the paper. The next morning, thousands of people—at home, over the breakfast table, and on buses and trains coming into New York—read about Chester.

The Bellinis got to the newsstand very early. Papa opened the *Times* bundle and thumbed through a copy looking for the letter. When he found it, he read it aloud to Mama and Mario. Then he folded the paper and put it back on the stack to be sold.

"So," said Papa. "We have a celebrity in our midst."

The celebrity was just at that moment having himself a big yawn in the cricket cage. He had been up most of the night with his manager and Harry Cat, learning new pieces. After eating breakfast and having another stretch, he tested his wings against each other, like a violinist making sure that his violin is in tune. The wings were fine. This time of year they almost itched to chirp. Chester ran over the scales a few times and started to play.

His first selection was something he had heard the night before called "A Little Night Music." It was by a man named Mozart. Chester and Tucker and Harry had all been delighted by "A Little Night Music." They thought it was a very good piece for the cricket to learn because they had heard it first at night, and also because Chester was quite a little person himself. It was lovely music too, with little tunes that sounded like insects hopping around and having a grand time.

As Chester played, the station began to fill up with the usual commuters. People collected around the newsstand—some drawn by the chirping, and

others because they wanted to see the cricket they'd
read about. And as always in New York, when a
little crowd formed, more people came just to see
what the others were looking at. Bees do that, and
so do human beings.

Somebody asked who was playing.

"A cricket," a man answered.

"Oh, stop joking!" the first man said and burst
out laughing.

In front of him a little lady with a feather in her
hat, who was enjoying the music, turned around and
whispered "Shhhh!" very angrily.

In another part of the station a man was reading
Mr. Smedley's letter, and two other men were also
reading it over his shoulders.

"My gosh!" said the one on the right. "A cricket.
Who would have believed it?"

"It's a fake," said the man on the left. "Probably
a record."

The man in the middle, who owned the paper,
snapped it shut. "It *isn't* a fake!" he said. "It's a little
living creature—and it sings beautifully! I'm going
to give up my season ticket at the Philharmonic."

Everywhere people were talking and arguing and
listening to Chester.

Mario made a pile of old magazines and put
the cricket cage on top of them so everyone could
see better and hear more clearly. When Chester
finished one number, a shout of "More! More!" rang
through the station. The cricket would catch his
breath, have a sip of water, flex his wings, and begin
a new selection as fast as he could.

And the crowd grew and grew. Mama Bellini
had never seen such a crowd around the newsstand.
But she wasn't one to be so dazed by good fortune
that she missed out on such a chance. Taking a
bundle of *Times* under one arm, she worked her
way around, murmuring softly—so as not to disturb
the music lovers—"Read about the cricket, read about
the cricket. It's in the New York *Times*."

People snapped up the papers like candy. Mama had to keep going back to the newsstand for new loads. And in less than half an hour the whole stock of the *Times* had been sold.

"Don't sit with your eyes shut," Mama whispered to Papa. (Papa Bellini was one of those people who enjoy listening to music most with their eyes closed.) She put a bunch of *Musical America* into his arms. "Try these. It's a good time now."

Papa sighed, but did as she asked him. And in a little while all the copies of *Musical America* were gone too. It is safe to say that there had never been such an interest in music in the Times Square subway station as there was on that morning.

Over in the drainpipe, Tucker Mouse and Harry Cat were listening too—Harry with his eyes closed like Papa Bellini. There were so many human beings that they couldn't even see the newsstand. But they could hear Chester chirping away on the other side of all the heads and legs and backs. His clear notes filled the station.

"Didn't I tell you?" said Tucker between pieces. "Look at them all. There's a fortune in this. I wish one of us was big enough to pass the hat."

But Harry only smiled. He was happy right where he was, just sitting, enjoying the music.

And the crowd kept on growing. That first day alone, there were seven hundred and eighty-three people late to work because they had stopped to listen to Chester.

During the next few days, other papers besides the *Times* began to run articles on the cricket. Even

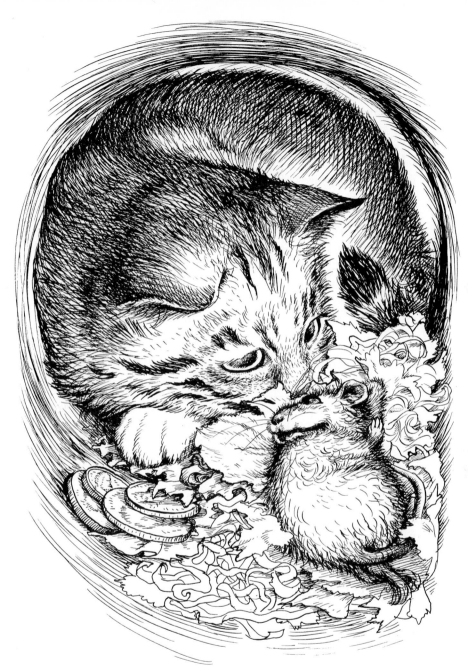

Musical America sent an editor (an assistant editor) down to hear a recital. And Chester was news on the radio and television. All the announcers were talking about the remarkable insect who was delighting throngs in the Times Square subway station.

The Bellinis decided that the best times for Chester to play were early in the morning and late in the afternoon, since that was when the station was the fullest. Concerts began at eight A.M. and four-thirty P.M. and usually lasted an hour and a half—not including encores.

Business boomed at the newsstand. Mama made sure that extra loads of magazines and newspapers were delivered. But even so, by closing time they had sold out completely. Mama Bellini, by the way, turned out to be the best friend a cricket ever had. At noon she would rush home and fix Chester some delicacy for lunch, like a midget fruit salad or an entire vegetable dinner so small you could serve it on a silver dollar. Chester really preferred his mulberry leaves, but he ate everything so as not to hurt her feelings.

Sai Fong, from whom Mario had bought a cage for Chester, had seen Chester's picture in the paper. He kept Mario supplied with leaves. He and another Chinese gentleman dug out two collapsible chairs from his attic and came uptown every day at eight and four-thirty to hear Chester's new programs.

Mr. Smedley was there at least once a day too. He brought a tape recorder and made recordings of all the new pieces Chester learned. And during the intermissions—there was always an intermission of ten minutes halfway through the concert—he delivered short talks on musical appreciation to the audiences.

So by Thursday, Chester Cricket was the most famous musician in New York City.

Questions

1. Why did the music editor of the New York *Times* print Mr. Smedley's unusual letter?

2. Why did Tucker Mouse and Harry Cat approve of Chester's selection "A Little Night Music"?

3. What is the story's main fantasy device—something not likely to be believed if it happened in "real" life?

4. What are two ways in which the author helps make this fantasy device believable?

5. Which word did the author use instead of each underlined word or phrase below?
   a. Chester lacked loudness; he played softly. (page 128)
   b. He loosened up his wings before he played. (page 126)
   c. He played a selection written for orchestra and solo instrument. (page 128)
   d. He impressed a person who studies music. (page 129)

Activity   Prepare a News Report

You are a television news reporter assigned to tell about the unusual event described on pages 131–134 in "A Very Talented Cricket." Your producer has assigned you a 40-second "spot" on the news to read your report while Chester's music plays in the background. Write your script, practice it, and deliver it as you would do it on the news show tonight. Also list the titles of the selections you will use as musical background.

A HERO'S PROMISE

A Greek legend retold by Ian Serraillier

Illustrated by Kinuko Craft

Stories about Theseus,[1] one of the greatest heroes of ancient Greece, have been told for centuries. The story of his struggle with the Minotaur[2] is but one of many tales about Theseus' strength and bravery.

---

1. **Theseus** (THEE·see·uhs).
2. **Minotaur** (MIN·uh·tawr).

Theseus was a long-lost son of King Aegeus[3] of the ancient Greek city of Athens. Many years before this story begins, King Aegeus had caused the death of Androgeus,[4] the son of King Minos[5] of Crete.[6] As punishment, Minos demanded a human sacrifice from the people of Athens. Every year for ten years the people of Athens had sent seven boys and seven girls to the island of Crete, where King Minos forced them to enter the Labyrinth.[7] The huge maze was the home of the terrible Minotaur, half man and half beast, who ate only human flesh. No one who entered the Labyrinth had ever escaped.

When Theseus came at last to his father's city, he was horrified to learn of this cruel punishment. Theseus felt that his father Aegeus and the people of Athens had paid far too much for one misdeed. He made a promise to the fourteen doomed young people: "Do not despair. I will go with you and kill the Minotaur. None of you will die."

---

3. **Aegeus** (EE·jee·uhs).
4. **Androgeus** (An·DRAH·jee·uhs).
5. **Minos** (MY·nuhs).
6. **Crete** (KREET).
7. **Labyrinth** (LAB·uh·rinth).

In the harbor the ship was already waiting. The helmsman was standing by the steering oar. The pilot at the prow and the thirty oarsmen on their benches were impatient to be off. As the victims embarked, their families and friends followed them up the gangplank, pressing on them food for the voyage, embracing them, clinging to them. And when the ship drew slowly away, they stretched out their hands to them over the water.

Outside the harbor the sailors hauled the black sail up to the masthead and unfurled it. The north wind filled it, and the ship sped away over the waves. But the victims, huddled together amidships, were cold and lonely as the sea, and the crying gulls above their heads echoed their misery.

They sailed past the islands of Aegina[8] and Milos,[9] and on the third day out they sighted far off the cliffs of Crete. A ship came out to meet them.

"She has a golden sail painted with royal dolphins," said the pilot. "King Minos himself must be on board."

The sails of both ships were lowered and the oarsmen took over. The Cretan ship drew alongside. King Minos was standing at the prow, splendid in a golden embroidered cloak that streamed behind him in the breeze. He was a great warlord and a lover of beautiful things, but he was also vain.

When the two ships were close enough for the oarsmen to touch hands, he leaped aboard the Greek

---

8. **Aegina** (ee·JY·nuh).
9. **Milos** (MEE·laws).

ship and asked to see the victims. Trembling with
fear, they stood up at the prow, with Theseus beside
them. At once a quarrel started. When King Minos
saw that there were fifteen and not fourteen of them,
he said he would keep one of them as his slave. And
he picked out Eriboia,[10] the most beautiful of the
girls, and touched her pale cheek with his hand as if
she were already his slave. She screamed to Theseus
to help her.

Theseus leaped up and stood chin to chin with
King Minos and said, "She is no slave but a noble's
daughter. If you touch her again I shall throw you
into the sea."

---

10. **Eriboia** (ehr·ih·BOY·uh).

Never before had anyone spoken to King Minos like that.

"Who are you that dare insult me so?" said King Minos, white with anger.

"I am Theseus, son of King Aegeus."

"I am the warlord of Cnossus,[11] king of the islands," said Minos. "Immortal Zeus,[12] the king of the gods, is my father." And stretching out his hands to heaven, he called on Zeus to confirm it with a flash of lightning.

At once the whole face of the sky was split with lightning, and there was a great drum roll of thunder.

"I have the blood of Poseidon,[13] the sea god, in my veins," said Theseus. "He will give me whatever help I need."

"Then fetch this," said King Minos. He threw his gold signet ring into the sea, and it sank at once.

Theseus climbed on to the stern rail and dived into the sea, deep down to the watery halls of Poseidon, the sea god. And a hundred dolphins, rolling and plunging, brought him to the palace of the Nereids,[14] the daughters of Ocean, who were shining with the splendor of fire. Thetis,[15] the loveliest of the sea nymphs, dressed him in a purple robe and gave him a jewelled crown. Meanwhile her sisters swam everywhere to find the golden ring. At last they found it in a cranny of rock and, in front of Poseidon the sea god, they gave it to Theseus. Then

---

11. **Cnossus** (NAHS·uhs).
12. **Zeus** (ZOOS).
13. **Poseidon** (puh·SY·duhn).
14. **Nereids** (NUR·ee·ids)
15. **Thetis** (THEE·tis).

he sped towards the sea roof, a long trail of bubbles
marking his path back to the ceiling of light. When
he broke the surface, the young men and girls hauled
him eagerly aboard. They were amazed to see him
dressed in a robe even more splendid than King
Minos's and not even wet. And when he handed
Minos the golden ring, how they shouted for joy!

As for Minos, he said not a word, but went back to his ship and returned to harbor.

In those days Cnossus was one of the great cities of the world. The nearby port of Heracleion[16] was crowded with shipping, with trading boats from Egypt and Asia as well as the King's own fleet. People had come from all over the island to see the Athenian[17] strangers. They stared at them as they disembarked and marched up the road to the palace.

And what a palace it was! It spread right over the hill. The halls and galleries and countless rooms were built of huge blocks of stone, framed in cypress wood cut from the forests inland. The wooden columns tapered downwards and were painted russet with blue capitals.[18] There was a grand staircase four stories high, lit by wells of light and thus protected from the hot summer sun and freezing winter winds.

As Theseus entered the hall at the foot of the staircase, he was startled to see a huge black bull in front of him. It had gold horns and white nostrils, red-rimmed eyes and a fierce mouth. At once he thought of the Minotaur. He drew his sword and waited for the charge.

"The beast is harmless," laughed King Minos. "Sheathe your sword."

Then Theseus saw it was only a painting on the wall, and he too laughed.

It was the custom for King Minos to entertain his Athenian guests to dinner; they were not shut in the

---

16. **Heracleion** (ee·RAH·klee·awn).
17. **Athenian** (uh·THEE·nee·uhn).
18. **capitals:** in this story, the upper parts of columns or pillars.

Labyrinth till the following day. The cups and dishes were all of solid gold; and the food was lavish and magnificent. Yet Theseus and his companions did not feel hungry. They were haunted by the thought of what lay in store for them next day.

In the middle of the dinner they were puzzled by a sudden growl of thunder that seemed to come from underneath their feet. King Minos was quick to explain it.

"The Minotaur is hungry tonight," he said. "Perhaps he has smelled human flesh and cannot wait till morning."

Then the floor began to tremble and the foundations of the palace quivered and shook.

"The Minotaur is trying out his paces," said the King. "His temper does not improve with waiting. But why should we cut short our entertainment to please him?"

King Minos clearly enjoyed his guests' dismay. Not so his daughter, Ariadne,[19] who admired Theseus's dignity and calm. She asked about his exploits on the road to Athens and listened entranced while he told her about them. She could not bear to think of the miserable death that awaited him and his companions next morning. So she decided to help him.

After the dinner she took Theseus to the Hall of Distaffs, where she did her weaving. The walls were bright with deep blue dolphins and starfish and spiky sea urchins painted against a pale blue ground, all lit with a soft light.

"Tomorrow I must wrestle with death," said Theseus.

"I can help you win and escape safely," said Ariadne. "Daedalus,[20] the master craftsman who built the Labyrinth, once told me how to find the way out."

She went to her spindle and picked up a ball of wool.

"As soon as you are inside the door, tie the loose end of the wool to the lintel," she said, "and unwind the ball as you go. Do not let it out of your hand or you will never find the way back. When you meet the Minotaur, seize him by the horn and stab him."

"But we are allowed no weapons," said Theseus.

---

19. **Ariadne** (ahr·ee·AD·nee).
20. **Daedalus** (DED·uh·luhs).

"Take this dagger and hide it in your tunic." She
gave it to him; the hilt was of solid gold and the
iron point sharp as a needle.

"Tomorrow I shall owe my life to you," said
Theseus. "Dearest princess, what can I do for you
in return?"

"Make me your wife and take me back to Greece,"
said Ariadne, and the tears welled up in her eyes.
"I am lonely and unhappy here. The palace is full of
soldiers; the talk is of nothing but wars and fighting.
And at night the monster bellows so loudly that I
cannot sleep. I beg you to take me away."

"With all my heart," said Theseus, much moved
by her beauty and goodness. And he took her in his
arms and kissed her.

Next morning the palace guards locked Theseus and his companions in the Labyrinth. The huge iron door shut behind them with a clang that echoed through the dark twisting passages, the numberless corridors. And when the last echo had faded, there was a dreadful stillness.

"You have nothing to fear," said Theseus. "I shall keep my promise. Wait here till I return."

He had hidden Ariadne's dagger under his cloak. And to light him on his way, he had the jewelled crown which Thetis had given him. He fastened one end of the ball of wool to the lintel above the door and set off into the darkness. Crouching by the door, his companions watched the splash of light on the walls till he turned a corner and vanished; then they listened in the pitch darkness to the echo of his footsteps fading into the distance.

On and on down the endless corridors went Theseus, hour after hour, unwinding the wool as he walked. The stone walls were ice cold and slimy; they glistened wet in the light of the jewels. Sometimes he stopped to look for signs of the monster, to listen for its footsteps.

He had come to a place where the corridor branched into three when he suddenly heard the sound of heavy breathing. He put down the ball of wool and gripped the hilt of his dagger. He peered round and turned his head slowly while the jewels on his crown, shining like a torch, floodlit the darkness.

The Minotaur was lying in the mouth of the third passage, curled up, asleep. The monstrous bull's head with its golden horns and white nostrils was nodding

over a human chest. Roused by the light, it opened
its eyes, red-rimmed and bloodshot, and for a whole
minute blinked at Theseus. Suddenly it let out so
great a bellow that it seemed as if the walls had
crumbled and fallen in. High above in the palace
Ariadne heard it as she sat weaving in her room, and
the distaff fell from her hand. The trees in the forest
trembled and a great wave rolled ashore and rocked
the ships in harbor.

Then the creature scrambled upright. It lowered
its head and, snorting smoke from its fiery nostrils,
charged. There was no room for Theseus to step

aside, but he remembered what Ariadne had told him to do. He reached up with his left hand, caught hold of a horn and wrenched the head backwards. With his right hand he plunged the dagger into its neck. The beast groaned and slumped forward on top of him, almost smothering him as they fell. For a long moment they rolled and wrestled on the stony floor. Then the Minotaur's muscles went limp and slack and it never moved again.

Theseus struggled to his feet. He picked up what was left of the ball of wool, and winding it up as he went, groped his way back to the mouth of the Labyrinth where his companions were waiting. They cheered when they saw him and kissed his hands.

But he silenced them at once, for they were not out of danger yet. "We must stay here till nightfall, till the guards are sure we are dead," he told them. "Then Ariadne will unlock the door and let us out."

At last they heard the key grate in the lock and the door creak open. The stars were shining as they tiptoed out into the warm night. He called softly to Ariadne. "I have killed the Minotaur," he whispered. He slipped her hand into his and they hurried down to the harbor, with the seven young men and the seven girls behind them.

The ship was waiting. They hoisted sail and cast off their moorings and steered past the sleeping ships. So that King Minos could not pursue them, they scuttled one of the ships in the harbor mouth to block the way out. Then joyfully they made for the open sea.

With his companions as witnesses, while the wind filled the sail and tugged at the rigging, Theseus made Ariadne his wife. And as a pledge that he would love her all his life, he gave her his jewelled crown and set it on her head, where it sparkled in the darkness as brightly as the stars.

Questions

1. *Legends* are stories that are handed down from the past. Legends often tell about heroes with amazing talents. What talents did Theseus have? How did he use them?

2. Some heroes are fortunate; they have "outside help." What "outside help" did Theseus have?

3. Do you think that Theseus would be a hero if he were alive today? Why or why not?

4. Find the underlined words in the story. Then choose the best answer to each question.
   a. Is a lintel a vegetable for making soup, a small piece of thread, or a support at the top of a door? (page 148)
   b. In this story is scuttled what Theseus did when he sank a ship, what Ariadne did when she made thread, or what happens when you stumble? (page 150)
   c. When King Minos asked Theseus to sheathe his sword, did King Minos want Theseus to draw his sword, discard it, or put it back in its case? (page 144)

Activity   Design a Maze

A *labyrinth* is a maze or a network of confusing paths. On a large sheet of paper, draw a *diagram,* or plan, for a labyrinth. (Make sure only one path is the exit and the other paths are "dead ends.") Then ask someone to try to escape from your labyrinth by tracing the way out of it. Give the person a time limit of forty-five seconds.

BOOKSHELF

Fledgling by Jane Langston. Harper & Row, 1980. Georgie, the youngest child in her family, wants to learn how to fly. Despite her family's feelings, she fulfills her wish with the help of an unusual goose.

The Dollhouse Caper by Jean S. O'Connell. T. Y. Crowell, 1975. The Dollhouse Family is worried about being thrown away by three boys in the Human Family. They hope to be saved by warning the boys of a burglary that is about to happen.

The Mightiest of Mortals: Heracles by Doris Gates. Viking Press, 1975. Heracles, the super-strong, half-god, half-human son of Zeus, is forced to perform twelve labors in order to gain immortality.

Adventures with the Giants by Catherine F. Sellew. Little, Brown, 1950. These stories of the adventures of the Norse gods include Thor's great battle with the giants.

The Piemakers by Helen Cresswell. Macmillan, 1980. The Roller family of Danby Dale in England have been piemakers for generations. Yet never before have the Rollers made such an enormous meat pie—a pie to feed two thousand people, including the King.

3 Never Give Up

Something for Davy

From the novel *Thank You, Jackie Robinson*

by Barbara Cohen

Illustrated by Lyle Miller

After his father died, Sam Greene was lonely. With his mother busy running the family's New Jersey inn and his sisters busy with their own interests, Sam spent long hours alone with his radio, listening to what he loved most—major league baseball games.

Then Davy came to be the new cook at the inn, and Sam and Davy discovered they loved the same things—baseball, the Brooklyn Dodgers, and Jackie Robinson, the Dodgers' star player in that year of 1947. Though Sam and Davy were fifty years apart in age, they became great friends, talking endlessly of baseball and going to the Dodgers' games together.

Davy's heart attack two years later was a terrible shock for Sam. Not only was his best friend in the hospital, but—because he wasn't a family member— Sam wasn't even allowed to visit Davy. When he heard that Davy was asking to see him, Sam made a decision. If he couldn't see Davy in person, at least he could do something to help Davy get well. As Sam tells the story, "I'd had it. I was going to do something spectacular. I was going to make him better all by myself. It would be like magic."

That afternoon I got on my bike and rode downtown. I went into Muldoon's Sporting Goods and bought a brand new Spalding regulation baseball. It cost one sixty-five. I couldn't count on catching one at the ball park. In all the time Davy and I had gone to the games that had never happened to us. It probably never would, if we went to a thousand million games. I had to take matters into my own hands, and then rough the ball up a little bit and persuade the players to autograph it, even if I hadn't caught it.

The day after that was Friday. I collected my allowance and got my mother to give me my three dollars and fifty cents that was in the safe.

"I think that's too much to spend on a present for Davy," Mother said. "A dollar would be plenty."

"Mother!" I exclaimed. I was shocked. "If I had a thousand dollars it wouldn't be too much to spend."

"Davy wouldn't want you to spend all your money on him. You know that."

"*I* want to spend all my money on Davy," I said. "Davy never has to know."

"It's your money, but I think you're crazy. You don't need to spend money to show love."

"It's the only way," I said. "The hospital won't let me in to see him."

"It's your money," she repeated, shaking her head, but then she gave it to me.

The next day, Saturday, was of course the busiest day of the week at the inn. Even during July and August, the slow months, Saturday was sometimes busy. I was lucky. On this particular Saturday there was a wedding reception. What with Davy sick and the new cook not quite up to preparing a whole banquet, my mother had to be in six places at once. She really didn't have time to worry about us. It was one of those days when she just wanted us to disappear somewhere and not bother her until it was time for my sister Sara and me to help dish out the meal. I obliged. I told her I was going over to my friend Mickey's house and that I would stay there for dinner, but I'd come home before dark. If she had time to think about it, she might have wondered why I spent so much time at Mickey's lately, but she didn't have time to think about it.

I suppose I could have told my mother where I was going. She might have been perfectly willing to let me go. She might have given me money for it.

But I couldn't be sure. A mother who worried so much about our crossing the highway after sunset might not want us to go all the way to Ebbets Field by ourselves. I couldn't risk her telling me not to go. So I just went.

I had gone into the kitchen real early in the morning, before anyone else was up, and made myself a couple of egg-salad sandwiches. I had them and my money and the baseball in its little cardboard box. I walked the mile and a half to the bus station because there'd be no place to leave my bike if I rode there. I took the bus into New York City and I took a subway to Ebbets Field. I didn't have to ask anyone anything, except the bus driver for a ticket to New York City and the man in the subway booth for change of a quarter.

There was one thing I'd learned from Sara, and that was that if you know how to read you can do anything. Right in the middle of the subway was this big map of the subway system and Ebbets Field was marked right on it in large black letters. BMT, Brighton Local, downtown, get off at the station near Ebbets Field. I didn't even have to change trains.

You could see flags flying above the ball park when you climbed up out of the subway station. You had to walk three blocks and there you were. Inside it was as it always had been, as bright and green as ever, remote from the sooty streets that surrounded it, remote from all the world. In the excitement of being there, I almost forgot about Davy for a moment. I almost forgot why I had come. But then, when the Cubs' pitcher, Warren Hacker, began to warm up, I turned to Davy to ask him if he thought Shotton was going to give Jackie's sore heel a rest that day. But Davy wasn't there, and I remembered.

I thought maybe I'd better start trying right away. My chances were probably better during batting practice than they would be later. I took my ball out of its box and stashed the box underneath my bleacher seat. Then I walked around to the first-base side and climbed all the way down to the box seats right behind the dugout. I leaned over the rail. Billy Cox was trotting back to the dugout from home plate, where Erskine had been throwing to him.

I swallowed my heart, which seemed to be beating in my throat, and called out, "Billy! Hey, Billy!" waving my ball as hard and high as I could. But I was scared, and my voice wasn't very loud, and I don't think Billy Cox heard me. He disappeared into the dugout.

Marv Rackley came out of the dugout and then Carl Furillo. I called to them too, but they didn't seem to hear me either.

This method was getting me nowhere. I had to try something else before the game began and I'd really lost my chance. I looked around to see if there were any ushers nearby, but none was in sight. It was kind of early and the place hadn't really started to fill up yet. I guess the ushers were loafing around the refreshment stands.

I climbed up on the railing and then hoisted myself onto the roof of the dugout. That was something you could not do at many places besides Ebbets Field. That was one of the few advantages of such a small ball park. Of course, you know, you couldn't go see Ebbets Field now if you wanted to. They tore it down and put an apartment building there.

I could have stood up and walked across the dugout roof to the edge, but I figured if I did that an usher surely would see me. I sneaked across the roof on my belly until I came to the edge and then I leaned over.

It was really very nice in the dugout. I had always kind of pictured it as being literally dug out of the dirt, like a trench in a war. But it had regular walls and a floor and benches and a water cooler. Only trouble was, there were just a couple of guys in there— Eddie Miksis, and Billy Cox whom I'd seen out on the field a few minutes before.

I was disappointed. I had certainly hoped for Campy's signature, and Gil Hodges', and Pee Wee

Reese's, and of course Jackie Robinson's. But I figured Davy would be thrilled with Miksis and Billy Cox, since their names on a ball would be more than he'd ever expected. And anyway a few more guys might come meandering in before I was through.

But no matter how hard I swallowed, my heart was still stuck in my throat. "Eddie!" I called. "Eddie! Billy!" Hardly any sound came out of my mouth at all.

And then all of a sudden I heard a voice calling real loud. Whoever it was didn't have any trouble getting the sound out of *his* mouth. "Hey you, kid, get down off that roof," the voice said. "What do you think you're doing?" I sat up and turned around. An angry usher was standing at the foot of the aisle, right by the railing, screaming at me. "Get yourself off that roof," he shouted. "Right now, or I'll throw you out of the ball park."

I scrambled down fast as I could. Boy, was I a mess. My chino pants and my striped jersey were absolutely covered with dust and grime from that roof. I guess my face and arms weren't any too clean either. I looked like a bum.

"I'm going to throw you out anyway," the usher said, "because you don't have a ticket."

I got real mad when I heard him say that. People had been throwing me out of places all week long and I was plenty sick of it. Especially since I certainly did have a ticket.

"You can't throw me out," I shouted back at him. "I've got as much right to be here as you have." I had suddenly found my voice. I was scared of the ball players, but this usher didn't frighten me one bit. I pulled my ticket stub out of my pocket. "See?" I said, thrusting it into his face. "I certainly do have a ticket."

He made as if to take it out of my hand. I guess he wanted to look at it close, to make sure it was a stub from that day and not an old one I carried around in my pocket for emergencies. But I pulled my hand back.

"Oh, no, you don't," I said. "You can't take this ticket away from me. You won't give it back to me and then you'll throw me out because I don't have a ticket!"

"You crazy, kid?" he asked, shaking his head. "This is what I get for working in Ebbets Field. A bunch of crazy people. Next year I'm applying for a job at the Polo Grounds."

"Go ahead," I said, "you traitor. Who needs you?" I turned away from him and leaned over the rail.

"I better not see you on that roof again," the usher said. "I'll have my eye out for you—and so will all the other ushers."

"Don't worry," I said.

Then I felt his hand on my shoulder. "As a matter of fact, kid," he said, "I think I'll escort you to your seat where you belong. Up in the bleachers where you can't make any trouble."

Well, right then and there the whole enterprise would have gone up in smoke if old Jackie Robinson himself had not come trotting out onto the field from the dugout that very second. "Hey, Jackie!" I called. "Hey, Jackie!" in a voice as loud as a thunderbolt. I mean there were two airplanes flying overhead right that minute and Jackie Robinson heard me anyway.

He glanced over in the direction he could tell my voice was coming from, and I began to wave frantically, still calling "Jackie! Hey, Jackie!"

He lifted up his hand, gave one wide wave, and smiled. "Hey, kid," he called, and continued on his way to the batting cage. In another instant he'd

have been too busy with batting practice to pay any attention to me.

"Sign my ball!" I screamed. "Sign my ball!"

He seemed to hesitate briefly. I took this as a good omen. "You gotta," I went on frantically. "Please, please, you gotta."

"He don't gotta do nothing," the usher said. "That's Jackie Robinson and everyone knows that he don't gotta do nothing."

I went right on screaming.

"Come on, kid," the usher said, "we're getting out of here." He was a big hulking usher who must have weighed about eight hundred pounds, and he began pulling on me. Even though I gripped the cement with my sneakers and held onto the rail with my hand, he managed to pull me loose. But he couldn't shut me up.

"Please, Jackie, please!" I went right on screaming.

It worked. Or something worked. If not my screaming, then maybe the sight of that monster usher trying to pull me up the aisle and scrungy old me pulling against him for dear life.

"Let the kid go," Jackie Robinson said when he got to the railing. "All he wants is an autograph."

"He's a fresh kid," the usher said, but he let me go.

"Kids are supposed to be fresh," Jackie Robinson said.

I thrust my ball into Jackie Robinson's face. "Gee, thanks, Mr. Robinson," I said. "Sign it, please."

"You got a pen?" he asked.

"A pen?" I could have kicked myself. "A pen?" I'd forgotten a pen! I turned to the usher. "You got a pen?"

"If I had," the usher said triumphantly, "I certainly wouldn't lend it to you!"

"Oh, come on," Jackie Robinson said. "Don't be so vindictive. What harm did the kid do, after all?"

"Well, as it happens, I don't have one," the usher replied smugly.

"Wait here," I said. "Wait right here, Mr. Robinson. I'll go find one."

Jackie Robinson laughed. "Sorry, kid, but I've got work to do. Another time, maybe."

"Please, Mr. Robinson," I said. "It's for my friend. My friend, Davy."

"Well, let Davy come and get his own autographs," he said. "Why should you do his dirty work for him?"

"He can't come," I said. The words came rushing out of me, tumbling one on top of the other. I had to tell Jackie Robinson all about it, before he went away. "Davy can't come because he's sick. He had a heart attack."

"A heart attack?" Jackie Robinson asked. "A kid had a heart attack?"

"He's not a kid," I explained. "He's sixty years old. He's my best friend. He's always loved the Dodgers, but lately he's loved them more than ever."

"How did this Davy get to be your best friend?" Jackie Robinson asked.

So I told him. I told him everything, or as near to everything as I could tell in five minutes. I told him how Davy worked for my mother, and how I had no father, so it was Davy who took me to my first ball game. I told him how they wouldn't let me into the hospital to see Davy, and how we had always talked about catching a ball that was hit into the stands and getting it autographed.

Jackie listened silently, nodding every once in a while. When I was done at last, he said, "Well, now, kid, I'll tell you what. You keep this ball you brought with you. Keep it to play with. And borrow a pen from someone. Come back to the dugout the minute, the very second, the game is over, and I'll get you a real ball, one we played with, and I'll get all the guys to autograph it for you."

"Make sure it's one you hit," I said.

What nerve. I should have fainted dead away just because Jackie Robinson had deigned to speak to me. But here he was, making me an offer beyond my wildest dreams, and for me it wasn't enough. I had to have more. However, he didn't seem to care.

"O.K.," he said, "*if* I hit one." He had been in a little slump lately.

"You will," I said, "you will."

And he did. He broke the ball game wide open in the sixth inning when he hit a double to left field, scoring Rackley and Duke Snider. He scored himself when the Cubs pitcher, Warren Hacker, tried to pick him off second base. But Hacker overthrew, and Jackie, with that incredible speed he had, ran all the way home. Besides, he worked two double plays

with Preacher Roe and Gil Hodges. On consecutive
pitches, Carl Furillo and Billy Cox both hit home
runs, shattering the 1930 Brooklyn home-run record
of 122 for a season. The Dodgers scored six runs,
and they scored them all in the sixth inning. They
beat the Cubs, 6–1. They were hot, really hot, that
day and that year.

But I really didn't watch the game as closely as I had all the others I'd been to see. I couldn't. My mind was on too many other things—on Jackie Robinson, on what was going to happen after the game was over, on that monster usher who I feared would yet find some way of spoiling things for me, but above all on Davy and the fact that he was missing all of the excitement.

And then I had to worry about getting hold of a pen. You could buy little pencils at the ball park for keeping box scores, but no pens. It was the first—and last—time in my life I walked into a ball park without something to write with. And I didn't see how I could borrow one from someone, since in all that mess of humanity I'd never find the person after the game to return it to him. Unless I took the guy's name and address and mailed it back to him later.

It didn't look to me like the guys in the bleachers where I was sitting had pens with them anyway. Most of them had on tee shirts, and tee shirts don't have pockets in them for pens. I decided to walk over to the seats along the first-base line to see if any of those fans looked more like pen owners. I had to go in that direction anyway to make sure I was at the dugout the second the ball game ended. I took with me my ball in its box.

On my way over I ran into this guy hawking soft drinks and I decided to buy one in order to wash down the two egg-salad sandwiches I had eaten during the third inning.

This guy had a pen in his pocket. As a matter of fact, he had two of them. "Look," I said to him, as I paid him for my soda, "could I borrow one of those pens?"

"Sure," he said, handing it to me after he had put my money into his change machine. He stood there, waiting, like he expected me to hand it back to him after I was done with it.

"Look," I said again, "maybe I could sort of buy it from you."

"Buy it from me? You mean the pen?"

"Yeah."

"What do you want my pen for?"

"I need it because Jackie Robinson promised me that after the game he and all the other guys would autograph a ball for me." Getting involved in all these explanations was really a pain in the neck.

"You don't say," the hawker remarked. I could tell he didn't believe me.

"It's true," I said. "Anyway, are you going to sell me your pen?"

"Sure. For a dollar."

I didn't have a dollar. Not anymore. I'd have to try something else. I started to walk away.

"Oh, don't be silly, kid," he called to me. "Here, take the pen. Keep it." It was a nice pen. It was shaped like a bat, and on it, it said, "Ebbets Field, Home of the Brooklyn Dodgers."

"Hey, mister, thanks," I said. "That's real nice of you." It seemed to me I ought to do something for him, so I added, "I think I'd like another soda." He sold me another soda, and between sipping first from one and then from the other and trying to watch the game, I made very slow progress down to the dugout.

I got there just before the game ended in the top of the ninth.

The Dodgers didn't have to come up to bat at all in that final inning, and I was only afraid that they'd all have disappeared into the clubhouse by the time I got there. I should have come down at the end of the eighth. But Jackie Robinson had said the end of the game. Although my nerve had grown by about seven thousand percent that day, I still didn't have enough to interrupt Jackie Robinson during a game.

I stood at the railing near the dugout, waiting, and sure enough, Jackie Robinson appeared around the corner of the building only a minute or two after Preacher Roe pitched that final out. All around me people were getting up to leave the ball park, but a lot of them stopped when they saw Jackie Robinson come to the rail to talk to me. Roy Campanella, Pee Wee Reese, and Gil Hodges were with him.

"Hi, kid," Jackie Robinson said. He was carrying a ball. It was covered with signatures. "Pee Wee here had a pen."

"And a good thing, too," Pee Wee said, "because most of the other guys left the field already."

"But these guys wanted to meet Davy's friend," Jackie Robinson said.

By that time, Preacher Roe had joined us at the railing. Jackie handed him the ball. "Hey, Preacher," he said, "got enough strength left in that arm to sign this ball for Davy's friend here?"

"Got a pen?" Preacher Roe asked.

I handed him the pen the hawker had given me.

I was glad I hadn't gone through all the trouble of getting it for nothing.

"Not much room left on this ball," Roe said. He squirmed his signature into a little empty space beneath Duke Snider's and then he handed me both the pen and the ball.

Everybody was waving programs and pens in the faces of the ballplayers who stood by the railing. But before they signed any of them, they all shook my hand. So did Jackie Robinson. I stood there, clutching Davy's ball and watching while those guys signed the programs of the other fans.

Finally, though, they'd had enough. They smiled and waved their hands and walked away, five big men in white uniforms, etched sharply against the bright green grass. Jackie Robinson was the last one into the dugout and before he disappeared around the corner, he turned and waved to me.

I waved back. "Thank you, Jackie Robinson," I called. "Thanks for everything." He nodded and smiled. I guess he heard me. I'm glad I remembered my manners before it was too late.

When everyone was gone, I looked down at the ball in my hands. Right between the rows of red seaming, Jackie Robinson had written, above his own signature, "For Davy. Get well soon." Then all the others had put their names around that.

I took the ball I had bought out of the box and put it in my pocket. I put the ball Jackie Robinson had given me in the box. Then I went home.

Questions

1. To get "something for Davy," Sam had to solve problems. In what order did Sam meet and solve the following problems in the story?
   a. how to ask the ball players for a favor
   b. how to get a regulation baseball
   c. how to get a pen
   d. how to get money for the game
   e. how to get to Ebbets Field
   f. how to get to the dugout on time

2. Why do you think that Jackie Robinson was willing to help Sam get what he wanted?

3. Two times in the story Sam "lost his voice," but another time, he "found his voice." What happened to cause Sam to lose or find his voice each time?

4. Sam *exaggerated* when he said that he and Davy wouldn't catch a ball if they went to "a thousand million games." Find another place in the story where Sam *exaggerates,* or makes something much greater than it is. Why did he exaggerate that time?

Activity   Write a Description

"Bit players" in a television play or a movie are characters who have small parts. List two bit players in the story who make a big difference in Sam's day. Then write a description of a bit player in your own life—someone who may have made a difference to you. Provide details describing the person's actions, appearance, and speech.

Today Song

A poem by Robert McGovern

Two days are never quite the same—
Yesterday's then, tomorrow is when.
If today is good, I'll remember it then
When now is when, and when was then,
Good morning.

FROZEN YOGURT

UMBRELLAS

Illustrated by Marie-Louise Gay

179

An Allergy Is a Bothersome Thing

From the novel *Philip Hall likes me. I reckon maybe.* by Bette Greene
Illustrated by Diane de Groat

*Lately, things have been changing for Beth Lambert.
Her best friend, Philip Hall, has been spending most
of his time with other friends, and Beth's family is too
busy getting ready for a new baby to think much
about her. What Beth wants right now is something
special—something just for her. And if that something
special just happened to be a dog, well, Beth Lambert
wouldn't mind that at all!*

Mr. Barnes stopped the school bus along the side of the highway just at that spot where the dirt road leading to our farm meets the blacktop. First Philip Hall got off. Then I jumped off in front of the faded black-and-white sign at the intersection which read:

1 mile
↑
Lambert Farm
good turkeys
good pigs

As I took a flying leap across the frozen drainage ditch that separated the road from the field, I heard Philip calling me.

"Hey, Beth!" He was still standing on the blacktop just where the bus left him. "You oughtna be going through the field. You might step into an ice puddle."

181

Of all days to have to stop and start explaining things to Philip Hall. But at any other time I'd be thinking that he wouldn't be fretting about my feet if he didn't really like me. Now would he? "Frosty feet ain't nothing," I told him, "when you have a spanking new puppy waiting to meet you."

"What if Mr. Grant wouldn't swap a collie dog for one of your pa's turkeys?" asked Philip, grinning as though he hoped it was so.

"That's all you know! When I left the house this morning, my pa was picking out six of our fattest turkeys for swapping." I turned and began running across the field.

"Well, one collie dog is worth more than six of your old turkeys," called Philip.

I kept on running, pretending not to hear. And, anyway, everybody loves to eat turkey. Don't they?

When I reached the rise in the field, I could see our house a nice pale green. As I came closer, I could see my mama on the porch. She was hanging work-worn overalls across the porch clothesline. I tiptoed up behind her and threw my arms around her.

"Ohhh!" She jumped. "What you mean scaring me clear out of my wits, girl?"

"Where is he?" I asked. "Where's the collie?"

She put on her I'm-not-fixing-to-listen-to-any-nonsense face and said, "I don't know nothing about no collie."

"Did Pa make the swap? Did he?"

"Get out of here, girl. Go on into the kitchen."

"Tell me if Pa got the collie," I pleaded. "Now did he?"

Her mouth was still set into that no-nonsense way of hers, but it was different with her eyes. Her eyes were filled up with pure pleasure. "And I told you," she said, "to get on into the kitchen, didn't I?"

Suddenly I understood. I threw open the screen door and, without waiting to close it gently behind me, ran in a straight line through the living room and into the kitchen.

And then I saw him. There in a cardboard carton next to the cookstove was a reddish-brown puppy with a circle of white fluffy hair ringing his neck and spilling down to his chest. I dropped to my knees and showed my open palms. "Hi, puppy. Beautiful little collie puppy."

"He's beautiful, sure enough," said Ma from behind.

The collie just looked at me for a few moments. Then he got to his feet and trotted over.

"And you're friendly too," I said, patting his back. "Hey, that would be a good name for you."

"Friendly," said Ma, smacking her lips like she was word tasting. "That's a right good name."

I gave Friendly a hug and a kiss. "I will now name you— *ah-choo!*" I tried again. "I will now name—*AHHHHhhhh-choo!!*"

Ma shook her head the way she does when she catches me at mischief. "You done gone and got yourself a cold, now, didn't you?"

"AHHHHhhhhhh-ha-ha-ha-choo! I now name you Friendly," I said at last.

By bedtime I was sneezing constantly and water kept pouring from my sore, itchy eyes. But, thank goodness, all my sneezing didn't seem to bother Friendly, who slept peacefully in his cardboard carton at the foot of my bed.

I could hear my folks in the kitchen talking about what they were always talking about these days—names for our soon-to-be-born baby. When they finally tired of that topic, Ma said, "Beth got me worried. All them wheezing sounds coming from her chest."

"I seen Doc Brenner in town this afternoon," said Pa. "He asked me to kill and clean one of our twenty-pound birds. Said he'd stop by this evening to pick it up."

"When he comes by," said Ma, "ask him to kindly take a look at our Beth."

I climbed out of bed to take off my raggedy tail of a nightgown and put on the one that Grandma had given me last Christmas. She had made it out of a sack of Fairy Flake flour, but she dyed it a bright, brilliant orange. It was nice.

Friendly started to bark.

"Don't you be frightened, little Friendly. It's only me, only Beth."

While I patted my new pet, I told him how glad I was that he had come to live with us. "You're going to like it here, you'll see. I'm going to bring all my friends to meet you. Philip Hall, Susan, Bon—*ahh-choo-whoo! Ahh choo!* Bonnie, Ginny, Esther. You're going to like all my friends, Friendly, but you're going to like me best of all . . . I reckon maybe."

Ma called out, "Is you out of bed, Beth?"

I jumped back into bed before answering. "No ma'm. I'm right here. Right here in bed."

I kept my eyes open, waiting for the doctor to come, but after a while my eyelids came together. Sleep stood by waiting for me to fall . . . fall asleep . . . sleep . . . sleep.

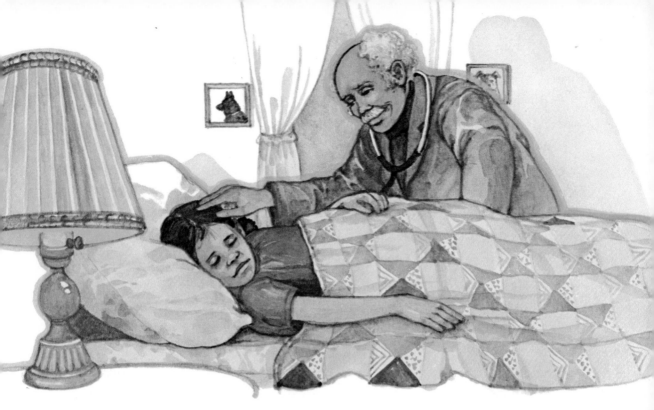

"Let me take a look at my old friend, Beth," said a big voice.

My cheeks were being patted. "Doctor's here, Beth honey," Ma was saying.

I pulled myself up to sitting and looked into the face of Dr. Brenner, who said, "This won't hurt," as he placed a stethoscope to my chest.

"Just breathe naturally," he said. He listened quietly without saying a word. Then he took the stethoscope from his ears. "I heard some wheezing sounds coming from your chest. Tell me, how do your eyes feel?"

"They feel like I want to grab them out of their sockets and give them a good scratching. They're so . . . so itchy."

"Uh-hun," answered Dr. Brenner, as though he knew all about itchy eyes. "Beth, can you remember when all this sneezing and wheezing began?"

"Yes, sir," I told the doctor. "It all started when I met Friendly."

Friendly must have heard his name called 'cause he jumped out of his carton and jogged floppily on over.

"Hi, little Friendly, little dog."

I picked him up and gave him a hug and a kiss. *"AHHHHhh-choo! Ah-choo!"*

"Beth," said Dr. Brenner, running his fingers through his silver hair. "I'm sorry to do this, but I'm going to have to tell you something. Something you're not going to like hearing. I believe you have an allergy to Friendly."

"Oh, no sir, I don't!" I cried. "I don't have one, honest. I never asked for no allergy. Why, I don't even know what that means."

Dr. Brenner took my hand. "It simply means that Friendly's dog hair is making you sick. And, furthermore, it means that he must be returned to wherever he came from."

"But Friendly is *my* dog. He belongs to me. And he's never *never* going to go back to that kennel!" I felt tears filling up my eyes. "I love Friendly. Friendly loves me."

"I know you love each other," agreed Dr. Brenner. "But all this sneezing, wheezing, and red eyes is your body's way of telling you something."

I shook my head no.

Doc Brenner nodded his head yes. "Bodies don't need to say fancy words like allergic rhinitis[1]— or any words at all, Beth. When your throat is dry, you don't wait to hear the word *water* before taking a drink. And do you really need the school's lunch bell to ring before you know when it's time to eat? Well, now your body is saying something just as important. Listen to it!" he said, cupping his hand around his ear. But the only sound in the room was the hissing noise coming from my own chest.

When the morning sun came flooding through my bedroom window, my eyes opened and I remembered about the allergy. Was it real or only a dream?

"Friendly," I called. "Come here, little Friendly."

But Friendly didn't come and I didn't hear him either. I jumped to the foot of my bed. The cardboard box was empty. They've

---

1. allergic rhinitis (uh•LUHR•jik ry•NY•tis): a sensitivity to something that causes sneezing and a painful, red swelling inside the nose.

taken him back to Mr. Grant's kennel!

I was just about to shout out for Friendly when outside the kitchen window I heard my brother Luther's and my sister Anne's voices: "Get that ball, Friendly. Friendly, you going to get that ball?"

Ma laughed. "That dog ain't fixing to do nothing he ain't a mind to do."

I went out the kitchen door still wearing my orange nightgown and sat down on the back steps next to her. She put her arm around me and gave me a quick squeeze. "How you feeling, honey babe?"

I thought about her question. My chest felt as though it was still filled up with old swamp water while my head carried around last night's headache. Finally, I gave my answer, "I'm OK, Mama. I reckon."

"After you come home from school, I want you to take a little nap. Never mind them chores. Just put your head down on the pillow and nap. 'Cause you spent half the night crying into your pillow."

"About what the doctor said ... about taking Friendly back to the kennel. We're not going to listen to that, are we?"

She looked past me, out to where Luther and Anne were playing with Friendly. "Life don't always be the way we want it to be. Life be the way it is. Ain't nothing we can do."

"You *can't* take him back!" I shouted. "Besides, Mr. Grant probably's eaten up all the turkeys."

"If he did, he did," answered Ma.

"You don't understand," I said, bringing my voice back down to size. "I *need* Friendly! Luther was three and Anne was two when I was born so they had me, but I never had nothing little and soft to—"

"And I told you," she said, "that life be the way it be. Ain't nothing we can do. But if you misses that school bus, there is something I can do. I can take a switch to you. So *get!*"

At school I felt better and worse. Better because I didn't sneeze or wheeze and even my

eyes stopped itching and watering. And worse because tonight, after supper, Friendly was going back to Mr. Grant's kennel.

If only I had some magic. One time I remembered my teacher, Miss Johnson, pointing to shelves of books and saying that they held many secrets. Could one of her books hold the secret of making the allergy go and the dog stay?

At recess, she stood on a three-step ladder to bring down a heavy book from the top shelf.

"This book may have the secret we're looking for," she said, pointing to a page. "Right here," she whispered, the way people do when they're telling secrets. "It says that people who have an allergy to long-haired dogs, like the collie, might not have an allergy to a short-haired dog, like the chihuahua."

At the kennel I held Friendly close to me while Pa explained about the allergy to Mr. Grant. "You are welcome to swap," he said, reaching out for Friendly.

"Wait!" I said. "A person has got to say good-bye, don't they?" I looked into Friendly's eyes and wondered how I could make him understand. "I never wanted to get rid of you, Friendly. I only wanted to get rid of the aller— *Her-her-choo!*—of the allergy."

He licked my ear almost as if to tell me not to worry because any dog as friendly as Friendly would get along just fine.

Again Mr. Grant reached out, only this time I gave him my Friendly. As he took him away, I heard him say, "Rest of the collies going to be mighty happy to see you again."

When he returned, Friendly wasn't with him. "An allergy sure is a bothersome thing," said Mr. Grant. "Reason I know that is because I've had an allergy ever since I was about your age."

It was so hard to believe. "You got yourself an allergy to collies too?" I asked.

"Nope." Mr. Grant pointed to the bend in his suntanned arm. "Tomatoes—that's what gets my allergy going. One tomato and my arm breaks out like a strawberry patch."

"Tomatoes don't bother me a bit," I said proudly.

"Reckon that's what an allergy is," said Mr. Grant. "It's what don't bother some folks, bothers other folks a whole lot."

When we stopped in front of the chihuahua's run, a tiny fellow came rushing to the gate, barking. "That's the dog for me," I said.

On the drive back home I held the chihuahua in my lap while my folks went back to trying to pick out a baby name. I was hoping they'd find a better name for the baby than they found for me.

When Pa turned off the highway onto the dirt road leading to our farm, the puppy jumped off my lap. He stood on his toes, pressing his nose against the truck's window. I hollered, "Looky there! Look at Tippietoes!"

"Ohhhh," said Ma, turning her head. "Now ain't that something?

And what a fine name for him too."

I put my hands against the little dog's cheeks and gave him a kiss between the eyes. "I now name you—*ah-ah*—I now name you—*ah-ah-ah-choo!*"

"Oh, *no!*" said Ma and Pa at exactly the same time.

But finally I was able to say, and say proudly, "I now name you Tippietoes."

By the time I crawled into bed, my eyes were red and itchy. My nose was sneezy and my chest was wheezy. Ma stood at my doorway. "Tippietoes going to sleep next to the cookstove tonight, but tomorrow evening we're going to take him back."

I shook my head no. "Mama, don't say that. I don't care nothing about no little allergy. Cross my heart I don't. All I care about is my little dog. My own little Tippietoes."

"Girl, you ain't talking nothing but a heap of foolishness. I ain't about to let you walk around sick. Not as long as I'm your mama, 'cause I ain't that kind of mama. Now you get yourself to sleep."

--»꩜«--

At first recess, I told Miss Johnson about having an allergy, not just to long-haired dogs but to short-haired ones too.

"Maybe I can find still another secret in that book," she said, bringing down the big book again. She fingered through a lot of pages before she finally began to read aloud: "People who have an allergy to both long-haired and short-haired dogs might not have an allergy to poodles, as they are the only dogs that never shed hair."

Pa explained to Mr. Grant what I had learned from the book. "So we'll be much obliged if you'll kindly swap Tippietoes here for one of your poodles."

"Fine with me," said Mr. Grant, reaching for Tippietoes.

"*Wait!*" I said, holding onto the little one for another moment. "A person still has to say good-bye." I patted his chin. He licked my fingers. "Good-bye, little boy, little Tippietoes. I'm sorry you couldn't be my dog."

I closed my eyes as I gave him over to Mr. Grant, who took him away. When he came back he said, "Come along, folks. Let me introduce you to my poodles."

We followed him until he stopped at the gate of a chain-link fence. "Poodles may be just the right dog for a girl with an allergy," he said, pointing to two white dogs that looked more like fluffy powder puffs than real dogs. "Because they never have dandruff or a doggy odor. And the book is right. They never shed a single hair."

He unhooked the gate and I walked in saying, "This time I'm going to be lucky. This time I *hope* I'm going to be lucky."

"Hope so," said Ma and Pa at exactly the same moment.

Both poodles walked over to say hello. They were quite polite. I bent down and one of the puppies came closer. "Is it you?" I asked him.

He took one step closer, resting his fluffy little head in my hand. I whispered, "I'm going to take real good care of you."

Inside the crowded cab of the pickup truck, I held the poodle puppy on my lap as Pa turned on the headlights and started for home. My patting must have relaxed the little dog 'cause he closed his eyes and went to sleep.

After a while Ma said, "I think we ought to name the baby after my great-aunt Alberta."

Pa's nose crinkled. "What you want to name our baby after her for?"

Ma's nose climbed. "Ain't she my grandma's sister? The oldest

living member of my family?"

"That nosy old lady!" said Pa.

"Aunt Alberta ain't one bit nosy," Ma corrected. "What she is, is interested. I'm disappointed in you, Mr. Eugene Lam—"

"Have you all noticed," I asked, hoping that my interruption would stop an argument from starting, "that I haven't sneezed even one time?"

Ma smiled. "Ain't it the truth."

"And Puffy will never have to go back to Mr. Grant's," I said.

"Puffy?" asked Pa, surprised.

"Don't you see," I asked, "how he's all puffy like cotton candy?"

Ma turned to look at Pa. "Beth has thought up three good names for three dogs while we is still fussing over one name for one baby."

Puffy opened his eyes and looked around. "You're here, Puffy," I said, putting my face into his white fluffiness. "And you're always going to be . . . my . . . my—*choo*! My—*ahhhhhhh-ey*!"

"Don't go telling me I heard what I think I heard," said Ma, fixing her eyes on the ceiling of the truck.

"It ain't what you think," I said quickly. "I really—*ahhh-choo! Ah-choo-who!* I really think I'm catching Billy Boy Williams's cold. He had one at school today. Sneezed all over the place—choo, choo, choo, like that! Spreading his germs about."

Pa drove the truck over to the side of the road and turned off the engine. "Beth, I is sorry to disappoint you. I know how much you wanted a pup, but there ain't nothing I can do."

"If you take him back," I warned, "I ain't never going to live home again. For the rest of my life I'm going to live in the kennel with Puffy."

My mama patted my hand. "In this life you got to be happy about the good things and brave about the bad ones."

"I don't want to be brave," I shouted. "All I want is my little dog."

Pa started up the truck, made a U-turn on the highway, and headed back toward the kennel. "Ain't nothing in this wide world we can do," he said, shaking his head.

The next morning I asked Miss Johnson to bring down the book again. But after a while we stopped reading. It didn't have any more secrets to tell. I walked away 'cause I didn't have a single word for a single solitary soul. But later in the afternoon I told her, "I guess it's nobody's fault. But I reckon I'm learning to be brave about things I don't like."

"And I want you to know," said Miss Johnson, taking off her glasses, "that I think you're learning very well."

When the school bus stopped in front of our sign, I jumped off and with a running leap crossed the ditch.

"How come you shortcutting through the field again?" called Philip Hall. "Ain't no dog waiting for you today."

"Guess I know that," I said, wondering how I could have forgotten. And yet for some reason I really was in a hurry to get home.

When I reached the rise, I could see the outline of my mother. But it didn't look like her, not exactly. After I passed the vegetable garden, I could see that it wasn't her. It was . . . my grandmother.

I started running my fast run. "Grandma, Grandma! Hello!"

"Howdy there, Beth babe," she called back.

I ran into her arms as she closed them around me. "How come you're here? All the way from Walnut Ridge?"

Grandma smiled. "I came to see my new grandbaby. Born this very morning, a few minutes after nine."

"Where are they?" I asked.

"Shhhhh," she said, pointing to the inside of the house. "They are both real fine, but they're resting just now."

I asked, "Is it a . . . is it a brother?"

"A brother for you, a grandson for me," she said, hugging me some more.

I danced a circle around her. "My own little brother. He's going to be fun to take care of and fun to play with. Sometimes boys are almost as much fun to play with as girls. I've noticed that."

"Reckon I've noticed that too," said Grandma, joining my dance.

"What's my brother's name?"

Grandma stopped dancing. "Your folks ain't come to no decision on that," she said.

"Don't fret about that," I told her. "I happen to be good at names."

Then I heard Pa calling from inside the house, "Beth, come on in and meet up with your brother."

I closed the screen door quietly behind me the way I always remember to do when there is a visitor in the house. Pa stood at the door of his and Ma's bedroom and waved me on. "I want you to see something real pretty," he said.

Ma was sitting up in bed, propped up by two pillows. As I came closer, I saw something in her arms that I had never seen there before. A baby.

Ma said, "Fold your arms."

"Like this?" I asked.

"Just like that," she said, placing my soft little brother in my arms.

"Ohhhhh," I said, touching my lips to his warm head. "You are a beautiful baby brother. Baby brother Benjamin."

"Benjamin?" asked Ma. "Benjamin? *Benjamin!*—Oh, yes. That's it. That's the name!"

Pa smiled. "Benjamin is a good strong name for a boy."

"Finally," said Grandma, coming into the room. "A name for the baby."

I put my face next to Baby Benjamin's and breathed in deep. I didn't sneeze. "You're always going to be our Baby Benjamin," I whispered in his ear. "And anyway, Mr. Grant wouldn't know what to do with a real baby."

Questions

1. Sometimes you want something, but something else gets in the way. There is a *conflict,* or a struggle, between the two things. What was Beth's conflict? How was the conflict finally solved?

2. Why did Beth and her family decide to get a poodle? Did the idea work? Why or why not?

3. What did Beth learn from her troubles? Do you think it is a useful lesson? Why?

4. If you could talk to Beth about getting a pet, what kind of pet would you recommend? Why?

5. The author has Beth tell the story in her own words. Throughout the story, the "I" is always Beth speaking. How does Beth's own way of telling what happened help you enjoy the story?

6. The doctor said that Beth had "allergic rhinitis." How would you explain the meaning and effects of this illness in your own words?

Activity   Write a Letter

Dear Reader,

I heard that you like a story character whose name is Beth Lambert. Well, I have decided to write a book. Please write and give me advice about how I can make my main character as interesting and likable as Beth Lambert. Thank you.

Sincerely,
An author

THE WORST MORNING

From the novel . . . *and now Miguel* by Joseph Krumgold
Illustrated by Don Bolognese

*Each summer in New Mexico the days become
very hot, and the lowland grass dies. It is then that
the men of the Chavez[1] family drive their sheep
high into the Sangre de Cristo[2] Mountains, where
the grass stays green. For several years young
Miguel[3] Chavez has been waiting for the time
when his father will allow him to join the summer
journey. During the past year, twelve-year-old
Miguel has tried to show that he is ready to make
the journey by working as hard as the adults.
When a group of sheep become lost, it is Miguel
who finds them and brings them safely home. And
when sheep-shearing days begin, Miguel is given
more responsible jobs than ever before. Miguel
begins to hope that he is accepted, at last, as a
working member of his family. Then comes the
worst morning. Here is how Miguel tells about it.*

---

1. **Chavez** (CHAH•bays).
2. **Sangre de Cristo** (SAHN•gray THAY KREES•toh).
3. **Miguel** (mee•GEHL).

Just to look at, the morning was all right. Or even, to tell the truth, it was a nice morning. The sun was shining and the shadows were long and heavy when we came out of the house. The sky was blue and big like there was more of it around than usual, more clear sky thin as deep water all around. Over the mountains there were clouds looking like a flock of clouds grazing around up there, big and little ones. And over the house, there were a couple of little ones, tramp clouds, like orphans. The Sangre de Cristo Mountains, they looked closer than I ever saw them before.

I felt good that morning when we all went out to finish the shearing. When we all walked out together, my grandfather told me to hang up the bag for the wool. The rest of the unshorn sheep had to be herded from the fields, where they had grazed all night, into the corral. All the other hands had to go out to round them up and bring them in. So it was up to me, my grandfather

said, to hang up the big sack. Me, that is, and
Uncle Eli.[4]

I was glad to do this because hanging the sack,
after all, is an important job which you don't ask
anyone at all to do and which I had never been
asked to do before. I knew how it worked, though,
from watching.

First, Uncle Eli and I, we got this iron hoop, like
a hoop off a barrel only thick and solid, and this

---

4. Eli (AY•lee).

hoop we put around the top outside the opening of the sack. Then we turned over the cloth of the sack, which is burlap, we turned it over the hoop all the way around. All that's left is to take some nails, which you use like they were pins, to fasten the turned-over burlap to the rest of the sack so that the hoop is all covered over and it can't fall off.

Once you do this, it's very easy to hang the sack. All you do then is to go up on the wall of the shed where is nailed this square wooden frame and drop the bottom of the empty sack through the frame. But the opening of the sack can't go through because the hoop is bigger than the wooden square and it rests on the square letting the sack hang down at its full length, six or seven feet. That's all there is to it.

But once we got the sack hung up, Uncle Eli said, "Stay up there, Miguelito.[5] We'll get started and sack up these fleeces from yesterday."

Down below there was a bin into which the fleeces are put by the men who tie them up, my father and grandfather. A dozen or so were left over from the afternoon before, covered by a tarpaulin to keep them from the wet and the dew during the night. Eli took off the tarp and started to hand up the fleeces to me standing high up where I was, on the wooden frame on top of the sack. I dropped the fleeces into the sack, one after another, as Eli handed them to me.

---

5. **Miguelito** (mee·gay·LEE·toh).

By this time the first bunch had been herded into the yard in front of the shearing shed, the clippers were working, the shearing was started. And through the window that is in the back of the shed more fleeces were already starting to come into the bin where Eli was. He kept handing them up to me. I kept dropping them into the sack.

I saw that my big brother Blasito[6] was sweeping with the broom, which was the job I did the day before. So I just stayed up on top there, sacking the wool. If anything, this is even a more important kind of work than sweeping, to stand way up on top there to take the fleeces the shearers had cut and my father had tied, and sack them up so we could take them to the buyer, Mr. Morrison. I never thought I'd be doing this for years yet. But no one said I shouldn't, so there I was up on top, sacking the wool. And by this time the fleeces were coming through the window pretty fast, and no one took any notice who was doing the work as long as it was getting done. Eli didn't have any more time to hand me the fleeces. He started throwing them up to me.

It was easy to catch them. And it was nothing at all to drop them in the sack. But this is not the important part of sacking the wool.

The important part is that the wool has to be packed tight. It must be stamped down so hard and solid that the sack gets to look like one big round sausage. It is not difficult to do. You wait

---

6. **Blasito** (blah·SEE·toh).

until the fleeces pile up and then you step in
the middle of the bag and stamp up and down
and jump with all your might until the wool is
hard beneath your feet. You don't have to be
afraid the bag will tear. It's made out of the best
burlap, the strongest kind, and can hold even
the biggest men, who are usually the ones that
do the sacking.

So there I was up on top. Fleeces flying up
from Uncle Eli. Everybody as busy and working as
fast as they could, like on the day before. And
soon the woolly fleeces filled up the sack to the
very top. I stepped in the middle to stamp them
down. And it was like the whole world gave way
from right under my feet.

I dropped slowly down to the bottom of the sack. One long drop, and then a soft bump. There had not been enough fleeces to hold me up, not enough soft wool. I just went down, slow, and there was nothing to do. The sides of the bag, the burlap, were hard and rough with nothing to catch, not even with fingernails. Like going down a smooth tunnel standing straight up. There was no way to save myself. And yell, I couldn't yell. How could I yell and tell everyone what a fool I was to be falling that second into the bag which was for the wool?

I didn't yell.

I didn't breathe.

Outside nothing stopped. The clippers went on. And the gasoline engine went on. The sheep went on bawling like before. One lamb there was who kept crying louder than all the others, again and again. From the shearers there came a shout, "Sheep up, sheep up!" Someone laughed. And there was one somewhere singing. It was a song called "Chiapanecas"[7] which is also a dance. They played it at the fiesta. The singing came from far away, outside there. All these noises, I heard them in the same second. I myself made no noise. Not even to breathe.

I looked up. As if I was climbing up the rough cloth with my eyes, I looked up all the little criss-crosses of the cloth, and at the end I reached the top. Way up, high above me, I saw the sky, still

---

7. Chiapanecas (chee·ah·pah·NAY·kahs).

blue like this morning but no longer big and wide. An eye, a round eye it was, way up at the end of the tunnel, still blue and with one tramp cloud, an orphan cloud.

I breathed. And then a shadow went past the eye. It was a fleece. And right away another. Eli, without looking, he was still throwing fleeces up to me and I wasn't there. The fleeces were going right over the top of the bag. Another came and another. And no one to catch them. I stretched my hands, high, high, knowing I couldn't stretch high enough but stretching up anyway if only to beg they should stop. But over it came, another shadow. I grabbed at the bag around me, wishing I was a cat with claws. But there was nothing, the cloth was too tight and hard to grab. And still it came, another fleece sailing over the opening of the bag way up above.

There was a shout. "Miguel!"

Someone yelled. "What are you doing with the fleeces, Eli? Throwing them away?"

"Eli!"

"What?" That was Eli. "What's wrong? Well, what do you know! Miguel! Where is he? Miguel!"

The fleeces stopped. And everywhere, shouts. For me, Miguel.

"Ai, Miguel!"

"Miguel, where are you?"

"Where'd he go, Miguel?"

"Miguel!"

"Did you see Miguel?"

"Hey Miguel, Miguel! Speak up! Miguel!"

I didn't say anything. I wished only that my name was something different from Miguel. Alexander, Joe, Babaloo—anyone, except me.

"Miguel!"

It was my big brother Blasito who thought of it first. "Maybe he fell into the bag?"

Said one of the shearers, "Yeah, you better look in the bag."

Eli yelled, "Miguel, are you in there? Answer me, Miguel!"

"He's in there all right." It was Salph, the big, round shearer. "How do you like that? The boy fell in the bag."

"What do you think?" Everyone started to laugh, they roared. "Miguel's in the bag!"

Then I heard Johnny Marquez.[8] The man I thought was my friend. Mr. Marquez. Johnny was laughing harder than all the rest.

"Did you ever see anything like that Miguel?" He hit somebody on the back. I could hear it. "He gets tired of being a big man up there. So he jumps back into the sack and goes to sleep."

They screamed and yelled and laughed at how funny this was. There were also other jokes. When I looked up again it was just in time to see the face of my father come into the round blue hole way up there, above my head.

"He's here all right!" yelled my father. He looked down at me again. "What in Heaven's name, Miguel, do you think you're doing down there?"

I was breathing. That's all. But there was no need to tell him this.

"Is this any time to start playing games, hide and seek, like you were a little boy?"

When he said this I stopped breathing again.

He put down his hand. It hung there, big fingers and a big thumb, right in front of my nose.

"Come on, Miguel, let me get you out of this!" The thumb and one of the other fingers, they

8. **Marquez** (MAHR·kays).

snapped. They made a loud noise, one, two, three times. "Miguel! Give me your hand. Up!"

I went back to breathing. But I didn't take the hand. Even when the fingers snapped again, loud and angry. I didn't want to go up. I wanted to stay down here, where there was a shadow and it was dark.

Out there it was bright and blue and the sky was big, and if I went up everyone could see from all around that it was me, Miguel. I could only stay down here, at the bottom of this tunnel. The fingers snapped again, and still I didn't move. The only thing I wanted now was that when I got pulled out I should be somebody different from who I was—Alexander, or Joe, or Babaloo. Not me, Miguel.

My father was angry. "Give me your hand, Miguel, or I'll pull you out by the scruff of your neck. Now come on! Up!"

The big finger, upside down, shook at me. I put up my hands and took the hand hanging there in front of my nose. As soon as I did, my father grabbed me by the wrist.

"Games," he said. "At a time like this."

He lifted me up into the bright day. He dropped me over the side. I fell into the dirt at the bottom of the sack. Up above my father yelled, "Gabriel, get over here! And get those fleeces out of the rubbish. Come on, hombres,[9] we got a day's shearing yet to do."

---

9. **hombres** (OHM·brays).

I didn't look around to see who watched me.
They were stopping to laugh and the clipping
machines started up again, loud. I sat there in the
dirt without moving because there was nowhere I
could think of to go. When I fell I picked up a
handful of dirt and now I let the dirt go out of my
hand, a little bit at a time. After a while I looked
up, and there was my nineteen-year-old brother
Gabriel high up in the sky, sticking out of the
sack. He was stamping down the wool with all his

might, and at the same time he caught the fleeces that Eli was throwing up to him. He turned round and round up there, pushing down the wool solid and tight the way it should be, Gabriel with all the blue and the clouds behind him.

Whatever dirt there was left in my hand, I threw it away.

I made myself small and I got up. I walked away from the shearing shed across the yard, without looking back. No one called me to look back, and there was no one I wanted to see.

Questions

1. Reread the first paragraph of the story. How did Miguel feel about the morning? How did his feelings about the morning change by the end of the story? What caused the change?

2. Be Miguel's father and answer this question: Why did you act angry with Miguel instead of glad that Miguel was rescued?

3. Why do you think the story is written as if Miguel were telling it instead of the author?

4. The story explained a *process,* how to do something. What process did it explain? Why do you think the author, using Miguel's words, explained the process so carefully?

5. Here are four pairs of words from the story. How are the words in each pair related to each other?
   a. fleeces–shearers
   b. Chiapanecas–fiesta
   c. burlap–crisscrosses
   d. tarpaulin–sack

Activity   Draw a Diagram and Write Directions

A new worker has arrived to help with the sheep shearing. Draw and label a diagram to tell the worker exactly what to do to fix the burlap sack so that it can hold the wool. Write step-by-step directions telling what to do to put the sack in its place and to store the wool in it. If necessary, add a CAUTION to your directions.

Running Away

A poem by Karla Kuskin

Running away
From the rest of today
Running away
From you
Running away
From "Don't do that"
From all of the things
I must constantly do.
I feel too tall
I feel too old
For a hundred helpings of being told.
Packing my head
Taking my feet
Galloping down the familiar street.
My head is a bird.
My heart is free again.
I might come back
When I feel like me again.

Illustrated by Nancy Schill

About KARLA KUSKIN

"Running Away," like many of Karla Kuskin's poems, came from a childhood memory. One day when she was nine, she got mad at her mother and decided to run away. "I was going to stay away until they were really scared," she writes, "maybe a week." She got no farther than the nearby woods. "Suddenly there was a very large spider web right in front of me," she remembers. "There was a very large spider in it. I've always been afraid of spiders, so I went home."

Karla Kuskin, who was born in New York City, has written more than twenty books of poetry. Some, like *James and the Rain,* tell complete stories in verse. Others are collections of separate poems. She has illustrated all but one of her books herself.

Karla Kuskin grew up hearing her parents and teachers read poetry aloud to her. Even when she didn't understand all the words, she loved the sounds they made. Today, she often teaches young people about poetry. Sometimes she asks them to write poems of their own. "You can write about anything," she believes. "You can write about things or feelings. When I have feelings that make me sad or angry, I try to write them down to get them outside myself."

Books of Poetry by Karla Kuskin

Near the Window Tree: Poems and Notes
Any Me I Want to Be: Poems
Dogs & Dragons, Trees & Dreams: A Collection of Poems

213

Characters to Remember

Think about some favorite characters in stories you have read. Were they brave? determined? clever? honest? wicked? These are all *traits*. A character's traits are what make that character stand out in your mind. They are what make a character someone you are likely to remember.

A character's traits may be learned from what that character says. What traits do you detect in Beth from what she says in the following section from the story "An Allergy Is a Bothersome Thing"? In this scene, Beth is saying goodbye to her dog, Friendly, because she is allergic to him.

At the kennel I held Friendly close to me while Pa explained about the allergy to Mr. Grant. "You are welcome to swap," he said, reaching out for Friendly.

"Wait!" I said. "A person has got to say good-bye, don't they?" I looked into Friendly's eyes and wondered how I could make him understand. "I never wanted to get rid of you, Friendly. I only wanted to get rid of the aller—*Her-her-choo!*—of the allergy."

Caring, sensitive, concerned—these are traits you may have observed in Beth from what she says.

A character's traits also may be learned from what the author tells us. Here is the way author Natalie Babbitt describes Egan as he begins to climb the mountain in the story "The Megrimum."

. . . Egan was half an hour ahead by that time. And he was young and strong, alone—and determined.

Later in that story, the traits of being *strong* and *determined* are shown in what Egan does—in his actions.

Egan, deep in the mist, heard nothing. He wandered up the final stony slope toward the top like a sleepwalker lost in dreams. . . . And then he stopped, chilled suddenly out of his trance. Just ahead there came a noise as of an animal thrashing about, and the low rumble of a voice.

He crept forward, grasping the nearly forgotten stick tightly, and his heart pounded. The Megrimum! At last, the Megrimum! Slay it, perhaps—perhaps; but at least he would see it.

More thrashing in the weeds ahead. "Owanna-ooowanna," the voice seemed to murmur.

Closer and closer crept Egan and then he saw it dimly, all flailing arms, rolling about on the ground.

You've seen that a character's traits can be shown in several ways—through the words and actions of the characters themselves and through the words of others. Now read some paragraphs about other characters from the stories in this book. Match the characters with one or more of the traits in the list on this page. Choose only those traits that describe the characters in the examples given here. You may want to use some traits more than once, but not all the traits need to be used. Add new ones if you need them.

Character Traits

cheerful	outspoken	wise	determined	curious
sensible	thoughtful	cautious	sensitive	caring
brave	careful	kind	honest	practical
funny	friendly	adventurous	bold	dignified

1. Mr. Wigg in "Laughing Gas"

"I'd better explain, I think," Mr. Wigg went on calmly. "You see, it's this way. I'm a cheerful sort of man and very disposed to laughter. You wouldn't believe, either of you, the number of things that strike me as being funny. I can laugh at pretty nearly everything, I can."

And with that Mr. Wigg began to bob up and down, shaking with laughter at the thought of his own cheerfulness.

216

2. Lucy in "Lucy's Adventure"

Lucy felt a little frightened, but she felt very inquisitive and excited as well. She looked back over her shoulder and there, between the dark tree trunks, she could still see the open doorway of the wardrobe and even catch a glimpse of the empty room from which she had set out. (She had, of course, left the door open, for she knew that it is a very silly thing to shut oneself into a wardrobe.) It seemed to be still daylight there. "I can always get back if anything goes wrong," thought Lucy. She began to walk forward, *crunch-crunch,* over the snow and through the wood towards the other light.

3. Katharine in "The Tournament"

"I wish I could fight ten times as well as you, you bully! Yah!" were the words that the valiant Sir Kath spoke upon the field. It was a cry of pure temper. . . . What followed would have to be seen to be believed. Katharine came down like several wolves on the fold.

Knowing a character's traits may help you describe that character to someone else. Imagine that you've been asked to introduce your favorite book character to your class. Write one paragraph in which you introduce the character. Before you write, make a list of the traits you may want to mention.

I Want That Dog

From the novel *Mine for Keeps* by Jean Little

Illustrated by Dan Siculan

> *For a long time, Sarah Jane Copeland, nicknamed Sally, has been living at a special school. Because Sally was born with cerebral palsy, she has needed special training to learn how to care for herself. However, Sally's teachers feel she is ready to live with her family again and to attend a regular school. So Sally returns to her family's home in Toronto, Canada, to begin her new life.*
>
> *Sally's parents and her younger sister Meg decide that Sally might like a dog. They promise Sally that she can choose a puppy on the way home from her doctor's visit. Sally cannot tell them that she is afraid to own a dog!*

In the morning, Dad drove Mother, Sally and Meg to Toronto to see Dr. Eastman. Dr. Eastman was Sally's specialist. Their family doctor had referred them to him as soon as they had realized that Sal had cerebral palsy.

After he had checked her over, watched her walk and lifted her onto a table while he examined her to see she was "still working properly" as he put it, the doctor turned to find Meg standing at his elbow, her face one big question.

"What's the matter with her, do you know?" Meg asked him.

"Do please," Mother said. "I've done it before

and I'll do it again, but you do it so much better
than I."

Dr. Eastman shook his head as though he did not
believe that, but he sat down facing Meg and Sally.

"Your brain is like a motor," he told them. "Part
of this motor makes you walk. Part of it makes you
talk. Part of it makes you able to use your hands
easily. Another part helps you to see, another to hear,
and so on. If you are going to be able to walk and
use your hands well, you have to have the motor part
of your brain in good working order besides having
well-built arms and legs."

"I walk just on legs," Meg remarked, not believing a word of it.

"Sure you do—just as a car runs on its wheels. But if the motor wasn't in the car too, or if the motor in the car was broken, then what would happen?"

Meg thought about it.

"It wouldn't go," she admitted.

Dr. Eastman smiled. "You're right. It wouldn't," he said. "And it's the same with the brain. Most babies are born with the motor part of their brain all ready to go. But once in a while a baby is born with part of its motor broken—or injured, in other words."

Sal's eyes were bright with excitement. So that was why children with cerebral palsy were handicapped in so many different ways!

"Do you fix the broken parts or do you buy new parts?" Meg had more questions ready.

"I wish we could buy new parts," Dr. Eastman said. "We can't fix the broken or injured parts, Meg, and there isn't any place where you can buy new brains. But sometimes we can get other parts of the brain to do the work of the injured or broken part. It's as though you had to fix your car motor by getting another motor and working with it and trying it over and over until it worked—not as well as the right motor would have, but well enough to get the car moving. You learned how to drive the motor part of your brain when you learned to walk. Now Sally has to do that too—but she has to start off with the wrong motor and work a lot harder at it and teach it how to work."

"Who is the teacher?" Meg asked, looking Sal over as though she expected to see some special little person peeking out of her ear.

"The therapists who give her treatment help," he answered, "but the person who does most of it is, as I said, Sally herself."

Sal stared at him, sure he was mixed up, but he only nodded, smiling.

"Yes, you. Every time you do something yourself, getting yourself dressed maybe, or walking across a room, or anything that means putting the brain to work for you, it gets more used to its new job and does it a bit better. Mind you, it takes years and years for it to learn. Brains aren't too brainy, I guess," he finished.

Sal was still thinking about what her doctor had said when they were out in the car. She wished somebody had told her about it years ago, but maybe it wouldn't have seemed so simple then. Meg still had it muddled.

"Be careful, Daddy," she said, as Dad lifted Sal down the steps. "You might break her brains more."

Halfway home, they began to notice the kennels.

"BOXERS: PUPPIES FOR SALE," Dad read out. "And there is a cocker kennel. We might just buy that dog of yours this afternoon, Sally."

For once, Sal was paying attention, and she opened her mouth to tell him, once and for all, that she did not want a dog, when suddenly Meg squealed, "Oh, stop, Daddy, STOP! Look at the tiny white puppies!"

Dad slowed down. Behind a wire fence, set well

back from the road, four balls of lively white fur were tumbling over each other in a spirited game of I'm the King of the Castle.

"What breed are they?" Mother wondered. "Oh, there's a sign. WEST HIGHLAND WHITE TERRIERS. They are sweet. Do you suppose they're for sale?"

"No time like the present for finding out." Dad swung the car into the driveway of the kennel. From inside the nearby house, a cheery voice called, "I'll be out in just a second. Make yourselves at home."

"Let's go look," Meg begged, her head already hanging out the window.

The Copelands piled out of the car just as a woman left the house and came to meet them, her hand out in welcome.

"Those pups lured us right in off the highway," Mother said, smiling warmly. "We're in the market for a dog just now . . ."

Sal drew a deep, protesting breath but it turned into a relieved sigh as the woman shook her head ruefully.

"I'm sorry, but they aren't for sale yet. In another month they'll be old enough. We keep some of our dogs to show and we like to be sure we don't lose a champion. I do have one dog for sale, but she's not a pup any longer. I'll show her to you, though."

"Oh, we'd want a pup . . ." Mother began, but the lady was off already back to the house. Sal studied Mother's face. She was safe. Mother had no intention of buying this dog.

The screen door slammed. Sal turned. And her eyes fixed on a bundle of shivering fur in the kennel-lady's arms.

"What's her name?" Meg asked, peering at the shaggy little dog.

"She has a fancy kennel name, but I've just been calling her Susie. You could give her any name you wanted. She's a bit timid with strangers yet, but she'd get over that in no time."

"No," Mother said, smiling and stretching out a

hand to pat Susie's back, which was all she could see of her. "I think Sal wants a puppy."

But Sal took a sudden step forward. She had been staring at Susie ever since the woman had brought her out. One thing was certain—Susie was scared stiff. She was shaking, and she kept burrowing her head into the woman's arm as though she wanted to hide. Her tail was tucked under her and her coat was all rubbed up the wrong way.

Just then, the woman reached down and set her on her feet. Susie cowered before them, head hanging. She didn't run. She curled up as though she hoped somehow she would drop into the earth and disappear. Meg had turned back to the pups, but Sal leaned over as far as she could and looked at this small dog. Then, all at once, Susie lifted her shaggy face. Through the mat of tangled hair that almost covered it, Sal saw her brown eyes gleaming, begging someone to rescue her, saying that she knew all about what a queer lost feeling in your stomach felt like.

Sal drew a shaking breath. Then—"I want that dog," said Sarah Jane Copeland.

And, stunned by what she had said, she said it again, her voice wobbling wildly. "I want that dog right there, for mine!"

"Sally, what in the world," Mother started, but before she could say more, Dad announced, "That settles it. We'll take her."

Sal stood there, a little dazed, watching the arrangements being made. Mrs. Miller told the Copelands a great deal more about Susie. She was already housebroken. She had a fine pedigree. Her kennel name was Roseneath Rosette.

Then they were back at the car. Dad helped Sally into the back seat.

"Here's your dog, Sal," he said, and placed Susie on the seat beside her.

At that moment, Sal understood what she had done. She wanted to dive to the other side of the car and yell: "No. I didn't mean it! Take her away!"

But Susie did not even look at her. She lay down on the seat with her nose plunged out of sight in the corner by the far door. The hump of her that she couldn't hide looked so miserable that Sal sat back and felt miserable along with her. The car swept out of the drive. They were bound for home—*and she had a dog!*

Before they had gone ten miles, Sal could not stand it any longer. Timidly, ready to jerk back if Susie so much as sneezed, she inched her way closer to the small lonely dog. Gently, her hand as light as a feather, she reached out and patted her. Susie lay still. Sal's touch grew surer, more comforting.

Susie didn't move away, although she was still shivering. At last, Sal cleared her throat and said huskily, "Don't be scared, Susie. Please, don't be scared."

When her mother glanced back at her ten minutes later, she was patting the shaggy little rump steadily and crooning, "Good girl . . . good little Susie. . . . Don't be scared. . . . I'll look after you."

Every so often, Sal caught the tip of Susie's ear flicking back just a little, as though she were hearing every single word. "There it goes again," she thought, her hand steadier, her voice soft as a spring wind. "She knows I'm talking to her."

In the front seat, Meg had fallen asleep. Her mother spoke very softly to her father.

"Blessings on you, Andrew," she said. "I think you were right. She's coming out of her shell already."

Sal wriggled over a little closer to Susie. Shyly, she moved her hand up to where the dog's head was turned into the corner of the seat cushion.

"Do you like to be scratched behind your ears?" she whispered to that one ear, flicking back at her. "All dogs in books like it."

Her fingers worked through the coarse coat till she could feel the short soft fur right next to the terrier's skin. Susie gave no signs of knowing her fingers were there, unless perhaps she trembled a little more. Sal scratched, and scratched—and went on scratching. At last, so slightly that Sal wondered if she might be imagining it, Susie moved her head. She pressed closer to the hand that felt so good, so consoling, just behind her ear.

Deep in the warm fur, Sal's fingers kept up their scratching, and above the little dog's head her voice still crooned. But now Sal's voice was breathless with excitement, and Susie was not the only one who trembled.

Then, unbelievably, Susie twisted her nose out of the crack between cushion and door, and a wet ribbon of tongue darted out for one hurried lick at Sal's hand. The hand was still. Sal could not move it. Susie, too, seemed frozen into a statue of a small wary dog, taken aback by her own daring. But then, she turned her body even further around with a rough little thud and began to sniff at Sal's fingers.

She's stopped trembling, Sal thought, dazed. She's stopped trembling. She's beginning to like me.

She looked out through the window at the October sky ablaze with blue and at the glowing maples. Everything seemed so bright, brighter than ever before, even at noon, as though someone had doubled the sunlight. The loveliness of it made her eyes sting, but although she blinked, the blurred, shining beauty did not vanish nor dim to an ordinary day.

Sal sat blinking and wondering why she was almost crying when, for once, she was happy clear down to her toes. Then she felt the rough, doggy tongue begin licking away at her hand with steady devotion.

As they neared Riverside, Meg wakened and, at once, her tousled head popped up over the front seat. For several seconds, she simply gazed at Susie, who went right on washing Sal's fingers as though nobody were watching.

"That's your dog, isn't it, Sally?" she said, at last.

"Yes, she is," Sal said, almost whispering lest she break the spell in the back seat.

"Is she Kent's dog too?"

"No," Sal said, suddenly looking at Meg instead of at Susie. "She's mine."

"Yours for keeps?" Meg sounded deeply impressed.

Then Sal remembered how short a time she had known this little dog—less than two hours—and how afraid she had been when they had turned in at the kennel, and she was amazed at the rush of love in her heart.

"Yes, Meggy," she said firmly. "Mine for keeps."

Questions

1. The story tells you that Sal has a serious medical problem. What is the problem?

2. Despite Sal's problem, at the end of the story she "was happy clear down to her toes." Why?

3. How did the puppy change Sal's mind about wanting a dog?

4. Sal's mother said, "Blessings on you, Andrew. . . . She's coming out of her shell already." What did Sal's mother mean by that?

5. Match the four words below with their meanings.

   cerebral   a. treatment of disease
   therapy   b. a place where dogs are kept
   pedigree   c. a line of ancestors
   kennel   d. relating to the brain

Activity Write Specific Questions

Sometimes, in order to help each other, family members must get information. At the start of the story, Sal's family is doing that: getting information about Sal's medical problem. As the story ends, they need more information to help care for Sal and also for her new puppy Susie.

Write six questions the family might ask: three about Sal and three about Susie. Write specific questions aimed at getting information the family will need. Then list at least one source that might help the family answer each set of questions.

About JEAN LITTLE

Jean Little was born in the
country of Formosa. She was born
blind and, though her sight improved, she has been almost totally
blind all her life. Yet her disability
did not prevent her from learning
to read. Her mother taught Jean to
read before she attended school,
and reading soon became a favorite
activity.

   When Jean was still a child, her
family moved to Canada. Jean
began attending public schools
with children who cruelly teased
her and chased her home from
school every day. Jean Little recalls that time by saying, "I had no armor
at hand so I gave up the fight and retreated to the public library. I read
and I daydreamed . . . so I prepared myself for becoming a writer."

   Jean Little had written poems, essays, and stories throughout her
school and college years. Yet she spent several years teaching children
with motor handicaps before writing became her fulltime career. In her
children's books, Jean Little often writes about children with disabilities.
She develops her characters and tells their stories with warmth and feeling.
In recognition of her talent, Jean Little and two of her books, *Mine for
Keeps* and *Listen for the Singing,* have been honored with Canadian book
awards.

More Books by Jean Little

From Anna
Listen for the Singing
Stand in the Wind

We Can Do Anything

Every day, many people lead useful lives despite great obstacles. Some of these people are the disabled, who live their lives in a world they cannot see, hear, touch, or move about in. A few of these disabled people have become heroes to others. Here are some of them.

Washington Roebling

The Brooklyn Bridge, connecting Brooklyn and New York City, is 1,595 feet long. When it was finished in 1883, it was the longest bridge in the world. During most of the thirteen years it took to build the bridge, Washington Roebling, the engineer in charge of the job, could not move from his chair.

The men who dug the foundations for the bridge's towers had to work inside air-tight structures called *caissons* (KAY·sahnz). Each caisson was pushed down to the bottom of the river and filled with air. When the workers returned to the surface, some were stricken with terrible pains. A few became paralyzed or even died.

232

Washington Roebling spent even more time in the caissons than his men. One day he, too, was stricken with "caisson disease." He suffered the effects for the rest of his life.

Washington did not stop his work on the bridge, however. He could see the bridge from the window of his home. Every day he sat in his chair and watched the work through field glasses. His wife, Emily, carried messages between Roebling and his foremen.

Washington Roebling could not go to the opening of the finished bridge. However, President Chester A. Arthur led a procession to Washington's house to thank him personally for his work.

Helen Keller

From babyhood, when an illness left her deaf and blind, Helen Keller lived in a dark, silent world. Then in 1887, when she was six, Helen's parents brought her a teacher named Annie Sullivan.

Annie Sullivan tried to teach Helen the sign alphabet that many deaf people use. Annie spelled the letters into Helen's hand so Helen could feel them. At first nothing happened. Helen could not understand that these hand movements were letters that could spell words and that words could name things.

Then one day, Annie took Helen outside to a well. She poured water over one of Helen's hands while she spelled "w-a-t-e-r" into Helen's other hand over and over.

Suddenly Helen understood. She knew that the hand movements she felt in one hand spelled the name of the water she felt in the other. "It was as if I had come back to life after being dead," she wrote later. She and "Teacher," as she called Annie Sullivan, were seldom apart after that.

Helen Keller learned to speak and to write. First, Annie Sullivan taught Helen the alphabet by having her touch raised letter shapes on cards. Then Helen learned to print letters using cards that had letter-shaped grooves. A piece of paper was placed over the grooves. Helen could follow each letter with her fingers, and the grooves guided her pencil point. Later, Helen learned to speak by imitating the movements of the lips of others.

As an adult, Helen became very active in public life. She wrote her life story and other books. She and Annie Sullivan gave lectures around the country. She helped persuade Congress to pay for reading services for the blind and to give blind people help through Social Security.

When she was eighty years old, Helen Keller was asked about her future plans. "I will always—as long as I have breath—work for the handicapped," she said.

Kitty O'Neil

The woman perched on the ledge of the twelve-story building for a moment, then leaped into space. As she fell, she curled her body into a somersault, then stretched it out in a dive. A few seconds later, she landed safely on an air bag.

The woman's name is Kitty O'Neil. She is one of the top stunt workers in Hollywood. Stunts, in movie-making, are feats of skill and daring that are difficult. Stunts include such dangerous actions as falling from high places, driving cars that must appear to crash or spin out of control, and escaping from burning buildings.

Someone who does stunts must be able to shut out the noise and confusion that go with making a movie. Kitty O'Neil has no trouble with that. She is totally deaf. Yet, although Kitty's deafness makes her work easier in some ways, it makes it more difficult in others. She can't hear directions or warnings of sudden danger. She must find ways around these obstacles to do her work well.

Like Helen Keller, Kitty O'Neil lost her hearing because of illness when she was only a few months old. Kitty's "Teacher" was her mother, who taught Kitty to read lips rather than use sign language.

When she was young, Kitty did not let her deafness keep her from pursuing her athletic goals. As a teenager, Kitty was a high-diving champion. She went on to race cars and motorcycles. In 1971, Kitty married a stunt worker who did falls, car crashes, and other dangerous acts as a stand-in for movie and TV performers. She asked him to teach her to do stunts, too. Soon Kitty had her own stunt career.

Kitty O'Neil has also driven rocket cars to become one of the fastest drivers on Earth. By 1979 she had boosted the women's land speed record to more than 618 miles per hour. She once told a reporter, "I like to do things people say I can't do because I'm deaf."

Questions

1. Which person seemed most interesting to you? Give at least one reason for your answer.

2. How did each of the people described show courage? What makes you think the way you do?

Activities

1. **Prepare a Report**

   Use books in the library to find out about other disabled people who have made important contributions to American life. Here are four you might look up and report on:

   a. Franklin D. Roosevelt, four-time President of the United States, who was stricken with polio at the age of 39.
   b. Wilma Rudolph, who could not walk as a child but won three gold medals in races in the 1960 Olympic Games.
   c. Carl Joseph, whose loss of a leg did not stop him from playing his favorite sport—football.
   d. Jim Brunotte, California ranch owner who teaches disabled people to ride horses and has several handicaps himself.

2. **Make a List**

   Find out and list the steps taken in your town or city to help disabled people in public places.

Metaphor

A poem by Eve Merriam

Morning is
a new sheet of paper
for you to write on.

Whatever you want to say,
all day,
until night
folds it up
and files it away.

The bright words and the dark words
are gone
until dawn
and a new day
to write on.

Illustrated by Sharon Harker

BOOKSHELF

All It Takes Is Practice by Betty Miles. Alfred A. Knopf, 1977. Peter and Stuart learn that being real friends can mean taking risks and standing up for one's beliefs.

The Great Gilly Hopkins by Katherine Paterson. T. Y. Crowell, 1978. Gilly Hopkins, just settled in her third foster home, is already trying her ''guaranteed-to-drive-you-crazy-techniques'' on her new foster mother, Maime Trotter. But in Mrs. Trotter, Gilly has finally met her match.

The Brooklyn Bridge: They Said It Couldn't Be Built by Judith St. George. G. P. Putnam's, 1982. This is the true story of John Roebling, the master engineer who designed the Brooklyn Bridge. The bridge was completed under the direction of his son, Washington.

Get on Out of Here, Philip Hall by Bette Greene. Dial Press, 1981. Beth is sure she is going to win her church leadership award. Then certain events happen that change both her feelings about leadership and her outlook on life.

Dear Mr. Henshaw by Beverly Cleary. William Morrow, 1983. Leigh is having problems adjusting to a new school, so he writes to his favorite author for advice.

Child of the Owl by Laurence Yep. Harper & Row, 1977. With her mother dead and her father in the hospital, Casey comes to live with her grandmother in San Francisco's Chinatown.

4 Facing the Unknown

Dinky

A poem by Theodore Roethke

O what's the weather in a Beard?
It's windy there, and rather weird,
And when you think the sky has cleared
    —Why, there is Dirty Dinky.

Suppose you walk out in a Storm,
With nothing on to keep you warm,
And then step barefoot on a Worm
    —Of course, it's Dirty Dinky.

As I was crossing a hot hot Plain,
I saw a sight that caused me pain,
You asked me before, I'll tell you again:
    —It *looked* like Dirty Dinky.

Last night you lay a-sleeping? No!
The room was thirty-five below;
The sheets and blankets turned to snow.
    —He'd got in: Dirty Dinky.

You'd better watch the things you do.
You'd better watch the things you do.
You're part of him; he's part of you
    —*You* may be Dirty Dinky.

243

Emergency in Space

From the science fiction novel *Farmer in the Sky* by Robert A. Heinlein

Illustrated by Lyle Miller

Some time in the future, the spaceship Mayflower *spins through space toward Ganymede,[1] a moon of the planet Jupiter more than half a billion miles from Earth. The 6,000 Earth people inside the* Mayflower, *like the Pilgrims on the original ship* Mayflower, *are traveling to settle a new colony in a new world.*

For Bill Lermer, one of the colonists, the decision to leave Earth had been a difficult one. He was leaving his high-school friends and the scout troop in which he had long been active to be with his father, George, who was emigrating with his new wife Molly and her daughter Peggy. With strict weight limits for each traveler, Bill had packed carefully—even going without food so that he could take one unnecessary item. As Bill tells it, "I began to wonder why I was going to all this trouble to hang on to a scout uniform I obviously wasn't going to use."

---

1. **Ganymede** (GAN•uh•meed): the third and largest satellite of Jupiter.

When we were fifty-three days out and about a week to go to reach Ganymede, Captain Harkness used the flywheel to precess[2] the ship so that we could see where we were going—so that the passengers could see, that is. It didn't make any difference to his astrogation.[3]

You see, the axis of the *Mayflower* had been pointed pretty much toward Jupiter and the torch had been pointed back at the Sun. Since the view ports were

_____

2. **precess** (PREE•ses): to change the direction of the axis of a rotating body, much like the movement of a spinning top as it loses speed.
3. **astrogation** (AS•truh•GAY•shun): the guiding of a spaceship in space.

spaced every ninety degrees around the sides, while we had been able to see most of the sky, we hadn't been able to see ahead to Jupiter nor behind to the Sun. Now he tilted the ship over ninety degrees and we were rolling, so to speak, along our line of flight. That way, you could see Jupiter and the Sun both, from any view port, though not both at the same time.

Jupiter was already a tiny, ruddy-orange disc. Some of the boys claimed they could make out the moons. Frankly, I couldn't, not for the first three days after the Captain precessed the ship. But it was mighty fine to be able to see Jupiter.

We hadn't seen Mars on the way out, because Mars happened to be on the far side of the Sun, three hundred million miles away. We hadn't seen anything but the same old stars you can see from Earth. We didn't even see any asteroids.

There was a reason for that. When we took off from the orbit of Supra-New-York, Captain Harkness had not aimed the *Mayflower* straight for where Jupiter was going to be when we got there; instead he had lifted her north of the ecliptic[4] high enough to give the asteroid[5] belt a wide berth. Now anybody knows that meteors are no real hazard in space. Unless a pilot does deliberately foolish things like driving his ship through the head of a comet it is almost impossible to get yourself hit by a meteor. They are too far between.

On the other hand the asteroid belt has more than its fair share of sky junk. The older power-pile ships used to drive straight through the belt, taking their chances, and none of them was ever hit to amount to anything. But Captain Harkness, having literally all the power in the world, preferred to go around and play it safe. By avoiding the belt there wasn't a chance in a blue moon that the *Mayflower* would be hit.

Well, it must have been a blue moon. We were hit.

---

4. **ecliptic** (ih•KLIP•tik): the plane, passing through the center of the sun, that contains the earth's orbit.
5. **asteroid** (AS•tuh•royd): any of several hundred small planets between Mars and Jupiter.

It was just after reveille,[6] "A" deck time, and I was standing by my bunk, making it up. I had my Scout uniform in my hands and was about to fold it up and put it under my pillow. I still didn't wear it. None of the others had uniforms to wear to Scout meetings so I didn't wear mine. But I still kept it tucked away in my bunk.

Suddenly I heard the strangest noise I ever heard in my life. It sounded like a rifle going off right by my ear, it sounded like a steel door being slammed, and it sounded like a giant tearing yards and yards of cloth, all at once.

Then I couldn't hear anything but a ringing in my ears and I was dazed. I shook my head and looked down and I was staring at a raw hole in the ship, almost between my feet and nearly as big as my fist. There was scorched insulation around it and in the middle of the hole I could see blackness—then a star whipped past and I realized that I was staring right out into space.

There was a hissing noise.

I don't remember thinking at all. I just wadded up my uniform, squatted down, and stuffed it in the hole. For a moment it seemed as if the suction would pull it on through the hole, then it jammed and stuck and didn't go any further. But we were still losing air. I think that was the point at which I first realized that we *were* losing air and that we might be suffocated in vacuum.

There was somebody yelling and screaming behind me that he was killed and alarm bells were going off all over the place. You couldn't hear yourself think. The

6. **reveille** (RE•vuh•lee): the sounding of a bugle early in the morning to awaken and call together people, usually in a camp or military post.

airtight door to our bunk room slid across automatically and settled into its gaskets and we were locked in.

That scared me to death.

I know it has to be done. I know that it is better to seal off one compartment and kill the people who are in it than to let a whole ship die—but, you see, *I* was in that compartment, personally. I guess I'm just not the hero type.

I could feel the pressure sucking away at the plug my uniform made. With one part of my mind I was recalling that it had been advertised as "tropical weave, self-ventilating" and wishing that it had been a solid plastic raincoat instead. I was afraid to stuff it in any harder, for fear it would go all the way through and leave us sitting there, chewing vacuum. I would have passed up desserts for the next ten years for just one rubber patch, the size of my hand.

The screaming had stopped; now it started up again. It was Noisy Edwards, beating on the airtight door and yelling, "Let me out of here! *Get me out of here!*"

On top of that I could hear Captain Harkness's voice coming through the bull horn. He was saying, "H-twelve! Report! H-twelve! Can you hear me?"

On top of that everybody was talking at once.

I yelled: "Quiet!" at the top of my voice—and for a second or so there *was* quiet.

Peewee Brunn, one of my Cubs, was standing in front of me, looking big-eyed. "What happened, Billy?" he said.

I said, "Grab me a pillow off one of the bunks. Jump!"

He gulped and did it. I said, "Peel off the cover, quick!"

He did, making quite a mess of it, and handed it to me—but I didn't have a hand free. I said, "Put it down on top of my hands."

It was the ordinary sort of pillow, soft foam rubber. I snatched one hand out and then the other, and then I was kneeling on it and pressing it down with the heels of my hands. It dimpled a little in the middle and I was scared we were going to have a blowout right through the pillow. But it held. Noisy was screaming again and

Captain Harkness was still asking for somebody, *any-body,* in compartment H-12 to tell him what was going on. I yelled "*Quiet!*" again, and added, "Somebody slug Noisy and shut him up."

That was a popular idea. About three of them jumped to it. Noisy got clipped in the side of the neck, then some-body poked him in the pit of his stomach and they swarmed over him. "Now everybody keep quiet," I said, "and keep on keeping quiet. If Noisy lets out a peep, slug him again." I gasped and tried to take a deep breath and said, "H-twelve, reporting!"

The Captain's voice answered, "What is the situation there?"

"There is a hole in the ship, Captain, but we got it corked up."

"How? And how big a hole?"

I told him and that is about all there was to it. They took a while to get to us because—I found this out afterward—they isolated that stretch of corridor first, with the airtight doors, and that meant they had to get everybody out of the rooms on each side of us and across the passageway. But presently two men in space suits opened the door and chased all the kids out, all but me. Then they came back. One of them was Mr. Ortega.[7] "You can get up now, kid," he said, his voice sounding strange and far away through his helmet. The other man squatted down and took over holding the pillow in place.

Mr. Ortega had a big metal patch under one arm. It had sticky padding on one side. I wanted to stay and watch him put it on but he chased me out and closed

---

7. **Ortega** (awr•TAY•guh).

the door. The corridor outside was empty but I banged on the airtight door and they let me through to where the rest were waiting. They wanted to know what was happening but I didn't have any news for them because I had been chased out.

After a while we started feeling light and Captain Harkness announced that spin would be off the ship for a short time. Mr. Ortega and the other man came back and went on up to the control room. Spin was off entirely soon after that and I got very sick. Captain Harkness kept the ship's speaker circuits cut in on his conversations with the men who had gone outside to repair the hole, but I didn't listen. I defy anybody to be interested in anything when he is drop sick.

Then spin came back on and everything was all right and we were allowed to go back into our bunk room. It looked just the same except that there was a plate welded over the place where the meteorite had come in.

Breakfast was two hours late and we didn't have school that morning.

That was how I happened to go up to Captain's mast for the second time. George was there and Molly and my sister Peggy and Dr. Archibald, the Scoutmaster of our deck, and all the fellows from my bunk room and all the ship's officers. The rest of the ship was cut in by visiplate. I wanted to wear my uniform but it was a mess— torn and covered with sticky stuff. I finally cut off the merit badges and put it in the ship's incinerator.

The First Officer shouted, "Captain's Mast for punishments and rewards!" Everybody sort of straightened up and Captain Harkness walked out and faced us. Dad shoved me forward.

The Captain looked at me. "William Lermer?" he said.

I said, "Yessir."

He said, "I will read from yesterday's log: 'On twenty-one August at oh-seven-oh-four system standard, while cruising in free fall according to plan, the ship was broached by a small meteorite. Safety interlocks worked satisfactorily and the punctured volume, compartment H-twelve, was isolated with no serious drop in pressure elsewhere in the ship.

"'Compartment H-twelve is a bunk room and was occupied at the time of the emergency by twenty passengers. One of the passengers, William J. Lermer, contrived a makeshift patch with materials at hand and succeeded in holding sufficient pressure for breathing until a repair party could take over.

"'His quick thinking and immediate action unquestionably saved the lives of all persons in compartment H-twelve.'"

The Captain looked up from the log and went on, "A certified copy of this entry, along with depositions of witnesses, will be sent to Interplanetary Red Cross with recommendation for appropriate action. Another copy will be furnished you. I have no way to reward you except to say that you have my heart-felt gratitude. I know that I speak not only for the officers but for all the passengers and most especially for the parents of your bunkmates."

He paused and waggled a finger for me to come closer. He went on in a low voice, to me alone, "That really was a slick piece of work. You were on your toes. You have a right to feel proud."

I said I guessed I had been lucky.

He said, "Maybe. But that sort of luck comes to the man who is prepared for it."

He waited a moment, then said, "Lermer, have you ever thought of putting in for space training?"

I said I suppose I had but I hadn't thought about it very seriously. He said, "Well, Lermer, if you ever do decide to, let me know. You can reach me care of the Pilots' Association, Luna City."

With that, mast was over and we went away, George and I together and Molly and Peggy following along. I heard Peggy saying, "That's *my* brother."

Molly said, "Hush, Peggy. And don't point."

Peggy said, "Why not? He *is* my brother—well, isn't he?"

Molly said, "Yes, but there's no need to embarrass him."

But I wasn't embarrassed.

Mr. Ortega looked me up later and handed me a little, black, twisted piece of metal, about as big as a button. "That's all there was left of it," he said, "but I thought you would like to have it—pay you for messing up your Scout suit, so to speak."

I thanked him and said I didn't mind losing the uniform; after all, it had saved my neck, too. I looked at the meteorite. "Mr. Ortega, is there any way to tell where this came from?"

"Not really," he told me, "though you can get the scientific johnnies to cut it up and then express an opinion—if you don't mind them destroying it."

I said no, I'd rather keep it—and I have. I've still got it as a pocket piece.

Questions

1. Why did William Lermer wad up his Scout uniform and stuff it in the hole?

2. Explain the delay in rescuing the passengers in compartment H–twelve. What had to be done before the rescue? Why?

3. When the compartment door slid shut, William was scared and said, "I guess I'm just not the hero type." Was he right or wrong? Explain.

4. If you had been William, would you have kept the meteorite as a pocket piece or would you have had the scientists analyze it? Explain your choice.

5. The ship's course was set high enough "to give the asteroid belt a wide berth." What is meant by that?
   a. The asteroid belt was really a wide bed.
   b. The ship allowed for a wide space between itself and the asteroid belt.
   c. The ship made its way into a wide dock.

Activity   Write Newspaper Headlines

Retell the story's main events in a series of newspaper headlines. Write a brief, but catchy, headline for each of these five events in the story: the space ship's take-off, the asteroid striking the ship, William stuffing the hole, the hole being repaired, William being rewarded for his bravery.

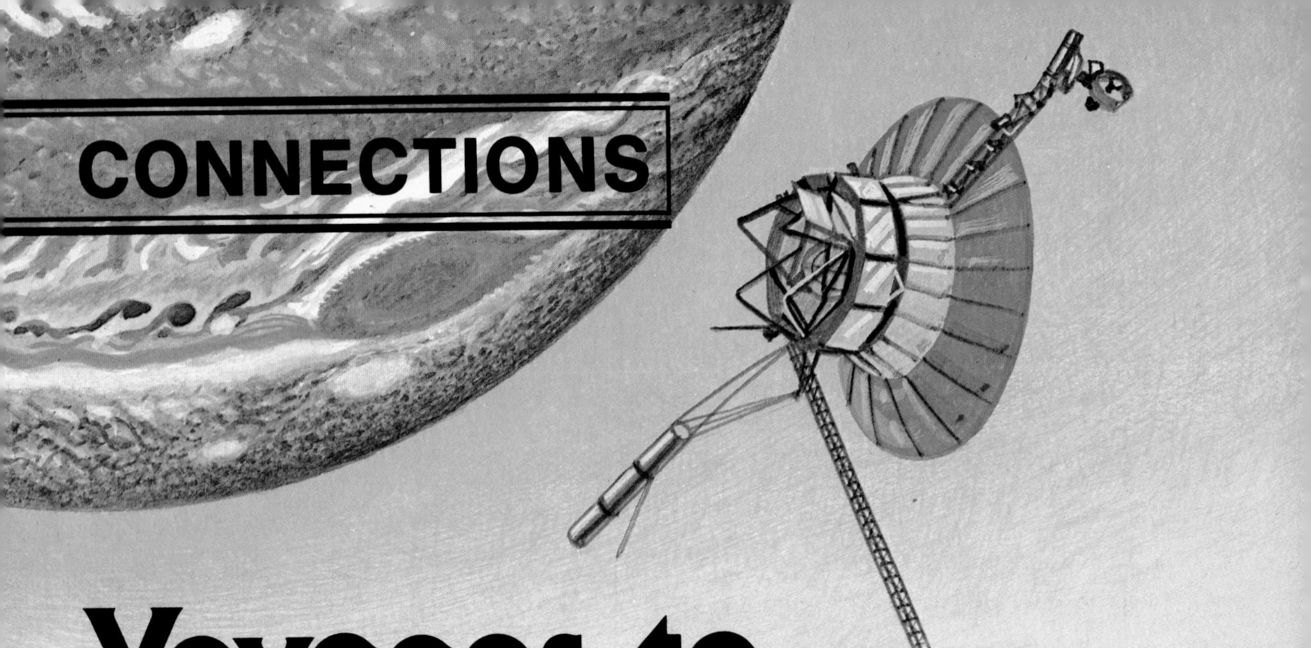

Voyages to the Planets

Nine planets, counting Earth, circle or *orbit* the sun. Seven of the planets have one or more moons orbiting them. The sun, its planets, and their moons are the major bodies in the *solar system*. In the last few years scientists have learned more about the solar system than at any other time since the telescope was invented, more than 350 years ago.

Solar System

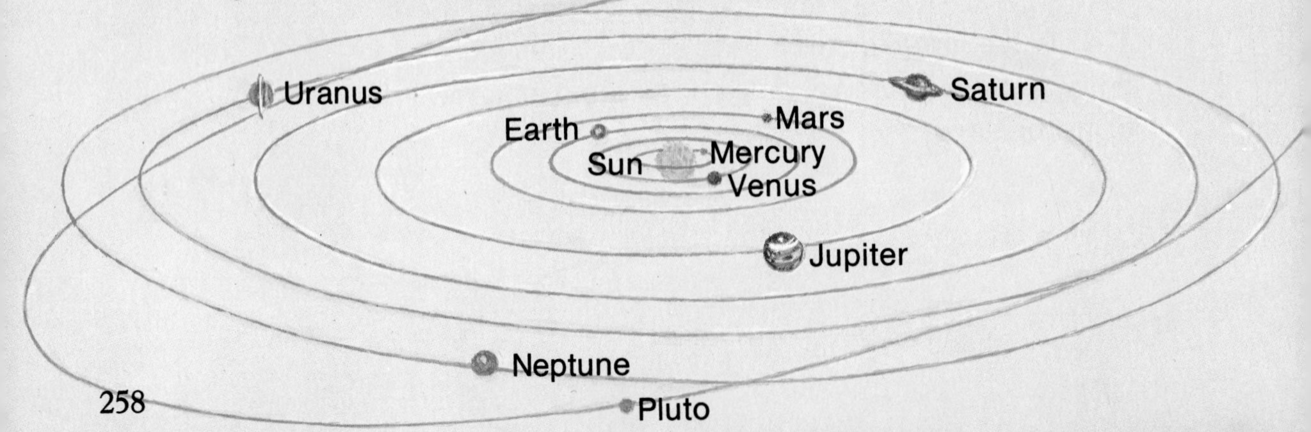

Uranus

Earth

Mars

Sun

Mercury

Venus

Saturn

Jupiter

Neptune

258

Pluto

What might it be like to orbit another planet, only a few hundred miles from its surface? What might it be like to land on another world and look around?

Scientists can answer these questions, even though no human has gone farther than the Moon. But scientists have sent spacecraft, called *space probes,* to five planets. Probes have landed on two of the planets. They have traveled near or orbited all five. Before 1990, probes will visit two more planets.

Probes can tell us much about the solar system. Television cameras on the probes have taken pictures of the planets and their moons. Other kinds of instruments pick up other information. All the information is radioed back to Earth. Computers help people understand the probes' information.

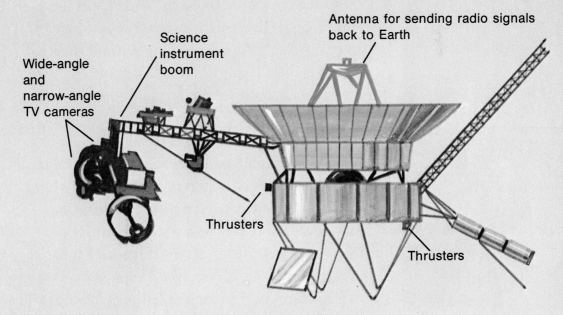

Wide-angle and narrow-angle TV cameras

Science instrument boom

Antenna for sending radio signals back to Earth

Thrusters

Thrusters

Voyager Space Probe

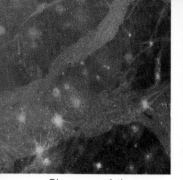

Close-up of the surface of Ganymede, one of Jupiter's moons

Jupiter with its satellites Io (1) and Callisto (2)

Volcanic explosion on Io (See arrow.)

The first space probes visited Mercury, Venus, and Mars during the 1960s and 1970s. People used to think Venus is like Earth, but the probes showed it is very different. Venus is boiling hot and covered with thick clouds of sulfuric acid. Two probes looked for life on Mars, but they did not find any.

Two space probes, *Voyagers 1* and *2*, were sent on longer journeys. They left Earth in 1977. Their first stop was Jupiter, the largest planet in the solar system. They found two rings of dust and ice circling Jupiter. No one had guessed that Jupiter had rings.

The Voyagers took close-up pictures of Jupiter's four largest moons. A scientist named Linda Morabito spotted one of Voyager 1's biggest surprises in pictures of the moon called *Io* (EYE•oh). She saw a plume rising like an open umbrella above Io's surface. Voyager scientists took a closer look.

Saturn with four of its satellites: Dione in front; Tethys above Dione; and Enceladus and Rhea to the right of Dione

Voyager flying by Saturn

They realized that the plume was gas from an erupting volcano! No one had ever seen a volcano erupt anywhere except on Earth. Io seems to have many active volcanoes.

The Voyagers went on to Saturn, the planet beyond Jupiter. Like Jupiter, Saturn is a giant planet covered with thick gases. Saturn has many rings made of bits of ice and rock. Some of the rings in the Voyager pictures have a "braided" look. Others have spokes like those in a bicycle wheel. At this time, scientists are not sure what causes the braiding or the spokes.

Voyager 2 is following a path that will take it past two more planets before it leaves the solar system. It should reach Uranus (yoo·RAY·nus) in 1986 and Neptune in 1989. Scientists know very little about these planets, so Voyager's report may surprise them.

Close-up of Saturn's rings

Our Solar System

1. Sun

2. Mercury

3. Venus

4. Earth

5. Mars

6. Asteroid belt

7. Jupiter

1. The **sun** is the star at the center of the solar system. In 1980, an Earth-orbiting probe called Solar Max went into space. It sent back information about *solar flares,* huge eruptions of glowing gases from the sun.

2. Mariner 10 visited **Mercury** in 1974. It showed that Mercury is covered with bowl-like holes, or *craters.* The craters were made when large rocks from space, called *meteorites,* hit the planet.

3. The two Pioneer Venus probes reached **Venus** in 1978. These probes and others studied the clouds of burning acid that hide Venus's surface. The surface is a plain broken by mountain ranges.

4. **Earth** is very different from the other planets. As far as scientists know, it is the only planet that has liquid water. It is also the only one known to have life.

5. Two Viking probes landed on **Mars** in 1976. They sent back pictures of Mars's red, rock-covered surface. They tested its soil for living things but found none.

6. Thousands of rocks, big and small, called **asteroids,** orbit the sun. Most lie in a belt between Mars and Jupiter. Some scientists think the asteroids may once have been part of a planet that broke up.

7. Voyagers 1 and 2 visited **Jupiter** in 1979. Jupiter is a giant ball of gas and liquid. The Voyagers saw a thin ring around Jupiter and found volcanoes on Io, one of its many moons.

8. The Voyagers flew by **Saturn** in 1980 and 1981. They took pictures of its rings and found new rings that had never been seen before.

9. Scientists projected that Voyager 2 should reach **Uranus** in 1986. Scientists discovered in 1977 that Uranus has rings, like Saturn and Jupiter.

10. Voyager 2 is expected to pass **Neptune** in 1989. Although Neptune is difficult to study, many scientists believe the planet is made of gases.

11. **Pluto** is the outermost planet of the solar system. At least, that's what most scientists think right now. Some scientists believe a tenth planet lies beyond Pluto.

8. Saturn

9. Uranus

10. Neptune

11. Pluto

As far as people know, Pluto is the farthest planet from the sun. It is an icy world about the size of the Moon. Its moon, Charon (KAIR·uhn), is about a third the size of Pluto.

Is there a tenth planet? Is there life on any of the other planets or their moons? Could humans make a home on any of these other worlds? Long before people go to other planets, space probes may answer these and other questions about the solar system.

Questions

1. How does information from space probes reach Earth?

2. Which planets have rings? What do scientists think the rings of these planets are made of?

3. Did the Viking probes find living things on Mars? Explain.

4. If you could send human beings to visit one planet besides Earth, which one would you choose? Why?

Activities

1. Complete a Fact Chart

Copy the chart below. Complete it to show information from pages 260–263 and from other books. Name at least one discovery for each planet visited by a space probe.

Space Probes and the Planets

Planet	Position from Sun	Size and Description	Space Probe Name and Year	Space Probe Discoveries
Mercury	nearest	a little bigger than the Moon	Mariner 10 1974	craters
Venus	second	same size as Earth	Pioneer Venus 1978	acid clouds, plains, mountains

2. Make Up a Mnemonic Device

"My Very Educated Mother Just Served Us Nine Pizzas." This sentence is a *mnemonic* (nih•MON•ik) *device.* It is a way to help people remember. The first letter of each word is the first letter of a planet in order from the sun. Try to name the planets in order using this mnemonic device.

Make up your own mnemonic sentence to help you remember the planets in order by size, from largest to smallest. Use the following order: Jupiter, Saturn, Uranus, Neptune, Earth, Venus, Mars, Mercury, Pluto.

HIEROGLYPHICS

From the novel *The Egypt Game* by Zilpha Keatley Snyder
Illustrated by Cheryl Arnemann

The Egypt Game began one September day in a weed-grown lot behind the junk store. In that old and forgotten place, April, Melanie, and Melanie's four-year-old brother Marshall found the statue of Nefertiti.[1] Finding the statue was only the beginning. Soon the three friends had transformed the old lot into Egypt and themselves into Egyptians. Marshall became the young pharaoh[2] Marshmosis. Their new friend, a shy fourth-grader named Elizabeth, reigned as Egypt's queen Neferbeth.

Sparked by April's leadership, the Egyptians played their game as often as they could, but only in the daytime. They had not been to Egypt for a while when Halloween came—and their chance for a nighttime visit.

However, the Egyptians were not alone that night. Toby Alvillar and Ken Kamata, two boys from April's class, followed them to Egypt. Suddenly, the Egypt Game no longer belonged to the four of them. Toby and Ken threatened to tell everybody at school about the Egyptians. In desperation, Elizabeth asked the boys to join their group. The boys were not sure—they wanted to visit Egypt in the daytime first.

---

1. **Nefertiti** (NEF·ur·TEE·tee): a queen of ancient Egypt.
2. **pharaoh** (FAY·roh): a ruler of ancient Egypt.

That afternoon, the girls and Marshall got to the
storage yard first, and they were all sitting on the
edge of the temple floor just waiting when Ken and
Toby arrived. Ken had to do a certain amount of
squeezing and inhaling to get through the fence, but
skinny Toby came through almost as easily as the
girls. They didn't say much at first, just "Hi," and
then the boys started looking around at the Egyptian
temple that the girls had constructed. The girls
watched warily, trying to figure out just what they
had in mind.

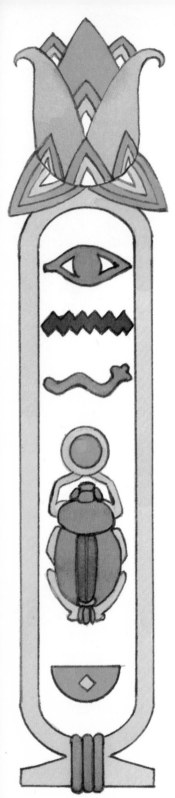

After a few minutes, Melanie decided that Ken really didn't have anything in mind at all. He looked reluctant and puzzled and a little bit embarrassed. She decided that Ken was only there because Toby was, so she started watching Toby.

It was easy to tell by looking at Toby's dark eyes that something important was going on behind them. They almost gave you the feeling that you could hear things inside his head going "whirr-clank-buzz," but for once it didn't seem to have anything to do with laughter. Melanie began to get the feeling that maybe Toby wasn't just there to tease and cut up after all.

So when Toby started asking questions about the temple and about Set[3] and Isis,[4] Melanie started giving straight answers. At first April poked her and frowned in a way that said not to give everything away, but after a while she changed her mind and started answering questions, too. She even took the secret scrolls out of their hiding place and showed the boys the partly finished hieroglyphic[5] alphabet. Finally Toby left the shed and walked to the middle of the yard.

Ken looked relieved. "Well, I guess that's all there is to see," he said to Toby. "We might as well split, huh? We'll still have time to get in the game up at school."

---

3. **Set**: in Egyptian mythology, the animal-headed god of darkness, night, and evil.
4. **Isis** (EYE·sis): an important goddess in Egyptian mythology. Her name is the Greek form of the ancient Egyptian *hieroglyph* (symbol) meaning "throne." Often Isis is pictured with the hieroglyphic sign of the throne on her head.
5. **hieroglyphics** (HY·ur·uh·GLIF·iks): a kind of writing that uses pictures or symbols to stand for words, syllables, or sounds. Ancient Egyptians and others used this writing system.

But Toby shook his head. "I don't feel like play-ing basketball," he said. "Besides, I sort of dig this Egypt stuff. Let's hang around a while. Okay?"

Ken shrugged. "Sheesh!" he said. "I don't care. But the whole scene's pretty kooky, if you ask me."

It turned out that Toby wasn't kidding—he really did dig the Egypt Game. Ken was pretty respectful about the whole thing, too. He kept hitting himself on the forehead and saying "Sheesh!" but his tone of voice seemed to indicate amazement more than any-thing else.

As they were all leaving, a little before 5:30, Toby asked the girls to write down the names of some of the best books about Egypt. He said he was going to the library that evening to check some out.

That night April and Melanie sat on Melanie's bed and, feeling very pleased with things in general,

they discussed the future. The first meeting of the enlarged Egypt gang had gone off much more smoothly than they had expected. They didn't admit it, even to each other, but they had both been flattered by Ken's and Toby's respectful interest.

"And maybe, after a week or two, they'll lose interest," Melanie said. "Maybe they'll play for a while and then they'll get homesick for their old ball games, and everything will be just like it used to be."

"Yeah," April agreed. "I'll bet they do. Or else, maybe they won't even come back at all. Maybe they were just curious, and now that they know all about it, they just might not bother to come back. You know, I wouldn't be surprised if they just don't show up tomorrow at all."

Ken and Toby showed up in Egypt the next day, all right. They showed up right on time, overflowing with ideas and loaded down with stuff. At least, Toby was overflowing with ideas, and Ken was carrying most of the stuff. Toby had also brought some pencils and paper. He said he'd been thinking it over, and he'd decided the first thing they ought to do was finish the alphabet of hieroglyphics the girls had started.

"Oh, is that right," April said. "Is that what you've decided? Whose Egypt Game do you think this is, anyway? Just because—"

She had a lot more things to say, but Toby interrupted. "Okay, okay. Cool it for a minute and let me finish. Let me tell you the rest of my idea before you start flipping your wig. Then if you don't dig it—" he shrugged, "we won't do it."

That seemed fair enough so April kept quiet, but she kept her eyes narrowed warily as Toby explained.

When they had the alphabet all made up, they could memorize it and use it to write secret messages—at school and everyplace. Then if the messages fell into enemy hands, no one would know what it was all about. Besides that, Toby thought they should each choose an Egyptian name—Marshall was already Marshmosis—and a hieroglyphic symbol that stood for the name. That way each one could sign his messages with his symbol and that would make the whole thing more mysterious. Toby took out a piece of paper all folded up into a tiny square and spread it out on the floor of the shed. On it were some hieroglyphics and some Egyptian names that he had copied out of books the night before. Everyone except April immediately got down on hands and knees and began to examine the paper eagerly and discuss possible names.

April was telling herself it was a crummy idea, when all of a sudden she remembered Bastet. Bastet had always seemed especially intriguing to April. She was a sort of cat goddess, and there was a famous statue of her as a cat, with cruel mysterious eyes and earrings in her ears. If you were to pick the name of Bastet, your symbol could be a cat's head with earrings. "Hey," she said, dropping down to join the group, "I've got a great one."

Everybody liked April's name and hieroglyph. In fact, Toby said it gave him an idea for a hieroglyph for himself. He'd already picked out his name. It was going to be Ramose, after a famous Egyptian wise

man. And since an owl was supposed to be wise, what could be better than an owl's head for a symbol.

Melanie knew right away what she wanted her name to be. She had gone once with her parents to hear Leontyne Price sing *Aïda*[6] and had been fascinated with the tragic story of the beautiful princess who had been a captive in ancient Egypt. As a matter of fact, she'd already thought of herself as Aïda, at times, when they were playing the Egypt Game, but she hadn't told anyone. A symbol to go with Aïda was a bit of a problem, but finally Melanie picked the bird hieroglyph because it stood for the letter A in the real Egyptian alphabet.

Ken had picked the name of Horemheb because Toby said Horemheb had been a great general and

---

6. **Aïda** (ah·EE·duh): an Italian opera in which the title character, Aïda, is an Ethiopian princess.

also a pharaoh. He thought up his own hieroglyph of a bloody sword. There wasn't anything particularly Egyptian about it, but it did seem to go with being a general. Elizabeth's symbol was April's idea. It was a real Egyptian hieroglyph and it meant "heart," to go with Nefertiti, which means "Beloved One." And of course Marshall's hieroglyph was the double crown of Egypt because he was already the boy-pharaoh—and that's what he liked to be best.

The next few meetings of the Egyptians were taken up with finishing the hieroglyphic alphabet and memorizing it. Some of the letters that they used in their alphabet were actual Egyptian hieroglyphs, but for the sounds that were missing in the Egyptian alphabet, as well as a few that were too difficult to draw in their original form, they made up their own. Then because their book on Egyptian writing told how hieroglyphics were considered works of art as well as writing, and because they were always done in many bright colors, it was decided that some sets of colored pens were necessary. So the game was suspended for a couple of afternoons while money was raised to buy the pens. Ken and Toby mowed a few lawns, and the girls and Marshall scouted the neighborhood for empty bottles to return to the grocery store.

Just buying the pens took most of another afternoon because it took so long to get waited on at Schmitt's Variety Store. Melanie said her mother said that the reason Mr. Schmitt never had a clerk for long was that he paid such low salaries. Except for Mr. Schmitt's cousin, a stocky red-headed young man with freckles, there was no one working in the store that day but Mr. Schmitt. The cousin never waited on customers, but only dusted shelves and brought stuff out from the backroom; and Mr. Schmitt, himself, never waited on kids until after all the grownups were taken care of, no matter who'd been there longest. So the Egypt gang waited and waited and it was all pretty frustrating.

But the pens were worth the effort, and during the next few days Egypt was full of scribes practicing the ancient art of hieroglyphic writing. In a short time all sorts of possibilities were suggested and explored. Letters were written and exchanged and deciphered. Decorative hieroglyphic borders were added to the poster-paint pictures that already adorned the walls of the temple. Secret mailing spots were picked out all around the neighborhood, such as a certain clump of weeds in an untended parkway or the trunk of a particular plum tree. A mysterious and beautifully drawn page of hieroglyphics got loose in the sixth-grade class at Wilson School and was passed around and puzzled over by everyone, including the teacher; but no one came even close to figuring it out. And of course, no one was as loudly and dramatically puzzled as the four sixth-grade members of the Egypt Game.

Questions

1. Why do you think the children in this story have such a great interest in ancient Egyptian hieroglyphics?

2. What might happen to the children in the story as a result of their interest in hieroglyphics?

3. How does the hieroglyphic writing system differ from our alphabet? List two ways mentioned in the story.

4. Toby says, "I sort of dig this Egypt stuff." What word in his speech is a *pun,* a play on different meanings of a word? What are the two meanings?

5. Match the three words below with their meanings.

   hieroglyph   a. a person who studies hieroglyphics

   hieroglyphist   b. the study of hieroglyphic writing

   hieroglyphology   c. a picture or symbol used in ancient Egypt

Activity   Write in Hieroglyphics

Using information about hieroglyphics in this story, compose a hieroglyph for your name and another one for the name of a friend. Put the two hieroglyphs at the top of a page. Then be a hieroglyphist a century from now. Write the hieroglyphist's report of how and where he or she found the two hieroglyphs and what they mean.

About ZILPHA KEATLEY SNYDER

Zilpha Keatley Snyder receives many letters asking her why she became a writer. In response, she tells of her California childhood in the country. She spent her time with animals and with books. "I think I read almost a book a day during my childhood," she says, "and loved every minute of it. . . . As soon as it occurred to me that books were written by ordinary human beings, I decided that was the kind of human being I'd like most to be." That happened when Zilpha Keatley Snyder was eight, and from then on she considered herself a writer.

Zilpha Keatley Snyder married, raised three children, and taught elementary school for nine years before she returned to her writing. While teaching, she met many wonderful students whose personalities and ideas inspired her. All six of the main characters in *The Egypt Game* are based on the boys and girls she taught.

Mrs. Snyder loves to write because it gives her the opportunity to "make things up." She chooses to write for boys and girls aged nine to fourteen because, she says, "they are magical people."

More Books by Zilpha Keatley Snyder

Blair's Nightmare
The Headless Cupid
And All Between

What a Fright!

Two limericks

A skeleton once in Khartoum
Asked a spirit up into his room;
    They spent the whole night
    In the eeriest fight
As to which should be frightened of whom.

—Anonymous

Wailed a ghost in a graveyard at Kew,
"Oh, my friends are so fleeting and few,
For it's gravely apparent
That if you're transparent
There is no one who knows if it's *you!*"

—Myra Cohn Livingston

Lucy's Adventure

Two chapters from the novel
The Lion, the Witch and the Wardrobe
by C. S. Lewis
Illustrated by Emanuel Schongut

*A fantasy story is often full of things
that seem impossible to imagine. If the
story is a good one, it makes the reader
believe in it even so. One of the most
popular fantasies ever written is C. S.
Lewis's* The Chronicles of Narnia. *This
collection of stories fills seven books.
The tale that follows is from the first book
in the series.*

Lucy Looks into a Wardrobe

Once there were four children whose names were Peter, Susan, Edmund, and Lucy. This story is about something that happened to them when they were sent away from London during the war because of the air raids. They were sent to the house of an old Professor who lived in the heart of the country, ten miles from the nearest railway station and two miles from the nearest post office. He had no wife and he lived in a very large house with a house-keeper called Mrs. Macready and three servants. (Their names were Ivy, Margaret, and Betty, but they do not come into the story much.)

He himself was a very old man with shaggy white hair, which grew over most of his face as well as on his head, and they liked him almost at once. But on the first evening when he came out to meet them at the front door, he was so odd-looking that Lucy (who was the youngest) was a little afraid of him, and Edmund (who was the next youngest) wanted to laugh and had to keep on pretending he was blowing his nose to hide it.

As soon as they had said good night to the Professor and gone upstairs on the first night, the boys came into the girls' room and they all talked it over.

"We've fallen on our feet and no mistake," said Peter. "This is going to be perfectly splendid. That old chap will let us do anything we like."

"I think he's an old dear," said Susan.

"Oh, come off it!" said Edmund, who was tired and pretending not to be tired, which always made him bad-tempered. "Don't go on talking like that."

"Like what?" said Susan. "And anyway, it's time you were in bed."

"Trying to talk like Mother," said Edmund. "And who are you

to say when I'm to go to bed? Go to bed yourself.''

"Hadn't we all better go to bed?'' said Lucy. "There's sure to be a row if we're heard talking here.''

"No there won't,'' said Peter. "I tell you this is the sort of house where no one's going to mind what we do. Anyway, they won't hear us. It's about ten minutes' walk from here down to that dining room, and any amount of stairs and passages in between.''

"What's that noise?'' said Lucy suddenly. It was a far larger house than she had ever been in before and the thought of all those long passages and rows of doors leading into empty rooms was beginning to make her feel a little creepy.

"It's only a bird, silly,'' said Edmund.

"It's an owl,'' said Peter. "This is going to be a wonderful place for birds. I shall go to bed now. I say, let's go and explore tomorrow. You might find anything in a place like this. Did you see those mountains as we came along? And the woods? There might be eagles. There might be stags. There'll be hawks.''

"Badgers!'' said Lucy.

"Snakes!'' said Edmund.

"Foxes!'' said Susan.

But when next morning came, there was a steady rain falling, so thick that when you looked out of the window you could see neither the mountains nor the woods nor even the stream in the garden.

"Of course it *would* be raining!'' said Edmund. They had just finished breakfast with the Professor and were upstairs in the room he had set apart for them— a long, low room with two windows looking out in one direction and two in another.

"Do stop grumbling, Ed,'' said Susan. "Ten to one it'll clear up in an hour or so. And in the meantime we're pretty well off. There's a wireless and lots of books.''

"Not for me,'' said Peter, "I'm going to explore in the house.''

Everyone agreed to this and that was how the adventures began. It was the sort of house that you never seem to come to the end of, and it was full of unexpected places. The first few doors they tried led only into spare bedrooms, as everyone had expected that they would. But soon they came to a very long room full of pictures and there they found

a suit of armor. After that was a
room all hung with green, with
a harp in one corner; and then
came three steps down and five
steps up, and then a kind of little
upstairs hall and a door that led

out onto a balcony, and then a
whole series of rooms that led into
each other and were lined with
books—most of them very old
books and some bigger than a
Bible in a church. And shortly after

that they looked into a room that was quite empty except for one big wardrobe, the sort that has a looking glass in the door. There was nothing else in the room at all except a dead bluebottle on the windowsill.

"Nothing there!" said Peter, and they all trooped out again—all except Lucy. She stayed behind because she thought it would be worthwhile trying the door of the wardrobe, even though she felt almost sure that it would be locked. To her surprise it opened quite easily, and two mothballs dropped out.

Looking inside, she saw several coats hanging up—mostly long fur coats. There was nothing Lucy liked so much as the smell and feel of fur. She immediately stepped into the wardrobe and got in among the coats and rubbed her face against them, leaving the door open, of course, because she knew that it is very foolish to shut oneself into any wardrobe. Soon she went further in and found that there was a second row of coats hanging up behind the first one. It was almost quite dark in there and she kept her arms stretched out in front of her so as not to bump her

face into the back of the wardrobe. She took a step further in—then two or three steps—always expecting to feel woodwork against the tips of her fingers. But she could not feel it.

"This must be a simply enormous wardrobe!" thought Lucy, going still further in and pushing the soft folds of the coats aside to make room for her. Then she noticed that there was something crunching under her feet. "I wonder is that more mothballs?" she thought, stooping down to feel it with her hands. But instead of feeling the hard, smooth wood of the floor of the wardrobe, she felt something soft and powdery and extremely cold. "This is very queer," she said, and went on a step or two further.

Next moment she found that what was rubbing against her face and hands was no longer soft fur but something hard and rough and even prickly. "Why, it is just like branches of trees!" exclaimed Lucy. And then she saw that there was a light ahead of her; not a few inches away where the back of the wardrobe ought to have been, but a long way off. Something cold and soft was falling on her. A moment later she found that she was standing in the middle of a wood at nighttime with snow under her feet and snowflakes falling through the air.

Lucy felt a little frightened, but she felt very inquisitive and excited as well. She looked back over her shoulder and there, between the dark tree trunks, she could still see the open doorway of the wardrobe and even catch a glimpse of the empty room from which she had set out. (She had, of course, left the door open, for she knew that it is a very silly thing to shut oneself into a wardrobe.) It seemed to be still daylight there. "I can always get back if anything goes wrong," thought Lucy. She began to walk forward, *crunch-crunch,* over the snow and through the wood towards the other light.

In about ten minutes she reached it and found that it was a lamppost. As she stood looking at it, wondering why there was a lamppost in the middle of a wood and wondering what to do next, she heard a pitter-patter of feet coming towards her. And soon after that a very strange person stepped out from among the trees into the light of the lamppost.

What Lucy Found There

He was only a little taller than Lucy herself and he carried over his head an umbrella, white with snow. From the waist upwards he was like a man, but his legs were shaped like a goat's (the hair on them was glossy black) and instead of feet he had goat's hoofs. He also had a tail, but Lucy did not notice this at first because it was neatly caught up over the arm that held the umbrella so as to keep it from trailing in the snow. He had a red woolen muffler round his neck and his skin was rather reddish too. He had a strange, but pleasant little face with a short pointed beard and curly hair, and out of the hair there stuck two horns, one on each side of his forehead. One of his hands, as I have said, held the umbrella. In the other arm he carried several brown paper parcels. What with the parcels and the snow it looked just as if he had been doing his Christmas shopping. He was a Faun. And when he saw Lucy he gave such a start of surprise that he dropped all his parcels.

"Goodness gracious me!" exclaimed the Faun.

"Good evening," said Lucy. But the Faun was so busy picking up his parcels that at first he did not reply. When he had finished he made her a little bow.

"Good evening, good evening," said the Faun. "Excuse me—I don't want to be inquisitive—but should I be right in thinking that you are a Daughter of Eve?"

"My name's Lucy," said she, not quite understanding him.

"But you are—forgive me—you are what they call a girl?" asked the Faun.

"Of course I'm a girl," said Lucy.

"You are in fact Human?"

"Of course I'm human," said Lucy, still a little puzzled.

"To be sure, to be sure," said the Faun. "How stupid of me! But I've never seen a Son of Adam or a Daughter of Eve before. I am delighted. That is to say—" and then he stopped as if he had been going to say something he had not intended but had remembered in time. "Delighted, delighted," he went on. "Allow me to introduce myself. My name is Tumnus."

"I am very pleased to meet you, Mr. Tumnus," said Lucy.

"And may I ask, O Lucy, Daughter of Eve," said Mr. Tumnus, "how you have come into Narnia?"

"Narnia? What's that?" said Lucy.

"This is the land of Narnia," said the Faun, "where we are now; all that lies between the lamppost and the great castle of Cair Paravel on the eastern sea. And you—you have come from the wild woods of the West?"

"I—I got in through the wardrobe in the spare room," said Lucy.

"Ah!" said Mr. Tumnus in a rather melancholy voice, "if only I had worked harder at geography when I was a little Faun, I should no doubt know all about those strange countries. It is too late now."

"But they aren't countries at all," said Lucy, almost laughing. "It's only just back there—at least—I'm not sure. It is summer there."

"Meanwhile," said Mr. Tumnus, "it is winter in Narnia, and has been for ever so long, and we shall both catch cold if we stand here talking in the snow. Daughter of Eve from the far land of Spare Oom where eternal summer reigns around the bright city of War Drobe, how would it be if you came and had tea with me?"

"Thank you very much, Mr. Tumnus," said Lucy. "But I was wondering whether I ought to be getting back."

"It's only just round the corner," said the Faun, "and there'll be a roaring fire—and toast—and sardines—and cake."

"Well, it's very kind of you," said Lucy. "But I shan't be able to stay long."

"If you will take my arm, Daughter of Eve," said Mr. Tumnus, "I shall be able to hold the umbrella over both of us. That's the way. Now—off we go."

And so Lucy found herself walking through the wood arm in arm with this strange creature as if they had known one another all their lives.

They had not gone far before they came to a place where the ground became rough and there were rocks all about and little hills up and little hills down. At the bottom of one small valley Mr. Tumnus turned suddenly aside as if he were going to walk straight into an unusually large rock, but at the last moment Lucy found he was leading her into the entrance of a cave. As soon as they were inside she found herself blinking in the light of a wood fire. Then Mr. Tumnus stooped and took a flaming piece of wood out of the fire with a neat little pair of tongs, and lit a lamp. "Now we shan't be long," he said, and immediately put a kettle on.

Lucy thought she had never been in a nicer place. It was a little, dry, clean cave of reddish stone with a carpet on the floor and two little chairs ("one for me and one for a friend," said Mr. Tumnus) and a table and a dresser

and a mantelpiece over the fire
and above that a picture of an old
Faun with a gray beard. In one
corner there was a door which
Lucy thought must lead to Mr.
Tumnus' bedroom, and on one
wall was a shelf full of books.
Lucy looked at these while he
was setting out the tea things.
They had titles like *The Life and
Letters of Silenus* or *Nymphs and
Their Ways* or *Men, Monks and
Gamekeepers; a Study in Popular
Legend* or *Is Man a Myth?*

"Now, Daughter of Eve!" said
the Faun.

And really it was a wonderful
tea. There was a nice brown egg,
lightly boiled, for each of them,
and then sardines on toast, and
then buttered toast, and then toast
with honey, and then a sugar-
topped cake. And when Lucy was
tired of eating the Faun began to
talk. He had wonderful tales to tell
of life in the forest. He told about
the midnight dances and how the
Nymphs who lived in the wells and
the Dryads who lived in the trees
came out to dance with the Fauns;
about long hunting parties after the
milk-white Stag who could give you
wishes if you caught him; about
feasting and treasure-seeking with

the wild Red Dwarfs in deep mines and caverns far beneath the forest floor; and then about summer when the woods were green and old Silenus on his fat donkey would come to visit them, and sometimes Bacchus himself, and then the streams would run with wine instead of water and the whole forest would give itself up to jollification for weeks on end. "Not that it isn't always winter now," he added gloomily. Then to cheer himself up he took out from its case on the dresser a strange little flute that looked as if it were made of straw and began to play. And the tune he played made Lucy want to cry and laugh and dance and go to sleep all at the same time. It must have been hours later when she shook herself and said,

"Oh, Mr. Tumnus—I'm so sorry to stop you, and I do love that tune—but really, I must go home. I only meant to stay for a few minutes."

"It's no good *now,* you know," said the Faun, laying down his flute and shaking his head at her very sorrowfully.

"No good?" said Lucy, jumping up and feeling rather frightened. "What do you mean? I've got to go home at once. The others will be wondering what has happened to me." But a moment later she asked, "Mr. Tumnus! Whatever is the matter?" for the Faun's brown eyes had filled with tears and then the tears began trickling down his cheeks, and soon they were running off the end of his nose; and at last he covered his face with his hands and began to howl.

"Mr. Tumnus! Mr. Tumnus!" said Lucy in great distress. "Don't! Don't! What is the matter? Aren't you well? Dear Mr. Tumnus, do tell me what is wrong." But the Faun continued sobbing as if his heart would break. And even when Lucy went over and put her arms round him and lent him her handkerchief, he did not stop. He merely took the handkerchief and kept on using it, wringing it out with both hands whenever it got too wet to be any more use, so that presently Lucy was standing in a damp patch.

"Mr. Tumnus!" bawled Lucy in his ear, shaking him. "Do stop. Stop it at once! You ought to be ashamed of yourself, a great big Faun like you. What on earth are you crying about?"

"Oh—oh—oh!" sobbed Mr. Tumnus, "I'm crying because I'm such a bad Faun."

"I don't think you're a bad Faun at all," said Lucy. "I think you are a very good Faun. You are the nicest Faun I've ever met."

"Oh—oh—you wouldn't say that if you knew," replied Mr. Tumnus between his sobs. "No, I'm a bad Faun. I don't suppose there ever was a worse Faun since the beginning of the world."

"But what have you done?" said Lucy.

"My old father, now," said Mr. Tumnus, "that's his picture over the mantelpiece. He would never have done a thing like this."

"A thing like what?" said Lucy.

"Like what I've done," said the Faun. "Taken service under the White Witch. That's what I am. I'm in the pay of the White Witch."

"The White Witch? Who is she?"

"Why, it is she that has got all Narnia under her thumb. It's she that makes it always winter. Always winter and never Christmas; think of that!"

"How awful!" said Lucy. "But what does she pay *you* for?"

"That's the worst of it," said Mr. Tumnus with a deep groan. "I'm a kidnapper for her, that's what I am. Look at me, Daughter of Eve. Would you believe that I'm the sort of Faun to meet a poor innocent child in the wood, one that had never done me any harm, and pretend to be friendly with it, and invite it home to my cave, all for the sake of lulling it asleep and then handing it over to the White Witch?"

"No," said Lucy. "I'm sure you wouldn't do anything of the sort."

"But I have," said the Faun.

"Well," said Lucy rather slowly (for she wanted to be truthful and yet not to be too hard on him), "well, that was pretty bad. But you're so sorry for it that I'm sure you will never do it again."

"Daughter of Eve, don't you understand?" said the Faun. "It isn't something I *have* done. I'm doing it now, this very moment."

"What do you mean?" cried Lucy, turning very white.

"You are the child," said Mr. Tumnus. "I had orders from the White Witch that if ever I saw a Son of Adam or a Daughter of Eve in the wood, I was to catch them and hand them over to her. And you are the first I ever met. And I've pretended to be your friend and asked you to tea, and all the time I've been meaning to wait till you were asleep and then go and tell *her*."

"Oh but you won't, Mr. Tumnus," said Lucy. "You won't, will you? Indeed, indeed you really musn't."

"And if I don't," said he, beginning to cry again, "she's sure to find out. And she'll have my tail cut off, and my horns sawn off, and my beard plucked out, and she'll wave her wand over my beautiful cloven hoofs and turn them into horrid solid hoofs like a wretched horse's. And if she is extra and specially angry she'll turn me into stone and I shall be only a statue of a Faun in her horrible house until the four thrones at Cair Paravel are filled— and goodness knows when that will happen, or whether it will ever happen at all."

"I'm very sorry, Mr. Tumnus," said Lucy. "But please let me go home."

"Of course I will," said the Faun. "Of course I've got to. I see that now. I hadn't known what Humans were like before I met you. Of course I can't give you up

to the Witch; not now that I know you. But we must be off at once. I'll see you back to the lamppost. I suppose you can find your own way from there back to Spare Oom and War Drobe?"

"I'm sure I can," said Lucy.

"We must go as quietly as we can," said Mr. Tumnus. "The whole wood is full of *her* spies. Even some of the trees are on her side."

They both got up and left the tea things on the table, and Mr. Tumnus once more put up his umbrella and gave Lucy his arm, and they went out into the snow. The journey back was not at all like the journey to the Faun's cave. They stole along as quickly as they could, without speaking a word, and Mr. Tumnus kept to the darkest places. Lucy was relieved when they reached the lamppost again.

"Do you know your way from here, Daughter of Eve?" said Tumnus.

Lucy looked very hard between the trees and could just see in the distance a patch of light that looked like daylight. "Yes," she said, "I can see the wardrobe door."

"Then be off home as quick as you can," said the Faun, "and— c-can you ever forgive me for what I meant to do?"

"Why, of course I can," said Lucy, shaking him heartily by the hand. "And I do hope you won't get into dreadful trouble on my account."

"Farewell, Daughter of Eve," said he. "Perhaps I may keep the handkerchief?"

"Rather!" said Lucy, and then ran towards the far-off patch of daylight as quickly as her legs would carry her. And presently instead of rough branches brushing past her she felt coats, and instead of crunching snow under her feet she felt wooden boards, and all at once she found herself jumping out of the wardrobe into the same empty room from which the whole adventure had started. She shut the wardrobe door tightly behind her and looked around, panting for breath. It was still raining and she could hear the voices of the others in the passage.

"I'm here," she shouted. "I'm here. I've come back, I'm all right."

Questions

1. Why did Mr. Tumnus say he was a bad faun?

2. Mr. Tumnus did not know what he should do about Lucy. What was his *conflict,* or struggle? How did he solve it?

3. Lucy was firm with Mr. Tumnus, but also kind. What is one event in the story that shows Lucy being both firm and kind?

4. When the story ends, who is still in trouble? What might happen to help that character?

5. Characters in stories may be brave or kind or afraid, or have any of a number of other qualities. What quality did Lucy have that led her into adventure? Explain your answer.

6. When Peter said, "We've fallen on our feet," what did he mean?
   a. Our feet are tired so we should go to bed.
   b. We were lucky.
   c. We were in serious trouble.
   d. We should have looked where we were walking.

Activity   Name the Imaginary Places

Mr. Tumnus was not familiar with Lucy's world. He thought of the spare room from which Lucy came as "the far land of Spare Oom." The wardrobe he saw as "the bright city of War Drobe." Find other words or phrases in the story that would make humorous names of places. Add other words or phrases from your imagination. Then use these place names in sentences that show your meaning.

The Megrimum

From the novel *Kneeknock Rise* by Natalie Babbitt

Illustrated by Arvis Stewart

The village of Instep lies at the foot of a huge cliff known as Kneeknock Rise. Though no one has ever seen it, on stormy nights people can hear unearthly moans coming from a creature called the Megrimum, who lives at the top of the Rise. Once a year people come from afar to the Instep Fair, to eat and dance, be entertained, and hear the Megrimum for themselves. When young Egan comes to his first Instep Fair, he finds everyone, including his Uncle Anson and Aunt Gertrude, talking of little else than the fearful monster. Cousin Ada says that the Megrimum has eaten foolish Uncle Ott, who went off some days ago leaving behind his old dog, Annabelle, and some of his verses. Aunt Gertrude claims she saw the Megrimum's horrible face at the window one night. Finally, on a dare from Ada, Egan decides to find out about the Megrimum for himself. He takes Annabelle and begins to climb the Rise.

Aunt Gertrude stood rigid as a post, her hand on her heart, staring at her daughter.

"It's Egan, Papa! Egan," sobbed Ada. "He did it! I teased him, Papa, and he did it. He wouldn't stop."

"*What* did he do, Ada? What did Egan *do?*" cried Uncle Anson, gripping her shoulders firmly.

"Oh, Papa," she gulped, turning her face away from the alarm in her father's eyes. "It's all my fault. I dared him and he's doing it now. He's climbing, Papa. Climbing Kneeknock Rise."

"Merciful heavens!" gasped Uncle Anson, and behind him Aunt Gertrude sagged and dropped in a faint to the floor.

And all the while Egan was climbing. Up and up over rocks and weeds, up between the twisted trees, panting with excitement. From time to time he paused, waiting for Annabelle to catch up with him. The dog's sides were heaving and her tongue dangled sidewise from her jaws, but her stiff old legs churned steadily along and her eyes were bright. Then all at once it began to rain in earnest, blurring the dim light and shellacking the rocks into slippery, treacherous jewels. Egan leaned against a tree trunk to catch his breath and Annabelle dropped down at his feet. He bent over to scratch her ears and then, suddenly, the moaning began. It was loud here, half-way up the Rise, loud and horrifying and desperate.

Down through the trees it twisted with the wind, a long, unearthly moaning that rose gradually till it wound into a high and hollow wail. Egan stood transfixed with his hand on Annabelle's head and for the first time he was afraid.

The Megrimum was awake at last. In the fields below, the chattering ceased. Faces peered out of tent flaps and windows, serious, frightened, eager. Here and there a man or a child came out into the rain and stood quietly, listening. An old woman dragged a stool from under a little cart and sat clutching an onion, nodding with her eyes tight shut, while the rain wilted her bonnet down around her ears.

But in the village there was frantic activity. Uncle Anson, a lantern bobbing from his hand, was rushing from neighbor to neighbor. "Quick! Quick! To my house at once! Yes, it's my nephew, my wife's sister's child. He's trying to climb the Rise. We've got to stop him. What do you mean, I'm crazy? We can't just let him go!"

Soon a wet and anxious group of men were arguing and shouting before the fire in the little house, while Ada snuffled miserably in a corner and Aunt Gertrude rushed back and forth, making coffee and spilling more than she served.

"But see here, Anson, that boy won't climb all the way up!" said one of the men.

"How do you know he won't?" answered Uncle Anson grimly. "He doesn't live in Instep. He doesn't understand."

"But good lord, man," cried another, "do you realize what you're saying? You're asking us to climb the Rise!"

"I know what I'm asking!" shouted Uncle Anson. "How can you think I don't? But can I let that boy stay out there now? The Megrimum is wide awake. I've never heard it moan so loud."

"Nobody would be fool enough to climb up there," growled another man.

"That boy is fool enough, bless him," said Uncle Anson. "And I know my brother Ott would have climbed in an instant to save him. There's fools and fools, my friend. I'm going. Gertrude, where's my cap? I'm going and I'll go alone if I have to."

"I'll go, then," said one man.

"I, too," said another. "And I'll bring along my bell." And then they were all going, hurrying out into the drenching rain while high above the moaning rose and fell, winding and rippling like ribbon down the night.

But Egan was half an hour ahead by that time. And he was young and strong, alone—and determined. After his first fear, he had clenched his fists and scowled. His early jealousy of the cliff's high pride returned. He searched about him among the trees and found a long, sharp stick.

"Look out up there!" he yelled into the rain. "I'm coming up!"

Off he went again, Annabelle struggling along behind him. And by the time his rescuers were beginning the climb, Egan had come nearly to the top, and the mist that hung there reached out gently and gathered him in.

--→≈≋≈←--

Egan stood uncertainly in the mist. The rain was easing off. There had been no sound from the Megrimum for many minutes now. A mumble of thunder complained from far away and then the clouds parted and the moon rode free. Instantly the mist was luminous, and Egan, with a gasp, felt as if he had suddenly been tucked inside a bubble. Looking up, he saw the moon as a shapeless radiance, like a candle seen through steamy glass. Each drop of moisture in the mist had become a tiny prism, filtering and fanning the dim light into a million pale rainbows of softest color. From a shrouded tree-top nearby came the soft, clear notes of a bird's call and, with the faintest of rustles, a small red kneeknock bird floated through the mist ahead of him. Egan held his breath and stared at the magic world around him, a nighttime world bewitched into seeming morning by the wizard moon. Annabelle stood silent at his feet, and then, all at once, the old dog stiffened and whined. Nudged in his trance, Egan bent to soothe her but she pulled away from his hand, her ears high. She whined again, moved forward, stopped with tilted head, listening. Then with a yelp she ran on into the mist and disappeared. From somewhere up ahead a low groan echoed and Egan, his stick in his hand, moved slowly after Annabelle, straight toward the very top of Kneeknock Rise.

On the cliffside below, the rescuers paused.

"The storm is over. Look, there's the moon!" said one of the men. "And the Megrimum's been quiet for quite a while now."

"Look here, Anson," said another. "I think we should search around a bit. That boy of yours can't have gone all the way up. He must be somewhere about."

"Perhaps," said Uncle Anson. "We'll divide up and look. But if we don't find him, I'm going on to the top."

With swaying arcs of lantern light washing the dark, the men spread out among the trees along the side of the Rise. Below, in her garden behind the little house, Aunt Gertrude stood wringing her hands. She could hear, faintly, the tinkling of the bell, warning away the Megrimum, and heard as well the

distant, muffled voice of her husband calling: "Egan! Egan! Where are you, Nephew? E-e-e-gan!"

Out in the fields, the visitors knew something had happened.

"A boy, you say?"

"What? Climbing up the Rise?"

"A terrible thing—terrible. It called the child, perhaps, called the child to climb."

"Where was the boy's mother, then, to let him run away?"

"They're climbing up to find him. Look—see the lights of the lanterns."

"Brave men, brave men all."

"Never come down again, ever."

Egan, deep in the mist, heard nothing. He wandered up the final stony slope toward the top like a sleepwalker lost in dreams. The heavy air around him, tinted and dim and moist, was growing unaccountably warmer, and a faint, unpleasant smell he could not quite recognize crept into his nostrils. And then he stopped, chilled suddenly out of his trance. Just ahead there came a noise as of an animal thrashing about, and the low rumble of a voice.

He crept forward, grasping the nearly forgotten stick tightly, and his heart pounded. The Megrimum! At last, the Megrimum! Slay it, perhaps—perhaps; but at least he would see it.

More thrashing in the weeds ahead. "Owanna-ooowanna," the voice seemed to murmur.

Closer and closer crept Egan and then he saw it dimly, all flailing arms, rolling about on the ground.

Another few cautious steps, and then:

"Oh, Anna, Anna, dear old dog!" crooned the voice. There before him, sitting on the ground, was a wild-haired, laughing man who had to be his Uncle Ott, engulfed and struggling happily in the wriggling, wagging ecstasy of Annabelle.

Egan stood with his mouth hanging open. The stick dropped from his hand, and at the sound the man and the dog paused in their greeting and looked toward him. Annabelle trotted over and beamed at him and then turned back.

"Hallo there, boy. Who might you be?" said the man warily.

Egan gulped. "Why, I'm your nephew. Sort of. That is, if you really *are* my Uncle Anson's brother. Are you? Are you Uncle Ott?"

"That's right!" said Uncle Ott in great surprise. "And you—you must be Anson's wife's sister's boy. I guess I've got that right. But what in the name of goodness are you doing up here?"

"I came . . . " Egan paused. "Well, I came to kill the Megrimum." He waited for his uncle to laugh or scold, but Ott did neither. He merely nodded as if it were all quite natural. "But where *is* the Megrimum?" asked Egan. "And why is it so awfully warm up here?"

Uncle Ott stood up and brushed bits of twigs and leaves from his clothes.

"The Megrimum. Yes. I came to find it, too." He paused and looked thoughtfully at Egan and then, in a rush, he said, "Boy, listen to me. There isn't any Megrimum. Never was. It's all been just a lot of—

megrimummery, if you will. It's too bad, that's what
it is. Too bad. Come along. I'll show you."

Close to the top of Kneeknock Rise lay a shallow
cave. At the mouth of the cave the mist was very
thick and as hot as steam, and the strange, unpleasant
smell was almost overwhelming.

"Phew!" said Egan. "What in the world is in
there? It must be something very rotten and dreadful!"

"No, not at all," said Uncle Ott. "It's only a
mineral spring. Sulphur. Nasty, but not unnatural."

"A spring?" puzzled Egan. "But how could it be
a spring? Springs aren't hot."

"Sometimes they are," said Uncle Ott. "This cliff
must have been a volcano long ago. The water boils

up to the top through a narrow hole, from far under the earth where it's very hot. And that makes this steamy mist. Usually the hole lets the steam through quietly, but when rain seeps into the hot places—more pressure, more steam. And the steam makes the whistling, whining, moaning sound as it shoots out the top of the hole. Just like a boiling kettle. The cave echoes and makes the sound even louder, and that, my dear boy, is the long-feared, long-loved Megrimum."

Egan stood and stared and then all at once he was very pleased. "I knew this old cliff wasn't so wonderful," he said. "Can I go in there and look at the spring?"

Uncle Ott shook his head. "Too hot," he said. "And anyway, there's not much to it. Just a hole in the ground and a lot of hot rocks." He shook his head again and sighed. "Too bad about that. Just a hole in the ground."

They turned away from the cave and walked back to where Annabelle sat waiting for them. "Come down to Instep with me and we'll tell them about it," said Egan. "We can both sleep in your room. I'll sleep on the floor with Annabelle."

"No, no, I think I won't go down to Instep," said Uncle Ott, running his fingers through his wild white hair. "Now that I've got my own dear Annabelle with me—and I do thank you for bringing her up—I guess I'll just go on down the other side."

"Have you been up here all the time?" asked Egan.

"Yes, as a matter of fact I have. I came up thinking I'd be going right back down again, so I didn't bring Annabelle along, and anyway, I was afraid she'd have trouble with the climbing. But when I got up here, the air was so wet and hot—well, it just did wonders for my wheezing. Absolute wonders. See? I can breathe perfectly well!" He took several deep breaths to show that it was true. "It's been a blessing. But now I guess I'll move along."

Egan had a sudden idea. "It was you that night, wasn't it? Tapping at the window?"

Uncle Ott looked embarrassed. "That was too bad. I thought I could get Annabelle to come to the window and then I could lift her out and take her away with me. But there was Gertrude all of a sudden, screaming, and I had to go away. I felt very bad about scaring her."

"But I don't see why you didn't just come into the house," said Egan. "During the day. And take Annabelle then."

"Because," said Uncle Ott slowly, "I didn't want to have to explain."

Egan was puzzled. "About the Megrimum, you mean?" he asked. "Why not? They're all scared to death of the Megrimum. They'd be happy to hear there isn't one after all."

"Do you think so?" said Uncle Ott. "I really don't know about that. I've been thinking and thinking about that." He looked at Egan sadly. "Is it better to be wise if it makes you solemn and practical, or is it better to be foolish so you can go on enjoying yourself?"

"The king and the fool!" said Egan, suddenly understanding.

"Exactly," said Uncle Ott. "Exactly. I see you've been reading my verses. I've been interested for years in this problem of kings and fools. Now here I am with a perfect example of the question and I really don't know the answer." He sat down on the ground beside Annabelle and stared off into the mist, rubbing his chin. "For me it's always been important to find out the why of things. To try to be wise. But I can't say it's ever made me happier. As for those people down below, they've had their Megrimum for years and years. And I don't know as I want to spoil it all for them. There's always the possibility that they're happier believing. Kind of a nice idea, this Megrimum." He stood up and pulled his jacket close around his chest, breathing the mist deeply. "Yes, it's kind of a nice idea in an odd kind of way," he said. "Do as you like about it. If I knew what was best, I'd certainly tell you, but the fact is I don't. Well, come along, Annabelle. Good-bye, Nephew. A pleasure to have seen you."

He started off and then he paused and stood thinking for a moment. At last he turned and came back. "I've just had another thought on the matter," he said. "It came to me in rhyme. Thoughts often come to me that way—I don't seem to be able to help it:

The cat attacked a bit of string
*   And dragged it by the head*
And tortured it beside the stove
*   And left it there for dead.*

"Excuse me, sir," I murmured when
*   He passed me in the hall,*
"But that was only string you had
*   And not a mouse at all!"*

He didn't even thank me when
*   I told him he was wrong.*
It's possible—just possible—
*   He knew it all along.*

"Well, there it is, for what it's worth. Good-bye." Uncle Ott smiled and then, with Annabelle wagging at his side, he turned and vanished into the mist.

Questions

1. What did the villagers think the Megrimum was?

2. What did Egan find out the Megrimum *really* was?

3. Why did Uncle Ott stay on Kneeknock Rise with the Megrimum? Give two reasons.

4. Should Egan tell the villagers the truth about the Megrimum? Why or why not?

5. Uncle Ott asks a question that underlies the story's *theme*, or main idea. What is the question? How would you answer it?

6. Which words did the author use to make each of these descriptions interesting?
   a. The rain _____ the rocks.

      shellacked   fell on   moistened
   b. The world was bewitched by the _____ moon.

      bright   wizard   cheese-colored

Activity   Write Explanations

Natural events that appear strange or magic usually have a natural explanation. Think of three examples— or find three examples in informational books. Then divide a paper into two columns. Label the first column *Megrimum Explanation.* Label the second column *Real Explanation.* When you have written your two-column report, share only the Megrimum Explanations with others. Ask them to figure out the real explanations from what you have described.

About NATALIE BABBITT

Natalie Babbitt's mother was an artist, and at first Natalie followed in her mother's footsteps. She studied art in high school and college. After she married, she and her husband worked on a children's book together. It was called *The 49th Magician.* Her husband wrote the story and she drew the pictures. Later, Natalie herself decided to try writing. "Now I am far more interested in writing than in illustrating," she says.

When Natalie Babbitt began to write *Kneeknock Rise,* she set out to write about the main character in *The 49th Magician.* "It was to have been only a funny story," she says, "but it got away from me." The magician character became a child, and Natalie Babbitt wondered what the child would find at the top of the mountain. "This led to the Kneeknock verse about the other side of the hill," she explains, "and eventually to the Megrimum."

Natalie Babbitt's story ideas begin with her interest in a word or phrase. Then she creates the characters, thinks about the adventures they would have, and begins to write.

More Books by Natalie Babbitt

Tuck Everlasting
The Eyes of the Amaryllis
The Search for Delicious

From
The House of Dies Drear

A novel by Virginia Hamilton

Illustrated by Jack White

Thomas Small and his family are on their way to a new home in Huntington, Ohio. Thomas's father is going to teach at a small college there. Thomas is so excited that he finds it almost as hard to keep still as his little twin brothers do. It is not his father's job, or the thoughts of a new town or a new school, that Thomas is excited about. Thomas is excited about the family's new house.

The house is not just any house. It is a house with a history. More than a hundred years ago, the house was a station on the Underground Railroad. The owner of the house, Dies Drear, had been one of the many "conductors" who had hidden run-away slaves and helped them escape to freedom.

Thomas finally falls asleep and misses crossing the Ohio River and coming into Huntington. When he wakes, the first thing Thomas sees is the house of Dies Drear.

Thomas did not wake in time to see the Ohio River. Mr. Small was glad he didn't, for through the gloom of mist and heavy rain, most of its expanse was hidden. What was visible looked much like a thick mud path, as the sedan crossed over it at Huntington.

Thomas lurched awake a long time after. The car went slowly; there was hardly any rain now. His mother spoke excitedly, and Thomas had to shake his head rapidly in order to understand what she was saying.

"Oh dear!" Mrs. Small said. "Why it's huge!"

Mr. Small broke in eagerly, turning around to face Thomas. "You've waited a long time," he said. "Take a good look, son. There's our new house!"

Thomas looked carefully out of his window. He opened the car door for a few seconds to see better, but found the moist air too warm and soft. The feel of it was not nice at all, and he quickly closed the door. He could see well enough out of the window, and what he saw made everything inside him grow quiet for the first time in weeks. It was more than he could have dreamed.

The house of Dies Drear loomed out of mist and murky sky, not only gray and formless, but huge and unnatural. It seemed to crouch on the side of a hill high above the highway. And it had a dark, isolated look about it that set it at odds with all that was living.

A chill passed over Thomas. He sighed with satisfaction. The house of Dies Drear was a haunted place, of that he was certain.

"Well," Mr. Small said, "what do you think of it, Thomas?"

"It must be the biggest house anyone ever built," Thomas said at last. "And to think—it's our new house! Papa, let's get closer, let's go inside!"

Smiling, Mr. Small kept the car on the highway that now curved up closer toward the house. In a short time they were quite near.

At the base of the hill on which the house sat, a stream ran parallel to the highway. It was muddy and swollen by rain; between it and the hill lay a reach of fertile land, lushly tangled with mullein weed and gold wildflower. The hill itself was rocky and mostly bare, although a thaw had come to the rest of the land and countryside. At the very top of the hill Thomas noticed a grove of trees, which looked like either pine or spruce.

The house of Dies Drear sat on an outcropping, much like a ledge, on the side of the hill. The face of the ledge was rock, from which gushed mineral springs. And these came together at the fertile land, making a narrow groove through it before emptying into the stream. Running down the face of the ledge, the springs coated the rock in their path with red and yellow rust.

Thomas stared so long at the ledge and springs, his eyes began to play tricks on him. It seemed as if the rust moved along with the spring waters.

"It's bleeding," he said softly. "It looks just like

somebody cut the house open underneath and let its blood run out! That's a nice hill though," he added. He looked at the clumps of skinny trees at each side of the house. Their branches were bare and twisted by wind.

Thomas cleared his throat. "I bet you can see a lot from the top of that hill." He felt he ought to say this. The hill was hardly anything compared to the mountains at home. Otherwise the land in every direction was mostly flat.

"You can see the college from the top of the hill," Mr. Small said. "And you can see the town. It's quite a view. On a clear day those springs and colored rock make the hill and house look like a fairyland."

"All those springs!" Thomas said. He shook his head. "Where do they come from? I've never seen anything like them."

"You'll get used to the look of the land," Mr. Small said. "This is limestone country, and always with limestone in this formation you'll find the water table percolating through rock into springs. There are caves, lakes and marshes all around us, all because of the rock formations and the way they fault."

Mrs. Small kept her eye on the house. It was her nature to concentrate on that which there was a chance of her changing.

"No, it's not," she said softly. "Oh, dear, no, it will never be pretty!"

"Everything is seeping with rain," Mr. Small said to her. "Just try to imagine those rocks, that stream and the springs on a bright, sunny day. Then it's really something to see."

Thomas could imagine how everything looked on a day such as his father described. His eyes shone as he said, "It must look just about perfect!"

They drove nearer. Thomas could see that the house lay far back from the highway. There was a gravel road branching from the highway and leading to the house. A weathered covered bridge crossed the stream at the base of the hill. Mr. Small turned off the highway and stopped the car.

"There's been quite a rain," he said, "I'd better check the bridge."

Now Thomas sat with his hands folded tightly beneath his chin, with his elbows on his knees. He had a moment to look at the house of Dies Drear, the hill and the stream all at once. He stared long and hard. By the time his father returned, he had everything figured out.

They continued up the winding road, the house with its opaque, watching windows drawing ever nearer.

The stream is the moat. The covered planks over it are the drawbridge, Thomas thought. And the house of Dies Drear is the castle.

But who is the king of all this? Who will win the war?

There was a war and there was a king. Thomas was as sure of this as he was certain the house was haunted, for the hill and house were bitten and frozen. They were separated from the rest of the land by something unkind.

"Oh dear," Mrs. Small was saying. "Oh dear. Dear!"

Suddenly the twins were scrambling over Thomas, wide awake and watching the house get closer. By some unspoken agreement, they set up a loud, pathetic wail at the same time.

"Look!" Thomas whispered to them. "See, over there is clear sky. All this mist will rise and get blown away soon. Then you'll feel better."

Sure enough, above the dark trees at the top of the hill was deep, clear sky. Thomas gently cradled the boys. "There are new kinds of trees here," he told them. "There will be nights with stars above trees like you've never known!" The twins hushed, as Thomas knew they would.

Up close the house seemed to Thomas even more huge, if that were possible. There were three floors. Above the top floor was a mansard roof with dormer windows jutting from its steep lower slopes. Eaves overhanging the second story dripped moisture to the ground in splattering beats. There was a veranda surrounding the ground floor, with pillars that rose to the eaves.

Thomas liked the house. But the chill he had felt on seeing it from the highway was still with him. Now he knew why.

It's not the gray day, he thought. It's not mist and damp that sets it off. There are things beyond weather. The house has secrets!

Thomas admired the house for keeping them so long.

But I'm here now, he thought happily. It won't keep anything from me.

The twins refused to get out of the car, so Thomas had to carry one while his mother carried the other. They cried loudly as soon as they were set on the veranda.

"They don't like the eaves dripping so close," Mr. Small said. "Move them back, Thomas."

Thomas placed the boys close to the oak door and then joined Mrs. Small in front of the house. His father was already busy unloading the trailer. The heavy furniture and trucks had come by van a week earlier. Thomas guessed all of it would be piled high in the foyer.

"It's old," Mrs. Small remarked, looking up at the dormers of the house. "Maybe when the sun comes out. . . ." Her voice trailed off.

Thomas placed his arm through hers. "Mama, it must be the biggest house for miles. And all the land! We can plant corn . . . we can have horses! Mama, it will be our own farm!"

"Oh, it's big," Mrs. Small said. "Big to clean and big to keep an eye on. How will I ever know where to find the boys?"

"I'll watch them," said Thomas. "Wait until it's warm weather for sure. They'll be with me all the time."

"Let's go inside now," Mr. Small said to them. He had unloaded cartons beside the twins on the veranda. "Thomas and I will have to set up the beds the first thing."

"And I'll have to get the kitchen ready," said Mrs. Small, "and you'll have to drive into town for food.

Goodness, there's so much to do, I won't have time to look around." Then she smiled, as though relieved.

Mr. Small went first, and Mrs. Small held the door for the twins and Thomas. At once the boys began to cry. Thomas watched them, noticing that they avoided touching the house, especially the oak door trimmed with carved quatrefoils. Mrs. Small hadn't noticed, and Thomas said nothing. He scooped up the boys and carried them inside.

When the heavy door closed behind them, they were instantly within a place of twilight and stillness.

While his parents are looking over the new house, Thomas goes back out on the veranda. His attention is caught by the intricate carvings on the heavy oaken front door. Thomas begins to study the door more closely and discovers a hidden button. When Thomas works the button, the front steps of the house move— revealing a large, dark hole. Thomas lies down on the edge of the hole to investigate, loses his grip, and falls in!

"Move slowly. Think fast," Thomas whispered. "Keep in mind what's behind and look closely at what's in front."

Thomas always carried a pencil-thin flashlight, which he sometimes used for reading in the car. He sat up suddenly and pulled out the flashlight. It wasn't broken from the fall, and he flicked it on. He sat in a kind of circle enclosed by brick walls. In some places, the brick had crumbled into powder, which was slowly filling up the circle of sod.

That will take a long time, thought Thomas. He looked up at the underside of the veranda steps.

Thomas got to his feet and made his way down the rock stairway into darkness. At the foot of the stairs was a path with walls of dirt and rock on either side of it. The walls were so close, Thomas could touch them by extending his arms a few inches. Above his head was a low ceiling carved out of rock. Such cramped space made him uneasy. The foundation of the house had to be somewhere above the natural rock. The idea of the whole three-story house of Dies Drear pressing down on him caused him to stop a moment on the path. Since he had fallen, he hadn't had time to be afraid. He wasn't now, but he did begin to worry a little about where the path led. He thought of ghosts, and yet he did not seriously believe in them. "No," he told himself, "not with the flashlight. Not when I can turn back . . . when I can run."

And besides, he thought, I'm strong. I can take care of myself.

Thomas continued along the path, flickering his tiny beam of light this way and that. Pools of water stood in some places. He felt a coldness, like the stream of air that came from around the button on the oak doorframe. His shoes were soon soaked. His socks grew cold and wet, and he thought about taking them off. He could hear water running a long way off. He stopped again to listen, but he couldn't tell from what direction the sound came.

"It's just one of the springs," he said. His voice bounced off the walls strangely.

Better not speak. There could be tunnels leading off this one. You can't tell what might hear you in a place like this.

Thomas was scaring himself. He decided not to think again about other tunnels or ghosts. He did think for the first time of how he would get out of this tunnel. He had fallen five feet, and he wasn't sure he would be able to climb back up the crumbling brick walls. Still, the path he walked had to lead somewhere. There had to be another way out.

Thomas felt his feet begin to climb; the path was slanting up. He walked slowly on the slippery rock; then suddenly the path was very wide. The walls were four feet away on either side, and there were long stone slabs against each wall. Thomas sat down on one of the slabs. It was wet, but he didn't even notice.

"Why these slabs?" he asked himself. "For the slaves, hiding and running?"

He opened and closed a moist hand around the flashlight. The light beam could not keep back the dark. Thomas had a lonely feeling, the kind of feeling running slaves must have had.

And they dared not use light, he thought. How long would they have to hide down here? How could they stand it?

Thomas got up and went on. He placed one foot carefully in front of the other on the path, which had narrowed again. He heard the faint sound of movement somewhere. Maybe it was a voice he heard, he couldn't be sure. He swirled the light around over the damp walls, and fumbled it. The flashlight slid out of his hand. For a long moment, he caught and held it between his knees before finally dropping it. He bent quickly to pick it up and stepped down on it. Then he accidentally kicked it with his heel, and it went rattling somewhere over the path. It hit the wall, but it had gone out before then. Now all was very dark.

"It's not far," Thomas said. "All I have to do is feel around."

He felt around with his hands over smooth, moist rock; his hands grew cold. He felt water, and it was icy, slimy. His hands trembled, they ached, feeling in the dark, but he could not find the flashlight.

"I couldn't have kicked it far because I wasn't moving." His voice bounced in a whisper off the walls. He tried crawling backward, hoping to hit the flashlight with his heels.

"It's got to be here . . . Papa?" Thomas stood, turning toward the way he had come, the way he had been crawling backward. He didn't at all like walking in the pitch blackness of the tunnel.

"I'll go on back," he said. "I'll just walk back as quick as I can. There'll be light coming from the veranda steps. I'll climb up that wall and then I'll be out of this. I'll get Papa and we'll do it together."

He went quickly now, with his hands extended to keep himself from hitting the close walls. But then something happened that caused him to stop in his tracks. He stood still, with his whole body tense and alert, the way he could be when he sensed a storm before there was any sign of it in the air or sky.

Thomas had the queerest notion that he was not alone. In front of him, between him and the steps of the veranda, something waited.

"Papa?" he said. He heard something.

The sound went, "Ahhh, ahhh, ahhh." It was not moaning, nor crying. It wasn't laughter, but something forlorn and lost and old.

Thomas backed away. "No," he said. "Oh please!"

"Ahhh, ahhh," something said. It was closer to him now. Thomas could hear no footsteps on the path. He could see nothing in the darkness.

He opened his mouth to yell, but his voice wouldn't come. Fear rose in him; he was cold, freezing, as though he had rolled in snow.

"Papa!" he managed to say. His voice was a whisper. "Papa, come get me . . . Papa!"

"Ahhhh." Whatever it was, was quite close now.

Thomas still backed away from it, then he turned around, away from the direction of the veranda. He started running up the path, with his arms outstretched in front of him. He ran and ran, his eyes wide in the darkness. At any moment, the thing would grab him and smother his face. At any time, the thing would paralyze him with cold. It would take him away. It would tie him in one of the tunnels, and no one would ever find him.

"Don't let it touch me! Don't let it catch me!"

Thomas ran smack into a wall. His arms and hands hit first; then, his head and chest. The impact jarred him from head to foot. He thought his wrists were broken, but ever so slowly, painful feeling flowed back into his hands. The ache moved dully up to the sockets of his shoulders. He opened and closed his hands. They hurt so much, his eyes began to tear, but he didn't seem to have broken anything.

Thomas felt frantically along the wall. The wall was wood. He knew the feel of it right away. It was heavy wood, perhaps oak, and it was man made, man hewn. Thomas pounded on it, hurting himself more, causing his head to spin. He kept on, because he knew he was about to be taken from behind by something ghostly and cold.

"Help me! It's going to get me!" he called. "Help me!"

Thomas heard a high, clear scream on the other side of the wall. Next came the sound of feet scurrying, and then the wall slid silently up.

"Thomas Small!" his mother said. "What do you think you are doing inside that wall!"

Questions

1. Stories often show a *conflict,* or a struggle, between one force and another. The conflict may be between or among people, within one person, or between a person and the *setting,* that is, the time and place. Which type of conflict do you find in this story? Explain your choice.

2. Why does the author describe the house of Dies Drear in great detail through Thomas's eyes?

3. What do you think made the frightening sound that Thomas heard in the tunnel? How might Thomas find out about it?

4. Which meaning best explains each underlined word used to describe the story's setting?
   a. If water percolates, it _____.
      oozes through   boils   runs free
   b. If windows are opaque, they _____.
      let light in   shut out the light   are closed

Activity   Diagram the Story Setting

The setting is important in stories of mystery and suspense. The setting of "The House of Dies Drear" is, of course, the house and its surroundings. Make a diagram such as the author might have used to plan the setting. Show what the author revealed about areas outside and under the house, as well as the house itself. Label important parts of the diagram. Compare your diagram with your classmates' diagrams.

About VIRGINIA HAMILTON

Virginia Hamilton was born in Yellow Springs, Ohio, where her grandfather and his mother had settled after traveling the Underground Railroad to freedom. She grew up in a large family that owned a small farm. As a child, Virginia Hamilton freely explored the farm land owned by her family and nearby relatives and kept notebooks in which she often wrote down her thoughts. Because she came from a family of storytellers, she also listened—and learned. Virginia Hamilton says that her brother Billy's stories of his life's dreams "taught me to dream large and lucky—which is something all young people should learn to do."

Virginia Hamilton left Yellow Springs to attend college at Ohio State, where she studied writing. After college she went to New York to work. She submitted many stories to magazines, but none were published. Then an old college friend urged her to rewrite a story she had written at Ohio State. That story, *Zeely,* became her first published book, followed by *The House of Dies Drear* and many others. Though her childhood is long past, Virginia Hamilton keeps the memory of it "very much alive. And it is from such memories . . . that the best of my writing comes."

More Books by Virginia Hamilton

Zeely
The Time-Ago Tales of Jahdu
Arilla Sun Down

The Secret Sits

A poem by Robert Frost

We dance round in a ring and suppose,
But the Secret sits in the middle and knows.

Illustrated by Jan Brett

BOOKSHELF

The Borrowers Aloft by Mary Norton. Harcourt Brace Jovanovich, 1961. Tiny people no taller than a pencil go on a voyage in a teakettle to search for a new home. This is the fourth book in a series of five.

I, Tut: The Boy Who Became Pharaoh by Miriam Schlein. Four Winds Press, 1979. A young boy tells how he became king of Egypt at the age of nine.

A Wrinkle in Time by Madeleine L'Engle. Farrar, Straus & Giroux, 1962. Meg Murray, her brother Charles Wallace, and their friend Calvin O'Keefe take a trip through time with the help of strangers from outer space. Their object is to find Mr. Murray, who disappeared while working on a secret government project.

Into the Dream by William Sleator. E. P. Dutton, 1979. Paul and Francine are troubled by identical nightmares in which a child's life seems threatened. They work together to end their nightmares and to solve a fantastic riddle.

The Selchie's Seed by Shulamith Oppenheim. Bradbury Press, 1975. For many years Marian has heard the legend of the seal people and her own enchanted family heritage. When she hears the call from the sea, she knows she must answer it.

The Ring in the Prairie: A Shawnee Legend edited by John Bierhorst. Dial Press, 1970. Enchanted by the youngest of the star princesses, Waupee cannot rest until he makes her his wife. But a star princess is not meant to live an earthly life.

5 To Live With Nature

You have to be careful with snakes—
some are dangerous, and some are
harmless, and you had better know the
difference. Take Old Ben, for example.
That old blacksnake was as harmless
as a kitten.

OLD BEN

A short story by Jesse Stuart

Illustrated by John Hamburger

One morning in July when I was walking across a clover field to a sweet-apple tree, I almost stepped on him. There he lay coiled like heavy strands of black rope. He was a big bull blacksnake. We looked at each other a minute, and then I stuck the toe of my shoe up to his mouth. He drew his head back in a friendly way. He didn't want trouble. Had he shown the least fight, I would have soon finished him. My father had always told me there was only one good snake—a dead one.

When the big fellow didn't show any fight, I reached down and picked him up by the neck. When I lifted him he was as long as I was tall. That was six feet. I started calling him Old Ben as I held him by the neck and rubbed his back. He enjoyed having his back rubbed and his head stroked. Then I lifted him into my arms. He was the first snake I'd ever been friendly with. I was afraid at first to let Old Ben wrap himself around me. I thought he might wrap himself around my neck and choke me.

The more I petted him, the more affectionate he became. He was so friendly I decided to trust him. I wrapped him around my neck a couple of times and let him loose. He crawled down one arm and went back to my neck, around and down the other arm and back again. He stuck out his forked tongue to the sound of my voice as I talked to him.

"I wouldn't kill you at all," I said. "You're a friendly snake. I'm taking you home with me."

I headed home with Old Ben wrapped around my neck and shoulders. When I started over the hill by the pine grove, I met my cousin Wayne Holbrook coming up the hill. He stopped suddenly when he saw me. He started backing down the hill.

"He's a pet, Wayne," I said. "Don't be afraid of Old Ben."

It was a minute before Wayne could tell me what he wanted. He had come to borrow a plow. He kept a safe distance as we walked on together.

Before we reached the barn, Wayne got brave enough to touch Old Ben's long body.

"What are you going to do with him?" Wayne asked. "Uncle Mick won't let you keep him!"

"Put him in the corncrib," I said. "He'll have plenty of delicate food in there. The cats we keep at this barn have grown fat and lazy on the milk we feed 'em."

I opened the corncrib door and took Old Ben from around my neck because he was beginning to get warm and a little heavy.

"This will be your home," I said. "You'd better hide under the corn."

Besides my father, I knew Old Ben would have another enemy at our home. He was our hunting dog, Blackie, who would trail a snake, same as a possum or mink. He had treed blacksnakes, and my father had shot them from the trees. I knew Blackie would find Old Ben, because he followed us to the barn each morning.

The first morning after I'd put Old Ben in the corncrib, Blackie followed us. He started toward the corncrib holding his head high, sniffing. He stuck his nose up to a crack in the crib and began to bark. Then he tried to tear a plank off.

"Stop it, Blackie," Pa scolded him. "What's the matter with you? Have you taken to barking at mice?"

"Blackie is not barking at a mouse," I said. "I put a blacksnake in there yesterday!"

"A blacksnake?" Pa asked, looking unbelievingly. "A blacksnake?"

"Yes, a pet blacksnake." I said.

"Have you gone crazy?" he said. "I'll move a thousand bushels of corn to get that snake!"

"You won't mind this one," I said. "You and Mom will love him."

My father said a few unprintable words before we started back to the house. After breakfast, when Pa and Mom came to the barn, I was already there. I had opened the crib door and there was Old Ben. He'd crawled up front and was coiled on a sack. I put my hand down and he crawled up my arm to my neck and over my shoulder. When Mom and Pa reached the crib, I thought Pa was going to faint.

"He has a pet snake," Mom said.

"Won't be a bird or a young chicken left on this place," Pa said. "Every time I pick up an ear of corn in that crib, I'll be jumping."

"Pa, he won't hurt you," I said, patting the snake's head. "He's a natural pet, or somebody has tamed him. And he's not going to bother birds and young chickens when there are so many mice in this crib."

"Mick, let him keep the snake," Mom said. "I won't be afraid of it."

This was the beginning of a long friendship.

Mom went to the corncrib morning after morning and shelled corn for her geese and chickens. Often Old Ben would be lying in front on his burlap sack. Mom watched him at first from the corner of her eye. Later she didn't bother to watch him any more than she did a cat that came up for his milk.

Later it occurred to us that Old Ben might like milk, too. We started leaving milk for him. We never saw him drink it, but his pan was always empty when we returned. We know the mice didn't drink it, because he took care of them.

"One thing is certain," Mom said one morning when she went to shell corn. "We don't find any more corn chewed up by the mice and left on the floor."

July passed and August came. My father got used to Old Ben, but not until he had proved his worth. Ben had done something our nine cats couldn't. He had cleaned the corncrib of mice.

Then my father began to worry about Old Ben's going after water, and Blackie's finding his track. So he put water in the crib.

September came and went. We began wondering where our pet would go when days grew colder. One morning in early October we left milk for Old Ben, and it was there when we went back that afternoon. But Old Ben wasn't there.

"Old Ben's a good pet for the warm months," Pa said. "But in the winter months, my cats will have to do the work. Maybe Blackie got him!"

"He might have holed up for the winter in the hayloft," I told Pa after we had removed all the corn and didn't find him. "I'm worried about him. I've had a lot of pets—ground hogs, crows, and hawks—but Old Ben's the best yet."

November, December, January, February, and March came and went. Of course we never expected to see Old Ben in one of those months. We doubted if we ever would see him again.

One day early in April I went to the corncrib, and Old Ben lay stretched across the floor. He looked taller than I was now. His skin was rough and his long body had a flabby appearance. I knew Old Ben needed mice and milk. I picked him up, petted him, and told him so. But the chill of early April was still with him. He got his tongue out slower to answer the kind words I was saying to him. He tried to crawl up my arm but he couldn't make it.

That spring and summer mice got scarce in the corncrib and Old Ben got daring. He went over to the barn and crawled up into the hayloft, where he had many feasts. But he made one mistake.

He crawled from the hayloft down into Fred's feed box, where it was cool. Old Fred was our horse.

There he lay coiled when the horse came in and put his nose down on top of Old Ben. Fred let out a big snort and started kicking. He kicked down a partition, and then turned his heels on his feed box and kicked it down. Lucky for Old Ben that he got out in one piece. But he got back to his crib.

Old Ben became a part of our barnyard family, a pet and darling of all. When children came to play with my brother and sisters, they always went to the crib and got Old Ben. He enjoyed the children, who were afraid of him at first but later learned to pet this kind old reptile.

Summer passed and the late days of September were very humid. Old Ben failed one morning to drink his milk. We knew it wasn't time for him to hole up for the winter.

We knew something had happened.

Pa and I moved the corn searching for him. Mom made a couple of trips to the barn lot to see if we had found him. But all we found was the rough skin he had shed last spring.

"Fred's never been very sociable with Old Ben since he got in his box that time," Pa said. "I wonder if he could have stomped Old Ben to death. Old Ben could've been crawling over the barn lot, and Fred saw his chance to get even!"

"We'll see," I said.

Pa and I left the crib and walked to the barn lot. He went one way and I went the other, each searching the ground.

Mom came through the gate and walked over where my father was looking. She started looking around, too.

"We think Fred might've got him," Pa said. "We're sure Fred's got it in for him over Old Ben getting in his feed box last summer."

"You're accusing Fred wrong," Mom said. "Here's Old Ben's track in the sand."

I ran over to where Mom had found the track. Pa went over to look, too.

"It's no use now," Pa said, softly. "Wouldn't have taken anything for that snake. I'll miss him on that burlap sack every morning when I come to feed the horses. Always looked up at me as if he understood."

The last trace Old Ben had left was in the corner of the lot near the hogpen. His track went straight to the woven wire fence and stopped.

"They've got him," Pa said. "Old Ben trusted everything and everybody. He went for a visit to the wrong place. He didn't last long among sixteen hogs. They go wild over a snake. Even a biting copperhead can't stop a hog. There won't be a trace of Old Ben left."

We stood silently for a minute looking at the broad, smooth track Old Ben had left in the sand.

Questions

1. How did people react to Old Ben when they first met him? How did they react to him later?

2. Tell two things that show how Old Ben reacted to people who were friendly to him.

3. The story has a sad ending. Would you rather that it had a happy ending? Why or why not?

4. Suppose that Old Ben were able to tell his own story. Based on his experiences in this story, what might he say he learned about humans?

5. The author is well known for the simple yet interesting way in which he retells events from his own life. Find and write the words he has used to make these ideas more interesting.
   a. Old Ben was like a rope. (page 339)
   b. Old Ben left a track in the sand. (page 347)

Activity   Write Notes

"Old Ben" is based on the *true story* of a pet black-snake the author once had. A true story or account is called *nonfiction*. The true story of one's own life is called an *autobiography*. Suppose that you are writing about an incident for your autobiography. The incident is about a time when you came upon something in nature, either an enemy or a friend. Write some notes to help you recall that incident. Your notes may include a diagram or sketch. They may also include a "word bank" of words or phrases that will make the incident true to life.

Riddle

A poem by Elizabeth Coatsworth

What is it cries without a mouth?
What buffets,[1] and yet has no hand?
And, footless, runs upon the waves
To drive them roaring up the sand?

Old as the world, unseen as Time,
Without beginning, without end,
What is it cries and has no mouth,
Wave-wrestler, and the sea gulls' friend?

---

1. **buffets** (BUF•its): to strike over and over.

I Called to the Wind

A haiku by Kyorai

Translated by Harry Behn

I called to the wind,
"Who's there?" . . . Whoever it was
still knocks at my gate.

Illustrated by Christa Keiffer

Wind Is a Ghost

A Dakota poem

Retold by Natalia Belting

Wind is a ghost
That whirls and turns,
Twists in fleet moccasins,
Sweeps up dust spinning
Across the dry flatlands.

Whirlwind
Is a ghost dancing.

Illustrated by Christa Keiffer

East O' the Sun and West O' the Moon

A Norwegian folk tale

Illustrated by Katie Thamer

Once on a time there lived a poor husbandman who had so many children that none had food or clothing enough. Kind and good children they were, but the kindest was the youngest daughter.

'Twas on a Thursday evening late in the fall of the year. The weather was wild outside. Rain fell and the wind blew till the walls of the cottage shook. There they all sat around the fire, busy with this thing and that. But all at once, something gave three taps on the windowpane—tap! tap! tap! The father went out to see what it was, and, when he got out of doors, what should he see but a big, White Bear.

"Good evening to you," said the Bear.

"The same to you," said the man.

"Will you give me your youngest daughter?" said the Bear. "If you will, I'll make you as rich as you are poor tonight."

Well, the man would be glad to be rich. But give up his daughter? No, that he wouldn't, he said. But the White Bear said, "Think it over. Next Thursday night I'll come back and then you can give me your answer."

So the father went into the house and told them all that had happened. Now when the lassie heard how she could lighten the poverty of her parents and brothers and sisters, she said at once she would go. Let her family beg never so hard, go she would, she said. I can't say her packing gave her much trouble. She washed and mended her rags and made herself ready to start.

Next Thursday evening the White Bear came. She got on his back with her bundle and off they went through the woods.

"Are you afraid?" said the Bear.

"No, not at all," said the lassie.

So she rode a long, long way till they came to a great steep hill. The White Bear knocked on the face of the hill, a little door opened, and they entered a castle, with rooms all lit up and gleaming, splendid with silver and gold. There, too, was a table laid. It was all as grand as could be. Then the White Bear gave the lassie a bell and told her to ring when she wanted anything.

Well, after she had eaten, she thought she would go to bed. Scarcely had she lifted the bell when she found herself in a room with a bed as fair and white as any one could wish to sleep in. But when she had put out her light she heard someone enter the room next to hers, and there someone stayed until dawn.

Night after night the same thing occurred. Not a single human being did the lassie see through the day, but, when all the lights were out, someone would enter the room next to hers and sleep there until dawn. But always before the daylight appeared, whoever it was was up and off, so as never to be seen.

Things went on well for a while. But all day long the lassie had not a soul to talk to except for the White Bear and she knew not whether it was man or beast who slept in the next room at night. So at last she grew silent and sorrowful. Then the White Bear came and said, "What troubles you, my lassie? Here you have everything a heart can wish. You have only to ring the bell and whatever you want is brought to you."

"Nay then," said the lassie. "I am lonely. Who is it that sleeps in the room next to mine?"

At that the Bear begged her to ask no such questions. "Trust me," he said. "Don't try to find out and in due time you will know."

Now the lassie was grateful to the Bear and fond of him. But in spite of what he said, she grew more and more sorrowful and more and more lonely. Who was it that shared the castle with her? Who was it? Who was it? Who was it? She was forever thinking of that one thing alone. All day long and all night long she wondered and fretted. Still for a long, long time she obeyed the Bear and did not try to find out. But at last she could stand it no longer. In the dead of night she got up, lit a candle, and slipped softly into the next room.

There asleep on a bed the lassie saw the loveliest Prince one ever set eyes on. Slowly she crept up to him, bent over, and kissed him. But as she did so, three drops of hot tallow fell from her candle onto his shirt and awoke him.

"Alas! What have you done?" he cried. "Now you have spoiled all that was gained by the months you were faithful to me. Had you held out only this one year, you would have set me free. For an evil queen has cast a spell upon me, so that I am a white bear by day and a man only at night. A year of good faith and you would have saved me. Now all is over between us. Back I must go to the castle *East o' the Sun and West o' the Moon*. There I must marry a princess with a nose three ells long. She must now be the wife for me."

The lassie wept, but there was no help for it. Go
he must, he said. Then she asked if she mightn't
go with him.

No, she mightn't, he said.

"Tell me the way there, then," said she, "and I'll
search you out over all the world, no matter how
hard is the journey."

"But there is no way to that place," cried the
Prince. "It lies *East o' the Sun and West o' the Moon*.
That is all I can tell you."

Next morning when the lassie awoke, both Prince and castle were gone. There she lay on a little green patch in the midst of the gloomy, thick wood. By her side lay the same bundle of rags which she had brought with her from home.

When she had rubbed the sleep out of her eyes and wept at her loss of the Prince, she set out on her journey. She walked for many days, until she came to a lofty crag under which an old woman sat tossing a golden apple. Her the lassie asked if she knew the way to the castle that lay *East o' the Sun and West o' the Moon*. But the old woman answered:

"All I know about it is that it lies *East o' the Sun and West o' the Moon* and thither you'll come late or never. But go on to my next neighbor. Maybe she will be able to tell you more." Then she gave the lassie her golden apple. "It might prove useful," she said.

So the lassie went on a long, long time till she came to another crag, under which sat another old woman with a golden carding-comb.[1] Her the lassie asked if she knew the way to the castle that lay *East o' the Sun and West o' the Moon*. But this old woman likewise knew nothing about the matter.

"Go on to my next neighbor," she said. "Maybe she can tell you." And she gave the lassie the carding-comb and bade her take it with her.

So the lassie went on and on, a far, far way and a weary, weary time till at last she came to another

---

1. **carding-comb:** a tool used to comb and untangle sheep's wool so the wool can be spun into yarn.

crag under which sat another old woman spinning with a golden spinning wheel. Her too she asked if she knew the way to the castle that lay *East o' the Sun and West o' the Moon*. It was the same thing over again. She knew nothing, but this old woman said:

"Go to the East Wind and ask him. Maybe he knows those parts and can blow you thither." Then she gave the lassie her golden spinning wheel, and bade her take it with her.

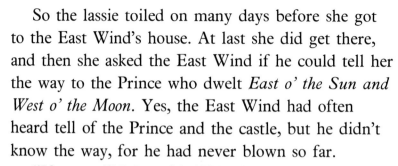

So the lassie toiled on many days before she got to the East Wind's house. At last she did get there, and then she asked the East Wind if he could tell her the way to the Prince who dwelt *East o' the Sun and West o' the Moon.* Yes, the East Wind had often heard tell of the Prince and the castle, but he didn't know the way, for he had never blown so far.

"If you will," he said, "I'll take you to my brother, the West Wind. Maybe he knows, for he's much stronger than I. Just get up on my back and I'll carry you thither."

Yes, she got on his back, and I should just think they went briskly along till they came to the West Wind's house. Then the lassie asked the West Wind if he knew how to get to the castle *East o' the Sun and West o' the Moon.*

"Nay," said the West Wind. "So far I've never blown. But if you'll get on my back, I'll carry you to our brother the South Wind. He has flapped his wings far and wide. Maybe he can tell you."

So she got on his back and travelled to the South Wind, and wasn't long on the way. And the lassie asked the South Wind if he knew the way to the castle *East o' the Sun and West o' the Moon.*

"Well, I've blustered about in most places in my time," answered the South Wind, "but so far I've never blown. Just get up on my back, and I'll carry you to my brother, the North Wind. He is the strongest of all of us, and if he doesn't know where it is, you'll never find anyone to tell you."

So she got on his back, and away he went.

When they got to the North Wind's house, he was so wild and cross that they felt his cold icy puffs when they were a long way off. "What do you want?" he roared in a voice that made them shiver. Then the lassie asked the North Wind if he knew the way to the castle *East o' the Sun and West o' the Moon*.

"Yes!" roared the North Wind. "I know well enough! Once in my life I blew an aspen leaf thither. I was so tired I couldn't blow a puff for ever so many days after. If you really wish to go so far and aren't afraid to come along, I'll take you on my back and see if I can blow you thither."

Yes, with all her heart! She must and would get there if she could possibly do it. And as for fear, no matter how madly he went, she wouldn't be afraid at all.

Early next morning they started. The North Wind puffed himself up and made himself so stout 'twas gruesome to look upon him. Off they went through the air, as if they would never stop till they got to the end of the world. Down below a storm raged.

They tore on and on—no one can believe how far they went—and all the time they still went over the sea. The North Wind got more and more weary, and so out of breath he could scarcely puff. His wings drooped and drooped, till he sunk so low that the crests of the waves went dashing over his heels.

"Are you afraid?" asked the North Wind.

No, she wasn't afraid.

But they weren't very far from the land, and the North Wind still had strength enough to throw her up on the shore. Now at last she was under the windows of the castle which lay *East o' the Sun and West o' the Moon*.

All through the day the lassie saw no one. But toward night she began to play with her golden apple, tossing it into the air. At that, out came Long-nose, who was going to marry the Prince.

"What do you want for your apple?" she asked.

"It's not for sale," answered the lassie. "But if I may visit the Prince, I will give it to you for nothing."

That she might, said Long-nose, and snatch! she seized the apple. But before Long-nose let the lassie in, she gave the Prince a drink that put him fast asleep, so though the lassie called him and shook him, she could not wake him up. Then along came Long-nose and drove her out again.

Next day the same thing happened. So long as it was light, the gloomy old castle was still as death and no one even looked out of it. But at nightfall signs of life awoke, and when the lassie began to card with the golden carding-comb, out came Long-nose to buy it.

"It's not for sale for gold or money," answered the lassie. "But if I may visit the Prince, you shall have it." Now when the lassie went up this time she found the Prince fast asleep as before, and all she called, and all she shook, she couldn't wake him up. Then along came Long-nose and chased her out again.

So the next night the lassie sat down under the castle window and began to spin with her golden spinning wheel. Long-nose must have the spinning wheel too. So in went the lassie once more. But this time, the Prince's servants had told him how a beautiful lassie had come and wept over him and called him two nights running. So, when Long-nose gave him his night drink, he poured it out secretly on the floor, and the lassie found, to her joy, that his eyes were wide open. Then she told him the whole long story of how she had made the far, far journey and the Prince wept and smiled and had great joy of her coming.

"You've got here just in the nick of time," cried he, "for tomorrow's to be my wedding. Be waiting at the gate and you'll see what you will see."

Well, the wedding was to be the next night in the dark, for neither Long-nose nor the trolls who had been invited could endure the daylight. But when the time came, the Prince announced:

"Ere I marry, I'll see what my bride can do. Here is my wedding shirt, but on it are three spots of tallow. I'll have no other for a bride save her who can wash it clean."

"No great thing to do," said Long-nose. So when the moon stood high, shining over the treetops, she hung a caldron of boiling lye in a clearing in the woods. Thither came running, tumbling, scolding, a whole pack of trolls, red-eyed, ugly, a hideous sight to see. First Long-nose began to wash. She washed as hard as she could. But the more she rubbed and scrubbed the bigger grew the spots. "Oh, you can't wash! Let me try!" a troll woman cried, and wash, wash, wash—every one in turn scrubbed away on that shirt. But the more they washed, the blacker and uglier grew the shirt, till at last it was black all over as if it had been up the chimney.

"Ah!" cried the Prince. "You're none of you worth a straw. I'll have none of you for my bride. Why look! Outside the gate there sits a beggar lass. I'll be bound she knows how to wash better than your whole pack. Come in, lassie!" he shouted.

So in came the lassie, and almost before she had taken the shirt and dipped it in the water, it was white as the driven snow.

"You are the lassie for me!" cried the Prince. Then the trolls rushed raging upon him, but ah! while they had been washing, the night had slowly waned. Just then the sun came up. The moment it pierced the mist and gloom and shone directly on Long-nose, she burst, like an empty bubble. The whole pack of trolls uttered horrid shrieks and hurried away toward the castle, but it was no use at all. The instant the sun struck them squarely, they every one of them vanished.

As for the Prince and Princess, they took hold of hands and ran away as far as they could from the castle that lay *East o' the Sun and West o' the Moon.*

Questions

1. How can you tell that this folk tale is meant to be told by a storyteller?

2. Suppose you are telling this story to someone. You will need to remember who helped the lass find her prince. List those who helped her, in the order in which they appear in the story.

3. Did the lass ever see her family again? Tell what you imagine happened *after* the story's end.

4. Illustrators may add details to folk tales to help readers imagine events. The illustrator of this story has added borders and decorations. Look at the borders and other illustrations again. What do they add to the telling of the story? Give at least two examples and the pages on which they appear.

Activity List Words That Describe Imagery

This story was composed long before movies and television. The storytellers who told it—and still tell it today—depended on words to show the *imagery,* or mental pictures, important to the story. What do you think is the story's most colorful and exciting image? If you were the storyteller describing that image, what words would you add? List them, or write the sentences you would use to show the image. Then list one other way (art, music, movement) in which you might make the image come alive for your audience.

World of Winds

For as long as people have lived on the earth, they have lived in a world of winds. As time has passed, people have wondered about the winds. They have found ways to explain them and to use their mysterious power.

Winds and Their Causes

The ancient Greeks explained the winds by thinking of them as *gods,* or spirits, each with a different power. About 2000 years ago, the Greeks built the eight-sided Tower of the Winds in the city of Athens. In this tall marble tower, each side faced a different compass point. On each side was a carved likeness of a different wind. The North Wind is wrapped up for protection against the cold he brings. The Northeast Wind rattles stones in his shield to bring hail. The South Wind pours water from a jar to make the rain fall. The West Wind, which brings good weather, has a lapful of flowers.

Thousands of years later, people still enjoy the old stories and beliefs about the winds. They know, however, that the winds are neither gods nor spirits. Winds, as science tells us, are nothing more than moving air. Air moves because heat from the sun makes it warmer in some places than in others. As

Illustrated by Joanna Adamska Koperska

the air warms, it rises, and cooler air rushes in to take its place. When warm air rises high enough, it loses its heat, becomes cooled, and sinks back to earth. This movement of warm air rising and cool air taking the place of warm air causes winds.

Earth's Prevailing Winds

The ancient Greeks were right when they thought that there were different *kinds* of winds. Scientists have named and classified the winds.

Prevailing winds are wide bands of winds that blow in the same direction and at much the same speed. Prevailing winds are caused by the rising and sinking of huge masses of warm and cold air.

HOW THE WINDS BLOW

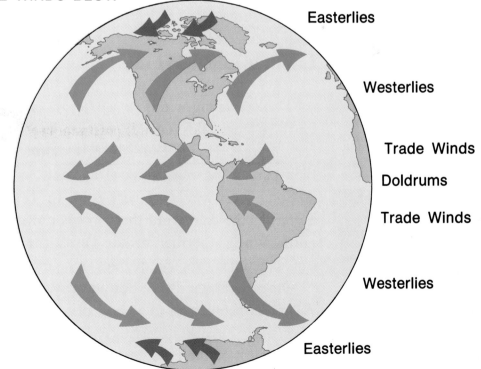

Easterlies

Westerlies

Trade Winds

Doldrums

Trade Winds

Westerlies

Easterlies

The *doldrums* are the winds that blow around the equator. The doldrums are very gentle, warm breezes.

The *trade winds* blow farther north and south of the equator than the doldrums. The trade winds are the steadiest and strongest of the winds.

Above and below the trade winds are the *westerly winds*. The westerlies are prevailing winds that blow from the west.

Cold air flowing away from both the North and South Poles creates the *easterlies,* the prevailing winds that blow from the east.

All of the winds are affected by the Earth's *rotation,* or turning. This rotation causes the winds to bend slightly instead of blowing directly north or south. In the Northern Hemisphere, the winds bend to the east. In the Southern Hemisphere, the winds bend to the west.

Earth's Local Winds

The prevailing winds sweep across large areas of Earth. Other winds, called *local winds,* blow only in certain areas. People have given the local winds in their part of the world special names.

Some local winds are very cold. In Texas, a *norther* is the cold wind that sweeps down from the north. When a norther strikes Texas, the temperature can sometimes drop 50 degrees in a few hours.

Other local winds are hot and dry. In Sydney, Australia, people call their hot, dry summer wind a *brickfielder* because it carries red dust from the brick fields south of the city.

Many winds blow across deserts, where they can cause sandstorms and make fires spread quickly. The Simoom (SIH·moom), or *poison wind*, crosses the Sahara, a desert in northern Africa. Simooms are called "poison" because they make some people feel nervous or sick.

A warm, dry wind called the *Chinook* (shih·NOOK) blows through western Canada in winter. People welcome the Chinook because it brings springlike weather. A Chinook melts the snow, exposing plants for hungry cattle to eat.

Destroying Winds

Much of people's fascination with the wind may come from the wind's destructive power. Winds can cause great harm. Giant storms called *hurricanes* are born over tropical seas during the summer and fall. Their whirling winds can move at speeds up to 200 miles an hour, bringing heavy rains. A hurricane pushes a wall of ocean water called a *storm surge* in front of it. When the surge reaches a shore, towns are buried under a great deal of water.

Another kind of whirlwind is the *tornado*. It moves across land rather than sea. A tornado is a smaller whirlwind than a hurricane, but it can be much more destructive.

Scientists cannot control these destructive winds, but they can study hurricanes and tornadoes. Specially trained researchers called Hurricane Hunters fly airplanes right into the center, or *eye*, of a hurricane. The eye is an area of little wind, where a plane is safe—for a little while. The plane flies along with the hurricane, and the researchers gather information on how powerful the hurricane is, where it might go, and how long it might last.

Tornado chasers, on the other hand, must follow their "twisters" on land. Researchers in Texas and Oklahoma, where tornadoes often happen, "chase" the whirlwinds in four-wheel-drive vehicles, gathering information. Scientists can also use information from weather satellites and weather stations to predict where hurricanes and tornadoes will strike. These studies and warnings save many lives.

Helping Winds

In days past, sailors would buy a "bag of winds" before they left on a voyage. Then, if the winds died, the sailors had a ready supply. They would open their bag of winds and be on their way.

The sailors were wasting their money, of course. They could not capture or control the winds. Over the centuries, however, people have learned to use the winds' energy. When the windmill was invented, for example, it became possible to do some jobs more easily with wind power than with human strength. Water was pumped out of the ground by windmills and grain was ground into flour. Today, scientists are exploring new ways to use windmills to get power from the wind.

Winds can also provide pleasure for people. Gentle winds fill the sails of small boats and move windsurfing boards on their way. Sailplanes and hang gliders can be used to carry people through the skies soaring on the wind.

Earth's winds do more than provide the power for work or sports. Winds have many effects on Earth. The wind moves heat from one place to another. Without wind, much of the Earth would be too hot—or too cold—to support life. Without wind, moisture from the oceans would not be brought over land to fall as rain. Without wind, the land itself would have a different look. Wind-blown sand and dust play a big part in shaping the landforms of Earth.

Many living things depend on the wind. Some plants release seeds into the wind. The wind carries the seeds to other areas. Some small animals, such as spiders, ride the wind to new homes. Many birds use the winds to "glide" or ride during their yearly migrations. Large animals on a hunt depend on the winds to bring them the scent of their prey.

Down through the ages, people have learned much about the winds. They have discovered the causes of winds and studied their effects. People have learned many ways to use the winds' power and energy. Yet no one has been able to tame or control the winds for very long. The world of winds, in some ways, remains a mystery.

Questions

1. What causes wind?

2. What are two ways that winds are important to life on Earth?

3. What are two local winds listed in the text?

4. What is the difference between a hurricane and a tornado?

Activities

1. **Keep a Record of the Winds**

   Keep a wind log for several weeks. Once or twice each day, go outside and observe the direction of the wind. Write down the direction of the wind in your log, as well as the date and time of each entry. Describe the weather at that time, too.

   As you fill in your log, try to answer some questions. From what direction does the wind usually come? Does it change direction often? From what direction does the wind usually come during a storm? How many times did you record winds from the east? the west? the south? the north?

2. **Give a Report**

   Use encyclopedias and other library books to find out about some of these local winds: dust devil, blizzard, mistral, nor'easter, cat's paw, waterspout. Write or give a report in which you explain these winds and where they blow. You may want to illustrate your report by using a map, a chart, or a diagram.

Direction

A poem by Alonzo Lopez

I was directed by my grandfather
To the East,
    so I might have the power of the bear;
To the South,
    so I might have the courage of the eagle;
To the West,
    so I might have the wisdom of the owl;
To the North,
    so I might have the craftiness of the fox;
To the Earth,
    so I might receive her fruit;
To the Sky,
    so I might lead a life of innocence.

Illustrated by Katrina Taylor

About ALONZO LOPEZ

Most American Indian stories, poems, and songs have been passed along by word of mouth for several thousand years. Many American Indian peoples regard this kind of artistic expression as an essential part of everyday life, special ceremonies, and religious experience. Such traditional literature has always depended upon participation and performance for its very existence. For this reason as well as many others, most American Indians required no written alphabet. But in recent years, ways have been devised to represent in written form the several hundred complex American Indian languages. American Indian writers who wish to do so, can now express themselves in their traditional languages.

Alonzo Lopez, a member of the Papago tribe in Arizona, is one American Indian poet who chooses to write in English. Mr. Lopez studied writing, drama, dance, and American Indian crafts at the Institute of American Arts in Santa Fe, New Mexico. Later he attended Yale University for a year, and then transferred to Wesleyan University in Connecticut, where he studied the Navajo language, helped organize an American Indian Festival, and worked to start a class in American Indian poetry. While attending Wesleyan University he made recordings of his own Papago language. He had to learn to read and write Papago to do this, and he said, "It is fun but I never knew that speaking my own language could be so difficult. It seems so unusual to see it written and try to read it, when I'm so used to speaking it only."

Mr. Lopez's poems appear in a book of poems by young American Indians called *The Whispering Wind.* Like "Direction," his writing often reflects the richness of his cultural heritage.

Dangerous Voyage

A chapter from the novel

Island of the Blue Dolphins by Scott O'Dell

Illustrated by Daniel San Souci

Off the coast of California there is an island shaped like a blue dolphin lying on its side, with its tail pointing toward sunrise. For centuries Indians had lived on the island. Then one day a party of sea-otter hunters landed there and tried to cheat the Indians. A bloody battle was fought. When the hunters left the island, only a few Indians remained alive.

The people of the island now shared one fear—that the hunters would return and kill them all. When sailors arrived and offered to carry them to safety, the Indians went aboard—all except six-year-old Ramo, who did not reach the ship in time, and twelve-year-old Karana,[1] who leaped from the ship and swam back to be with her brother. Two days later, Ramo was killed by wild dogs and Karana found herself alone.

As the seasons passed, Karana waited. She hoped for a ship to rescue her. To survive she made her own weapons, built a shelter, and defended herself against her enemies—the wild dogs. But Karana realized that for as long as she was trapped on the island, her worst enemy would be loneliness. In the story that follows, Karana tells her plan for escaping the lonely Island of the Blue Dolphins.

---

1. **Karana** (kuh·RAH·nuh).

Summer is the best time on the Island of the Blue Dolphins. The sun is warm then and the winds blow milder out of the west, sometimes out of the south.

It was during these days that the ship might return and now I spent most of my time on the rock, looking out from the high headland into the east, toward the country where my people had gone, across the sea that was never-ending.

Once while I watched I saw a small object which I took to be the ship, but a stream of water rose from it and I knew that it was a whale spouting. During those summer days I saw nothing else.

The first storm of winter ended my hopes. If the white men's ship were coming for me it would have come during the time of good weather. Now I would have to wait until winter was gone, maybe longer.

The thought of being alone on the island while so many suns rose from the sea and went slowly back into the sea filled my heart with loneliness. I had not felt so lonely before because I was sure that the ship would return as Chief Matasaip had said it would. Now my hopes were dead. Now I was really alone. I could not eat much, nor could I sleep without dreaming terrible dreams.

The storm blew out of the north, sending big waves against the island and winds so strong that I was unable to stay on the rock. I moved my bed to the foot of the rock and for protection kept a fire going throughout the night. I slept there five times. The first night the wild dogs came and stood outside the ring made by the fire. I killed three of them with arrows, but not the leader, and they did not come again.

On the sixth day, when the storm had ended, I
went to the place where my people had hidden their
canoes, filled with supplies, and let myself down over
the cliff. This part of the shore was sheltered from
the wind and I found the canoes just as they had
been left. The dried food was still good, but the
water was stale, so I went back to the spring and
filled a fresh basket.

I had decided during the days of the storm, when
I had given up hope of seeing the ship, that I would
take one of the canoes and go to the country that

lay toward the east. I knew that my ancestors had crossed the sea in their canoes, coming from that place which lay beyond. I was not nearly so skilled with a canoe as these men, but I must say that whatever might befall me on the endless waters did not trouble me. It meant far less than the thought of staying on the island alone, without a home or companions, pursued by wild dogs, where everything reminded me of those who were dead and those who had gone away.

Of the four canoes stored there against the cliff, I chose the smallest, which was still very heavy because it could carry six people. The task that faced me was to push it down the rocky shore and into the water, a distance four or five times its length.

This I did by first removing all the large rocks in front of the canoe. I then filled in all these holes with pebbles and along this path laid down long strips of kelp, making a slippery bed. The shore was steep and, once I got the canoe to move with its own weight, it slid down the path and into the water.

The sun was in the west when I left the shore. The sea was calm behind the high cliffs. Using the two-bladed paddle I quickly skirted the south part of the island. As I reached the sandspit the wind struck. I was paddling from the back of the canoe because you can go faster kneeling there, but I could not handle it in the wind.

Kneeling in the middle of the canoe, I paddled hard and did not pause until I had gone through the tides that run fast around the sandspit. There were many small waves and I was soon wet, but as I came out from behind the spit the spray lessened and the waves grew long and rolling. Though it would have been easier to go the way they slanted, this would have taken me in the wrong direction. I therefore kept them on my left hand, as well as the island, which grew smaller and smaller, behind me.

At dusk I looked back. The Island of the Blue Dolphins had disappeared. This was the first time that I felt afraid.

There were only hills and valleys of water around me now. When I was in a valley I could see nothing and when the canoe rose out of it, only the ocean stretching away and away.

Night fell and I drank from the basket. The water cooled my throat.

The sea was black and there was no difference between it and the sky. The waves made no sound among themselves, only faint noises as they went under the canoe or struck against it. Sometimes the noises seemed angry and at other times like people laughing. I was not hungry because of my fear.

The first star made me feel less afraid. It came out low in the sky and it was in front of me, toward the east. Other stars began to appear all around, but it was this one I kept my gaze upon. It was in the figure that we call a serpent, a star which shone green and which I knew. Now and then it was hidden by mist, yet it always came out brightly again.

Without this star I would have been lost, for the
waves never changed. They came always from the
same direction and in a manner that kept pushing me
away from the place I wanted to reach. For this
reason the canoe made a path in the black water like
a snake. But somehow I kept moving toward the star
which shone in the east.

This star rose high and then I kept the North
Star on my left hand, the one we call "the star that
does not move." The wind grew quiet. Since it always died down when the night was half over, I
knew how long I had been traveling and how far
away the dawn was.

About this time I found that the canoe was leak-
ing. Before dark I had emptied one of the baskets in
which food was stored and used it to dip out the
water that came over the sides. The water that now
moved around my knees was not from the waves.

I stopped paddling and worked with the basket
until the bottom of the canoe was almost dry. Then I
searched around, feeling in the dark along the smooth
planks, and found the place near the bow where the
water was seeping through a crack as long as my
hand and the width of a finger. Most of the time it
was out of the sea, but it leaked whenever the canoe
dipped forward in the waves.

The places between the planks were filled with
black pitch which we gather along the shore. Lacking

this, I tore a piece of fiber from my skirt and pressed it into the crack, which held back the water.

Dawn broke in a clear sky and as the sun came out of the waves I saw that it was far off on my left. During the night I had drifted south of the place I wished to go, so I changed my direction and paddled along the path made by the rising sun.

There was no wind on this morning and the long waves went quietly under the canoe. I therefore moved faster than during the night.

I was very tired, but more hopeful than I had been since I left the island. If the good weather did not change, I would cover many leagues before dark. Another night and another day might bring me within sight of the shore toward which I was going.

Not long after dawn, while I was thinking of this strange place and what it would look like, the canoe began to leak again. This crack was between the same planks, but was a larger one and close to where I was kneeling.

The fiber I tore from my skirt and pushed into the crack held back most of the water which seeped in whenever the canoe rose and fell with the waves. Yet I could see that the planks were weak from one end to the other, probably from the canoe being stored so long in the sun, and that they might open along their whole length if the waves grew rougher.

It was suddenly clear to me that it was dangerous to go on. The voyage would take two more days, perhaps longer. By turning back to the island I would not have nearly so far to travel.

Still I could not make up my mind to do so. The sea was calm and I had come far. The thought of turning back after all this labor was more than I could bear. Even greater was the thought of the deserted island I would return to, of living there alone and forgotten. For how many suns and how many moons?

The canoe drifted idly on the calm sea while these thoughts went over and over in my mind, but when I saw the water seeping through the crack again, I picked up the paddle. There was no choice except to turn back toward the island.

I knew that only by the best of fortune would I ever reach it.

The wind did not blow until the sun was overhead. Before that time I covered a good distance, pausing only when it was necessary to dip water from the canoe. With the wind I went more slowly and had to stop more often because of the water spilling over the sides, but the leak did not grow worse.

This was my first good fortune. The next was when a swarm of dolphins appeared. They came swimming out of the west, but as they saw the canoe they turned around in a great circle and began to follow me. They swam up slowly and so close that I could see their eyes, which are large and the color of the ocean. Then they swam on ahead of the canoe, crossing back and forth in front of it, diving in and out, as if they were weaving a piece of cloth with their broad snouts.

Dolphins are animals of good omen. It made me happy to have them swimming around the canoe, and though my hands had begun to bleed from the chafing of the paddle, just watching them made me forget the pain. I was very lonely before they appeared, but now I felt that I had friends with me and did not feel the same.

The blue dolphins left me shortly before dusk. They left as quickly as they had come, going on into the west, but for a long time I could see the last of the sun shining on them. After night fell I could still see them in my thoughts, and it was because of this that I kept on paddling when I wanted to lie down and sleep.

More than anything, it was the blue dolphins that took me back home.

Fog came with the night, yet from time to time I could see the star that stands high in the west, the red star called Magat which is part of the figure that looks like a crawfish and is known by that name. The crack in the planks grew wider so I had to stop often to fill it with fiber and to dip out the water.

The night was very long, longer than the night before. Twice I dozed kneeling there in the canoe, though I was more afraid than I had ever been. But the morning broke clear and in front of me lay the dim line of the island like a great fish sunning itself on the sea.

I reached it before the sun was high, the sandspit and its tides that bore me into the shore. My legs were stiff from kneeling and as the canoe struck the sand I fell when I rose to climb out. I crawled through the shallow water and up the beach. There I lay for a long time, hugging the sand in happiness.

Questions

1. The feelings of Karana, the girl who tells the story, are important to what happens in the story. Finish the following sentences to help tell what happens.
   a. Loneliness caused Karana to _____.
   b. Hopefulness caused her to _____.
   c. Fear caused Karana to _____.
   d. Happiness came when she _____.

2. What three things in nature might Karana have said were friendly? What three things in nature might Karana have said were unfriendly?

3. In "Dangerous Voyage" Karana makes decisions. She decides to leave the island and later decides to turn back again. What is another decision that she may make in the days ahead?

4. Karana's story is written as if she were telling it. Find a paragraph to read aloud to show the strength of Karana's language. Which paragraph will you select—and why?

Activity   Make a Pictomap

Make a *pictomap*—a map with drawings or pictures—using clues from the story. Show the island, the rock where Karana camped, and the place where the canoes were kept. Show where Karana began her voyage, including the sandspit she passed, where she turned back, and where the dolphins met her. Label those places on your pictomap. You might want to use arrows or dotted lines to trace Karana's journey.

About SCOTT O'DELL

Scott O'Dell was born in Los Angeles when it still had the flavor of a frontier town. His father worked for the railroad, and his family moved a lot. One time they lived on an island in a house on stilts above the ocean. "That is why," he says, "the feel of the frontier and the sound of the sea are in my books."

Scott O'Dell spent his early career as a movie cameraman and as a book editor for a newspaper. Then he began writing adventure stories, first for adults and then for children. His books for children have won many prizes and awards. For each book, Scott O'Dell spends about three or four months doing research and six months writing.

According to Scott O'Dell, *Island of the Blue Dolphins* "is based upon the true story of a girl who was left upon an island near the coast of southern California and lived there for eighteen years, alone." But *Island of the Blue Dolphins* also reflects Scott O'Dell's memories of living on an island. On summer days, he and his friends found big logs and paddled out to sea. The logs were their "proud canoes," taking them wherever they wished to explore.

More Books by Scott O'Dell

Zia
The 290
Sing Down the Moon

Song

An Eskimo poem

Translated by Knud Rasmussen

And I think over again
My small adventures
When with a shore wind I drifted out
In my kayak
And thought I was in danger.
My fears,
Those I thought so big,
For all the vital things
I had to·get and to reach.

And yet, there is only
One great thing,
The only thing:
To live to see in huts and on journeys
The great day that dawns,
And the light that fills the world.

Illustrated by Christa Keiffer

Sea Calm

A poem by Langston Hughes

How still,
How strangely still
The water is today.
It is not good
For water
To be so still that way.

Illustrated by Christa Keiffer

All Things Are Connected

From a letter by Chief Sealth

In 1855 Chief Sealth[1] of the Duwamish tribe of the State of Washington sent a letter to President Franklin Pierce. The letter was in response to an offer by the government to buy the tribe's land. Here is part of that letter.

---

1. Sealth (SELTH).

How can you buy or sell the sky—the warmth of the land? The idea is strange to us. We do not own the freshness of the air or the sparkle of the water. How can you buy them from us?

We will decide in our time. Every part of this earth is sacred to my people. Every shining pine needle, every sandy shore, every mist in the dark woods, every clearing and humming insect is holy in the memory and experience of my people. . . .

If I decide to accept, I will make one condition. The white man must treat the beasts of this land as his brothers. . . . What is man without the beasts? If all the beasts were gone, men would die from a great loneliness of spirit, for whatever happens to the beast also happens to man. All things are connected. Whatever befalls the earth befalls the sons of the earth. . . .

If we sell you our land, love it as we've loved it. Care for it, as we've cared for it. Hold in your mind the memory of the land, as it is when you take it. And with all your strength, with all your might, and with all your heart—preserve it for your children.

Illustrated by Daniel San Souci

BANDO

From the novel *My Side of the Mountain*
by Jean Craighead George
Illustrated by Lyle Miller

It was late spring when Sam Gribley left his family's
crowded New York City apartment home and set out
for some land in the Catskill Mountains that his great-
grandfather had once tried to farm. He carried only a
penknife, a ball of string, an ax, a flint with steel,[1]
and forty dollars. He knew how to fish and build fires,
and he figured that was all he needed for a new life.

During his first few days in the wilds, Sam was
hungry, cold, and confused. But he learned from his
early mistakes, and the mountain soon provided him
with food, shelter, and company—Frightful, a baby
falcon; The Baron, a weasel; and Jesse C. James, a
young raccoon.

Midsummer brought easy living, but also the
threat of discovery, as Sam tells it in his diary.

---

1. **flint with steel:** tools used for making sparks to start a fire.

Life was leisurely. I was warm, well fed. One day while I was down the mountain, I returned home by way of the old farmhouse site to check the apple crop. They were summer apples, and were about ready to be picked. I had gathered a pouchful and had sat down under the tree to eat a few and think about how I would dry them for use in the winter when Frightful dug her talons into my shoulder so hard I winced.

"Be gentle, bird!" I said to her.

I got her talons out and put her on a log, where I watched her with some alarm. She was as alert as a high tension wire, her head cocked so that her ears, just membranes under her feathers, were pointed east. She evidently heard a sound that pained her. She opened her beak. Whatever it was, I could hear nothing, though I strained my ears, cupped them, and wished she would speak.

Frightful was my ears as well as my eyes. She could hear things long before I. When she grew tense, I listened or looked. She was scared this time. She turned round and round on the log, looked up in the tree for a perch,

lifted her wings to fly, and then stood still and listened.

Then I heard it. A police siren sounded far down the road. The sound grew louder and louder, and I grew afraid. Then I said, "No, Frightful, if they are after me there won't be a siren. They'll just slip up on me quietly."

No sooner had I said this than the siren wound down, and apparently stopped on the road at the foot of the mountain. I got up to run to my tree, but had not gotten past the walnut before the patrol cars started up and screamed away.

We started home although it was not late in the afternoon. However, it was hot, and thunderheads were building up. I decided to take a swim in the spring and work on the moccasins I had cut out several days before.

With the squad car still on my mind, we slipped quietly into the hemlock forest. Once again Frightful almost sent me through the crown of the forest by digging her talons into my shoulder. I looked at her. She was staring at our home. I looked, too. Then I stopped, for I could make out the form of a man stretched between the sleeping house and the store tree.

Softly, tree by tree, Frightful and I approached him. The man was asleep. I could have left and camped in the gorge, but my enormous desire to see another human being overcame my fear of being discovered.

We stood above the man. He did not move, so Frightful lost interest in my fellow being. She tried to hop to her stump and preen. I grabbed her leash, however, as I wanted to think before awakening him. Frightful flapped. I held her wings to her body as her flapping was noisy to me. Apparently not so to the man. The man did not stir. It is hard to realize that the rustle of a falcon's wings is not much of a noise to a man from the city, because by now, one beat of her wings and I would awaken from a sound sleep as if a shot had gone off. The stranger slept on. I realized how long I'd been in the mountains.

Right at that moment, as I looked into his unshaven face, his close-cropped hair, and his torn clothes, I thought of the police siren, and put two and two together.

"An outlaw!" I said to myself. "Wow!" I had to think what to do with an outlaw before I awoke him.

Would he be troublesome? Would he be mean? Should I go live in the gorge until he moved on? How I wanted to hear his voice, to tell him about The Baron and Jessie C. James, to say words out loud. I really did not want to hide from him; besides, he might be hungry, I thought. Finally I spoke.

"Hi!" I said. I was delighted to see him roll over, open his eyes, and look up. He seemed startled, so I reassured him. "It's all right. They've gone. If you don't tell on me I won't tell on you." When he heard this, he sat up and seemed to relax.

"Oh," he said. Then he leaned against the tree and added, "Thanks." He evidently was thinking this over, for he propped his head on his elbow and studied me closely.

"You're a sight for sore eyes," he said, and smiled. He had a nice smile. In fact, he looked nice and not like an outlaw at all. His eyes were very blue and, although tired, they did not look scared or hunted.

However, I talked quickly before he could get up and run away.

"I don't know anything about you, and I don't want to. You don't know anything about me and don't want to, but you may stay here if you like. No one is going to find you here. Would you like some supper?" It was still early, but he looked hungry.

"Do you have some?"

"Yes, venison or rabbit?"

"Well . . . venison." His eyebrows puckered in question marks. I went to work.

He arose, turned around and around, and looked at his surroundings. He whistled softly when I kindled a spark with the flint and steel. I was now quite quick at this, and had a tidy fire blazing in a very few minutes. I was so used to myself doing this that it had not occurred to me that it would be interesting to a stranger.

"Desdemondia!" he said. I judged this to be some underworld phrase. At this moment Frightful, who had been sitting quietly on her stump, began to preen. The outlaw jumped back, then saw she was tied and said, "And who is this ferocious-looking character?"

402

"That is Frightful; don't be afraid. She's quite wonderful and gentle. She would be glad to catch you a rabbit for supper if you would prefer that to venison."

"Am I dreaming?" said the man. "I go to sleep by a campfire that looked like it was built by a boy scout, and I awaken in the middle of the eighteenth century."

I crawled into the store tree to get the smoked venison and some cattail tubers. When I came out again, he was speechless.

"My storehouse," I explained.

"I see," he answered. From that moment on he did not talk much. He just watched me. I was so busy cooking the best meal that I could possibly get together that I didn't say much either. Later I wrote down that menu, as it was excellent.

"Brown puffballs in deer fat with a little wild garlic, fill pot with water, put venison in, boil. Wrap tubers in leaves and stick in coals. Cut up apples and boil in can with dogtooth violet bulbs. Raspberries to finish meal."

When the meal was ready, I served it to the man in my nicest turtle shell. I had to whittle him a fork out of the crotch of a twig, as Jessie Coon James had gone off with the others. He ate and ate and ate, and when he was done he said, "May I call you Thoreau?"[2]

"That will do nicely," I said. Then I paused—just to let him know that I knew a little bit about him too. I smiled and said, "I will call you Bando."

His eyebrows went up, he cocked his head, shrugged his shoulders and answered, "That's close enough."

With this he sat and thought. I felt I had offended him, so I spoke. "I will be glad to help. I will teach you how to live off the land. It is very easy. No one need find you."

His eyebrows gathered together again. This was characteristic of Bando when he was concerned, and so I was sorry I had mentioned his past. After all, outlaw or no outlaw, he was an adult, and I still felt unsure of myself around adults. I changed the subject.

"Let's get some sleep," I said.

"Where do you sleep?" he asked. All this time sitting and talking with me, and he had not seen the entrance to my tree. I was pleased. Then I beckoned, walked a few feet to the left, pushed back the deer-hide door, and showed Bando my secret.

"Thoreau," he said. "You are quite wonderful." He went in. I lit the turtle candle for him, he explored, tried the bed, came out and shook his head until I thought it would roll off.

We didn't say much more that night. I let him sleep on my bed. His feet hung off, but he was comfortable, he said. I stretched out by the fire. The ground was dry, the night warm, and I could sleep on anything now.

I got up early and had breakfast ready when Bando came stumbling out of the tree. We ate crayfish, and he really honestly seemed to like them. It takes a little time to acquire a taste for wild foods, so Bando surprised me the way he liked the menu. Of course he was hungry, and that helped.

That day we didn't talk much,

---

2. **Henry David Thoreau** (thuh•ROH): an American writer (1817–1862) who lived alone for a time at Walden Pond in Concord, Massachusetts. In his best-known book, *Walden*, Thoreau spoke of going into the woods to live with nature and to learn about life.

just went over the mountain collecting foods. I wanted to dig up the tubers of the Solomon's-seal from a big garden of them on the other side of the gorge. We fished, we swam a little, and I told him I hoped to make a raft pretty soon, so I could float into deeper water and perhaps catch bigger fish.

When Bando heard this, he took my ax and immediately began to cut young trees for this purpose. I watched him and said, "You must have lived on a farm or something."

At that moment a bird sang.

"The wood peewee," said Bando, stopping his work. He stepped into the woods, seeking it. Now I was astonished.

"How would you know about a wood peewee in your business?" I grew bold enough to ask.

"And just what do you think my business is?" he said as I followed him.

"Well, you're not a minister."

"Right!"

"And you're not a doctor or a lawyer."

"Correct."

"You're not a businessman or a sailor."

"No, I am not."

"Nor do you dig ditches."

"I do not."

"Well . . ."

"Guess."

Suddenly I wanted to know for sure. So I said it.

"You are a murderer or a thief or a racketeer, and you are hiding out."

Bando stopped looking for the peewee. He turned and stared at me. At first I was frightened. A bandit might do anything. But he wasn't mad. He was laughing. He had a good deep laugh and it kept coming out of him. I smiled, then grinned and laughed with him.

"What's funny, Bando?" I asked.

"I like that," he finally said. "I like that a lot." The tickle deep inside him kept him chuckling. I had no more to say, so I ground my heel in the dirt while I waited for him to get over the fun and explain it all to me.

"Thoreau, my friend, I am just a college English teacher lost in the Catskills. I came out to hike around the woods, got completely lost yesterday, found your fire, and fell asleep beside it. I was hoping the scoutmaster and his troop would

be back for supper and help me home."

"Oh, no." My comment. Then I laughed. "You see, Bando, before I found you, I heard squad cars screaming up the road. Occasionally you read about bandits that hide out in the forest, and I was just so sure that you were someone they were looking for."

We gave up the peewee and went back to the raft-making, talking very fast now, and laughing a lot. He was fun. Then something sad occurred to me.

"Well, if you're not a bandit, you will have to go home very soon, and there is no point in teaching you how to live on fish and bark and plants."

"I can stay a little while," he said. "This is summer vacation. I must admit I had not planned to eat crayfish on my vacation, but I am rather getting to like it.

"Maybe I can stay until your school opens," he went on. "That's after Labor Day, isn't it?"

I was very still, thinking how to answer that.

Bando sensed this. Then he turned to me with a big grin.

"You really mean you are going to try to winter it out here?"

"I think I can."

"Well!" He sat down, rubbed his forehead in his hands, and looked at me. "Thoreau, I have led a varied life—dishwasher, sax player, teacher. To me it has been an interesting life. Just now it seems very dull." He sat awhile with his head down, then looked up at the mountains and the rocks and trees. I heard him sigh.

"Let's go fish. We can finish this another day."

That is how I came to know Bando. We became very good friends in the week or ten days that he stayed with me, and he helped me a lot. We spent several days gathering white oak acorns and groundnuts, harvesting the blueberry crop and smoking fish.

We flew Frightful every day just for the pleasure of lying on our backs in the meadow and watching her mastery of the sky. I had lots of meat, so what she caught those days was all hers. It was a pleasant time, warm, with occasional thunder showers, some of which we stayed out in. We talked about books. He did know a lot of books, and could quote exciting things from them.

One day Bando went to town and came back with five pounds of sugar.

"I want to make blueberry jam," he announced. "All those excellent berries and no jam."

He worked two days at this. He knew how to make jam. He'd watched his Pa make it in Mississippi, but we got stuck on what to put it in.

I wrote this one night:

"August 29

"The raft is almost done. Bando has promised to stay until we can sail out into the deep fishing holes.

"Bando and I found some clay along the stream bank. It was as slick as ice. Bando thought it would make good pottery. He shaped some jars and lids. They look good—not Wedgwood, he said, but containers. We dried them on the rock in the meadow, and later Bando made a clay oven and baked them in it. He thinks they might hold the blueberry jam he has been making.

"Bando got the fire hot by blowing on it with some homemade bellows that he fashioned from one of my skins that he tied together like a balloon. A reed is the nozzle.

"It was a terribly hot day for Bando to be firing clay jars, but he stuck with it. They look jam-worthy, as he says, and he filled three of them tonight. The jam is good, the pots remind me of crude flower pots without the hole in the bottom. Some of the lids don't fit. Bando says he will go home and read more about pottery-making so that he can do a better job next time.

"We like the jam. We eat it on hard acorn pancakes.

"Later. Bando met The Baron Weasel today for the first time. I don't know where The Baron has been this past week, but suddenly he appeared on the rock, and nearly jumped down Bando's shirt collar. Bando said he liked The Baron best when he was in his hole.

"Bando taught me how to make willow whistles today. He and I went to the stream and cut two whistles about eight inches long. He slipped the bark on them. That means he pulled the wood out of the bark, leaving a tube. He made a mouthpiece at one end, cut a hole beneath it, and used the wood to slide up and down like a trombone.

"We played music until the moon came up. Bando could even play jazz on the willow whistles. They are wonderful instruments, sounding much like the wind in the top of the hemlocks. Sad tunes are best suited to willow whistles. When we played 'The Young Voyageur' tears came to our eyes, it was so sad."

There were no more notes for many days. Bando had left me saying: "Good-bye, I'll see you at Christmas." I was so lonely that I kept sewing on my moccasins to keep myself busy. I sewed every free minute for four days, and when they were finished, I began a glove to protect my hand from

Frightful's sharp talons.

One day when I was thinking very hard about being alone, Frightful gave her gentle call of love and contentment. I looked up.

"Bird," I said. "I had almost forgotten how we used to talk." She made tiny movements with her beak and fluffed her feathers. This was a language I had forgotten since Bando came. It meant she was glad to see me and hear me, that she was well fed and content.

I picked her up and squeaked into her neck feathers. She moved her beak, turned her bright head, and bit my nose very gently.

Jessie Coon James came down from the trees for the first time in ten days. He finished my fish dinner. Then just before dusk, The Baron came up on his boulder and scratched and cleaned and played with a fern leaf.

I had the feeling we were all back together again.

411

Questions

1. What are three things that Sam could *teach* Bando about living on the mountain? What are three things that Sam might *learn* from Bando about living on the mountain?

2. Why does the author have Sam tell *how* he fixed dinner instead of just saying, "I fixed dinner"?

3. Will Bando's visit make a difference in how Sam spends the winter on the mountain? Explain.

4. How do you think Sam's experience on the mountain will change him if he returns to the city?

5. Match each word from the story with its meaning.
   talon   a. a deep, narrow passage between mountains
   gorge   b. grassland
   meadow   c. claw
   preen   d. to smooth or clean feathers

Activity   Write Directions for Teaching

Sam and Bando taught each other different things. What could you teach someone to do? Build a model? Tell a story? Prepare a meal? Excel in a sport? Figure out what you could teach someone your age or younger and then write how you would do it. You could write step-by-step directions, accompanied by diagrams or pictures. You could write the steps in paragraph form. Identify what you will teach and write your teaching plan.

BOOKSHELF

The First Travels to the Bottom of the Sea by Rhoda Blumberg. Lothrop, Lee & Shepard, 1983. Imagine that you're going to vacation at the bottom of the sea. The make-believe submarine *Sea Dragon* will take you there.

Alice and the Boa Constrictor by Laurie Adams and Alison Coudert. Houghton Mifflin, 1983. After learning in science class that boa constrictors make wonderful pets, Alice saves her money until she can buy "Sir Lancelot."

Children of the Incas by David Mangurian. Four Winds Press, 1979. In this true story, a modern-day boy and his family struggle to survive in the mountains of Peru by raising sheep, knitting sweaters, and harvesting potatoes.

The Cry of the Crow by Jean Craighead George. Harper & Row, 1980. Mandy learns about the nature of wild things when she finds a helpless baby crow in the woods and tames it in secret.

Snowshoe Trek to Otter River by David Budbill. Dial Press. 1976. Three short stories about two boys backpacking in the Vermont woods, learning the skills necessary for enjoyment and survival.

All Upon a Sidewalk by Jean Craighead George. E. P. Dutton, 1974. An account of one day in the life of Lasius Flavus, or the yellow ant, who is sent on a food gathering mission by the Queen Ant.

Tornado by Hilary Milton. Franklin Watts, 1983. Janet Carson and her two children learn how to survive floods, high winds, and a poisonous snake.

413

6 From America's Past

From

Where Was Patrick Henry on the 29th of May?

An historical biography by Jean Fritz

Illustrated by George Ulrich

On the 29th of May, 1736, Patrick Henry had just been born in Hanover County, Virginia. In those days, Virginia was still a colony of England and a wilderness of woodlands, creeks, and rivers. As a boy, Patrick often went off to the woods to hunt or fish. He even developed a good ear for birdcalls.

Patrick wasn't much interested in school or work. It seemed to people who knew him that Patrick had no useful talents except one: he "could send his voice out so that it could be heard clearly at a distance." Patrick's Uncle Langloo also had such a "sending voice"; when he gave a political speech, he could make people's hair stand on end. No one would have guessed that one day Patrick Henry's voice would do even more.

On May 29th, 1752, Patrick Henry became sixteen. He was six feet tall, a lanky, sharp-boned young man with flashing blue eyes, generally dressed in checked breeches and a jumpshirt, generally in his bare feet. He was old enough now to be counted among the men in Virginia and old enough to make his own living. And where was he?

Well, he may have been stretched out on a sack of salt. People claimed this was Patrick's favorite resting place and he rested a good deal. His father had set up his two boys as storekeepers on the Pamunkey River, but William paid little attention to the store and although people came in to pass the time of day, they seldom put down hard cash for the goods they bought. Besides, the store wasn't always open. Come a nice spring day with redbirds calling and Patrick might be at the store and then again he might be down at the river or off in the woods. Or he might be across the county, courting. Patrick was sweet on young Sarah Shelton whose father operated a tavern at Hanover Courthouse.

As it turned out, Patrick's storekeeping was a failure but his courting was a success. When he was eighteen years old, he got rid of the store and married sixteen-year-old Sarah. As a wedding present, Sarah's father gave them three hundred acres of land cut off from his own estate. So Patrick became a tobacco farmer. For three years he went through the business of planting, cultivating, leafing, worming, and curing tobacco, and then his house burned down and he gave up the farm.

He and Sarah moved to Hanover Courthouse and decided to give storekeeping another try, but when they had only twenty-six customers in six months, they quit altogether. Patrick and Sarah had two children now, Martha and John, but they had little else. They lived with Sarah's father at the tavern and Patrick helped take care of the guests, many of them lawyers and their clients doing business at the courthouse across the road. Patrick handed out refreshment, made friends, and sometimes entertained guests with his fiddle.

At the quarter sessions of the court in March, June, September, and December, the most important cases were tried and then every bed in the tavern would be taken. (It cost 75¢ a night for a bed with clean sheets.) Traveling troupes of acrobats and jugglers came to town at that time; peddlers came to sell their wares; there were horse races, cockfights, and wrestling matches. From all over the county people came to see the shows, do their trading, and hear the cases argued.

Patrick attended court as often as possible. He liked to watch a lawyer run his opposition up a tree. He liked to listen to him roll out his words, the way his Uncle Langloo did on Election Day. The more he listened, the more he thought he might like to have a try at it himself. After all, he was twenty-four years old now; he no longer had a farm or a store or even a house. He had to try *something*. So he got a few books and began studying on his own.

This was the winter of 1760, about the same time as young seventeen-year-old Thomas Jefferson met him at a houseparty and was struck by Patrick's "passion for fiddling, dancing and pleasantry." But Patrick read at least two heavy law books that winter and in the middle of April he hung up a sign at John Shelton's tavern. *Patrick Henry,* the sign said, *Attorney at Law.* Patrick had been to Williamsburg, the capital of Virginia; he'd been examined by three prominent lawyers and he'd been issued a license to practice law. (He had also been told that he needed to study some more.)

In his first year Patrick represented 60 clients (many of them relatives) in 176 cases, but the cases didn't amount to much and he collected less than half what was owed him. Much of the time he had so little to do, he'd ride into the piney woods for a week or more of hunting—"sleeping under a tent," according to Thomas Jefferson, "wearing the same shirt the whole time." Then likely as not, he'd go directly to court in his greasy leather breeches and a pair of saddle bags on his arm.

What Patrick Henry needed to prove himself as a lawyer was a big case at one of the quarter sessions of court when the whole county would take an interest.

At the December session in 1763 Patrick had his chance. There was an argument between a group of preachers (or parsons, as they were called) and the people, but in one sense it was an argument between the people of Virginia and England. For a long time England had been so busy fighting wars that she had left America relatively free to manage her own affairs. But now the French and Indian War was over, a new king was on the throne, and there were rumors that England had a plan to rule the colonies more strictly. With the Parsons' Case, it looked as if England had already started.

The case went back to a year when the tobacco crop in Virginia failed. Instead of selling for the normal rate of two cents a pound, tobacco was so scarce, it sold for six cents. This should have been good news for the parsons because, according to law, they were paid in tobacco, but this year the people felt they couldn't afford it. So they passed a new law which allowed them to pay the parsons in cash at the two-cent rate. The parsons took their case to the king; the king vetoed the law and now a group of parsons were suing the people for damages and back pay. And Patrick Henry was representing the people.

On the day of the trial Patrick was uneasy. Not only were there more spectators than he'd ever seen at the courthouse, there were two men that he wished were not there. The first was his Uncle Patrick who was one of the parsons. Patrick met his uncle at his carriage when he arrived at the courthouse and asked him if he wouldn't turn his carriage around.

He had never spoken in public, Patrick explained, and his uncle's presence would overawe him. Besides, he might say something about the parsons that his uncle wouldn't like. So wouldn't he please just go home? His uncle complied.

But Patrick couldn't ask the same of his father. Colonel John Henry was the presiding justice of the day and all through the trial he'd be sitting on a bench in front of the courtroom, right before Patrick's eyes.

Actually Colonel Henry was as uneasy as his son. He prayed that Patrick, who had failed in so many things, would not be an embarrassment today. But when Patrick stood up to argue the case, he was stooped, awkward, unable to look at the audience. When he spoke, he fumbled for words, halted, started sentences, stopped them as if he'd forgotten where he was going.

Colonel Henry sank down in his chair. He studied his hands. He looked out the window. Patrick's friends in the courtroom stared at the floor. What on earth had Patrick done with his voice, they asked themselves. Why didn't he *send* it?

Then all at once something seemed to come over Patrick. He stopped thinking about the people in the courtroom and about his father looking out the window and he began thinking about the King of England and how he could, if he wanted, change the character of the cheerful, independent world that Patrick lived in. Patrick Henry straightened up, he threw back his head, and sent his voice out in anger. How did the king know how much Virginians could pay their parsons? he asked. What right did he have to interfere?

Patrick was rolling his words out now like his Uncle Langloo. He was doing things with his voice that he had never known he could do—lowering it, raising it not only to fit his emotions but in such a way as to stir the emotions of everyone in the courtroom. The crowd sat transfixed. So did Colonel Henry. And why not? Here was Patrick Henry, a poor country lawyer, turning himself into an orator right before their eyes.

He talked for an hour. What about the parsons? he asked. Were they feeding the hungry and clothing the naked as the Scriptures told them to? No, he said. They were getting the king's permission to grab the last hoecake from the honest farmer, to take the milk cow from the poor widow.

When Patrick had finished, the jury took just five minutes to reach a decision. They could not deny the parsons all damages since a previous court had ruled they had to be paid something, but after hearing Patrick, they allowed the parsons so much less than they had asked for that the parsons demanded a retrial. They were refused.

The people in the courthouse were beside themselves with excitement at Patrick's success. As soon as court was adjourned, they raised him to their shoulders and carried him around the courtyard, hip-hip-hooraying him all the while. As for Colonel Henry, when asked about his son's performance, he smiled. He'd been pleasantly surprised, he said.

It was a good thing for America, as it turned out, that Patrick Henry became an orator at the same time that England was unfolding her new plan. Taxation was England's next step. Although Americans had always managed their own money, suddenly in 1765 the English government, without any kind of by-your-leave from America, slapped down a stamp tax on the colonies. It had provisions for taxing fifty-five separate items and Patrick Henry was ready to fight every one of them.

On May 29th, 1765, Patrick became twenty-nine years old. He and Sarah had four children now and were living in a four-room house on top of a hill in Louisa County. And on the 29th of May, what was he doing?

Well, he was bawling out the king again. He had become a member of the House of Burgesses, Virginia's governing body, only nine days before and now he was standing up in his buckskin breeches before the finest men of Virginia, using such bold language that at one point there was a cry of "Treason!" But Patrick went right on reeling off resolutions. Later these resolutions were printed and sent out through the colonies, giving other Americans courage to oppose the taxation. Indeed, there was so much opposition to the Stamp Tax that after a year the king repealed it.

But England did not give up the idea of taxation nor did Patrick give up talking. In 1773, when England decided to enforce a tax on tea, Patrick went right to the floor of the House. He was so spellbinding that in the middle of one speech the spectators rushed from the gallery to the cupola of the capitol to pull down the English flag. The members of the House, noticing the commotion, thought there was a fire and ran for safety.

Patrick and Sarah had six children now and were back in Hanover County in an eighteen-room house set on a thousand acres. Patrick was a public figure. When he went out, he wore a black suit or perhaps his peach-blossom-colored one, silver buckled shoes, and a tie wig which he was said to twirl around his head when he was excited.

Yet his private life contained much sadness. After the birth of their sixth child, Sarah became seriously ill. Her illness was so severe that, until she died in 1775, she had to be confined to her room. Unfortunately the years of Sarah's illness were also the critical years for the country and again and again Patrick was obliged to leave home. During one of her most severe spells, he was with George Washington in Philadelphia, attending the Continental Congress.

On March 23rd, 1775, just a few weeks after Sarah's death, Patrick delivered his most famous speech at St. John's Church in Richmond, Virginia. By this time everyone knew who Mr. Henry was; they had all heard of his passion for liberty and of the extraordinary quality of his voice. There were those who swore that Patrick Henry could not even announce that it was a cold evening without inspiring awe. So of course on March 23rd St. John's Church was filled to overflowing—people standing in the aisles, in doorways, sitting on window ledges.

Patrick Henry was angry not only at the king who was disregarding America's petitions, insisting on taxation, and preparing for war, but he was also angry at those people in America who still wanted to be friendly to the king and keep peace. Patrick stood up and pushed his glasses back on his head which was what he did when he was ready to use his fighting words.

"Gentlemen may cry peace, peace," he thundered, "but there is no peace . . . Is life so dear or peace so sweet, as to be purchased at the price of chains and slavery?" Patrick bowed his body and locked his hands together as if he, himself, were in chains. Then suddenly he raised his chained hands over his head.

"Forbid it, Almighty God!" he cried. "I know not what course others may take but as for me—" Patrick dropped his arms, threw back his body and strained against his imaginary chains until the tendons of his neck stood out like whipcords and the chains seemed to break. Then he raised his right hand in which he held an ivory letter opener. "As for me," he cried, "give me liberty or give me death!" And he plunged the letter opener in such a way it looked as if he were plunging it into his heart.

The crowd went wild with excitement. One man, leaning over the balcony, was so aroused that he forgot where he was and spit tobacco juice into the audience below. Another man jumped down from the window ledge and declared that when he died, he wanted to be buried on the very spot that Patrick Henry had delivered those words. (And so he was, twenty-five years later.)

The next year war came and Virginia volunteers marched off to battle with *Liberty or Death* embroidered on their shirtfronts. As for Patrick Henry, the people elected him governor.

On May 29th, 1777, he was elected for the second time. He was forty-one years old now, living in the luxurious palace where the royal governors had lived for fifty-five years. And he was busy, so busy that if a nice spring day came along, he wouldn't even have heard a redbird call.

Questions

1. At the trial of his first big case, Patrick Henry wished two people would *not* be there. Who were these two people? Tell why one of these people went home and why one stayed.

2. Patrick's life changed in the middle of a court case. Find the paragraph that describes that important moment. With what sentence does that paragraph begin? If Patrick were to tell the reason for the change, what might he say?

3. Patrick Henry became a great speaker, or *orator.* What did his speeches persuade the people of the colonies to do?

4. Why was the crowd so excited when Patrick Henry cried, "Give me liberty or give me death"?

5. Match these words with their definitions.
   client   a. obeyed
   attorney   b. revoked
   complied   c. lawyer
   repealed   d. customer

Activity   Make a Time Line

The biography of Patrick Henry begins on May 29, 1752. It closes on May 29, 1777. Draw a long line with one of those dates at each end. Find five very important happenings in Patrick Henry's life between those two dates. Write these five events on the time line you have drawn to show the order in which they happened. You could also illustrate each event with a small drawing.

A ghillie cap? What's that? And what is a gripsack? Those are two examples of *authentic*, or genuine, details one author used to help her readers picture life in the 1800s. (Read on to find out more about the ghillie cap and gripsack.) You'll find many such details, as well as more important facts, in every good biography you read. Authentic details give a sense of truthfulness to a biography. In a biography, truth and accuracy are essential, for a biography is the history of a person's life.

Writers of biographies may spend months or even years tracking down important facts and details about people and events, times and places. Such research helps biographers make their writings true to life.

Read the following paragraph from the biography *Where Was Patrick Henry on the 29th of May?* by Jean Fritz. Look for authentic details that give you the feeling of the time and place in which Patrick Henry lived.

At the quarter sessions of the court in March, June, September, and December, the most important cases were tried and then every bed in the tavern would be taken. (It cost 75¢ a night for a bed with clean sheets.) Traveling troupes of acrobats and jugglers came to town at that time; peddlers came to sell their wares; there were horse races, cockfights, and wrestling matches. From all over the county people came to see the shows, do their trading, and hear the cases argued.

Illustrations may play an important role in biographies by showing details of how people and things looked at a particular time or in a particular place. Illustrations, then, also need to be accurate. Look closely at the two illustrations on page 433. Can you find one detail that is wrong in each picture?

In 1932, Amelia Earhart flew her red Vega monoplane—a single-winged plane—across the Atlantic from Newfoundland to Ireland. She was the first woman, and the second pilot, to make this solo flight.

In 1752, Benjamin Franklin flew a kite in a thunderstorm to prove that lightning is electricity.

(Answers: biplane—a double-winged plane; TV antenna.)

But what about the ghillie cap and gripsack? They belonged to Elizabeth Cochrane who, using the pen name[1] of Nellie Bly, was an American newspaper reporter during the late 1800s. As a reporter for the New York *World*, Nellie Bly became known for her articles exposing some of the terrible living and working conditions of that time. But she became famous for another reason. In 1890, before airplanes or automobiles were invented, Nellie Bly went around the world by train and ship in a little over seventy-two

days—faster than anyone else had ever traveled. That's where the ghillie cap and the gripsack came in. On her historic trip around the world, Nellie wore one and carried her belongings in the other.

The pictures on pages 435 to 439 show some events in Nellie Bly's trip around the world. Imagine that you are Nellie Bly's biographer. You are writing a book for people your age about Nellie's trip. Choose one or more of the scenes pictured and describe what is happening. Make each event, and Nellie Bly's part in it, true-to-life and interesting for your readers. You can do this by including authentic details from the pictures as well as the facts given in the text below them. You may also want to include *dialogue,* or conversation, used in a picture, or you may want to add some of your own. Although such conversations are made up, they help to explain what really happened.

---

1. **pen name:** a made-up name an author uses to sign his or her work.

1. Nellie's Plan

Characters: Nellie Bly, a reporter; Julius Chambers—managing editor of the New York *World,* Nellie's employer.
Setting: Julius Chambers's office at the *World* newspaper.
Time: November, 1889
Facts: Few women traveled alone then; main forms of transportation—trains, ships, stagecoaches.

2. Starting Out—New Jersey

Characters: Nellie Bly; Julius Chambers—managing editor of the *World* newspaper; other newspaper editors; steamship-company officials; Nellie's mother.
Setting: Pier in Hoboken, New Jersey.

Time: November 14, 1889.
Facts: Ship was the *Augusta Victoria;* destination—England; articles in Nellie's gripsack included only one other dress and hat, lots of paper and pencils.

3. First Stop—England

Characters: Nellie Bly; London reporter for the *World* newspaper.
Setting: Hotel in London, England.

Facts: Nellie made the trip to Jules Verne's house and wrote a story about it. She didn't miss her boat.

4. At the Market—Singapore

Characters: Nellie Bly; Chinese merchant.
Setting: Singapore.
Facts: Nellie rode in a jinriksha—a small two-wheeled carriage pulled by one or two men. The captain of Nellie's boat considered it bad luck to have a monkey on his ship. Nellie and the captain argued. Nellie kept the monkey.

5. Homecoming—New Jersey

Characters: Nellie Bly; Mayor of Jersey City, New Jersey; timekeepers; huge crowd of people.
Setting: Railroad station in Jersey City, New Jersey.
Time: 3:15 P.M. on January 26, 1890.

Facts: All factory whistles in New Jersey blew. Official time recorded by three stopwatches: 72 days, 6 hours, 11 minutes, and 14 seconds. The *World* headlines read: FATHER TIME OUTDONE!

439

I brought to the New World the gift of devotion

Harriet Tubman was born a slave in Maryland in 1820. She escaped from slavery in 1849. She then began the very dangerous work of acting as a "conductor" on the Underground Railroad, a secret system of helping slaves escape from the South to freedom in the northern United States or Canada. Harriet Tubman risked her life again and again, helping more than three hundred slaves travel the Underground Railroad to freedom. She came to be called the Black Moses because she led so many people out of slavery, just as Moses is said to have led the people of Israel to freedom from the Egyptian pharaoh, many centuries ago.

I was Harriet Tubman, who would not stay in bondage.
I followed the devious, uncharted trails to the North,
I followed the light of the North Star,
    I ran away to freedom in 1849.
I was Harriet Tubman who could not stay in freedom,
    While her brothers were enslaved.
"Go down, Moses," back into Egypt,
    Back to the land of the bloodhound and the pateroller,
"Tell old Pharaoh, let my people go!"

Everywhere they waited for my coming,
    Tiny treasures hid against my coming—
I was the lone call of an owl in the darkness,
I was the blurred line of a Spiritual under a slave-cabin window,
I was the last, faint tremor of hope upon the wind.
    I was Harriet Tubman,
    Who "never run my train off the track,
    And never lost a passenger."

—Hildegarde Hoyt Swift   441

SAVED BY A WHISKER

From the novel *By the Great Horn Spoon!* by Sid Fleischman

Illustrated by Willi Baum

The year is 1849. Gold has been discovered in California. The scramble for quick fortunes is on. A paddle-wheeled sailing ship churns out of Boston Harbor bound for San Francisco by way of Cape Horn. Below the creaking decks two stowaways hide in potato barrels, while the thief who stole their money travels in comfort above. In one barrel is twelve-year-old Jack Flagg, an orphan on his way to strike it rich so his penniless Aunt Arabella can keep the family mansion. In the other is Praiseworthy, Aunt Arabella's loyal butler.

After a long voyage, during which they cleverly catch the thief, the two gold-seekers arrive in San Francisco—where survival itself requires cleverness.

In his pea jacket and stocking cap Jack felt fourteen years old at least. Maybe fifteen. He stood in the bow of the whale boat and watched the Long Wharf come closer. They bumped against the boat-stairs and Jack was the first out. His heart raced with the excitement of the moment. They had arrived, and he was ready to start digging.

"Not so fast, Master Jack," said Praiseworthy. "Don't forget your pick and shovel."

A hilltop telegraph had signaled the arrival of a side-wheeler and now it seemed as if all of San Francisco had turned out. The wharf was alive with men, women and children—not to mention dogs, mules, and chickens. Sea gulls flocked in the air like confetti.

Weighted down with their belongings, Praiseworthy and Jack started along the wharf. There were barrels and boxes piled everywhere. Peddlers and hawkers and hotel runners mixed through the crowd and shouted at the newcomers.

"Welcome, boys! Welcome to the fastest growing city in the world!"

"Flannel shirts for sale! Red flannel shirts, gents! They don't show the dirt!"

"Try the Niantic Hotel. The cleanest beds in town."

"Horn spoons! You'll need 'em at the diggin's. Carved from genuine ox horn!"

"Stay at the Parker House. None better!"

The wharf seemed a mile long and the noisiest place on earth. Beyond, the city rang to the sound of hammers. Buildings were going up everywhere and a sand dredger was pounding the air. Men stood in the doorways of the shops ringing hand bells.

"Auction! Auction going on! Fresh eggs just arrived from Panama!"

"Onions at auction! Fifty bushels just come in from the Sandwich Islands! Also calomel pills, castor oil, and carpet tacks!"

Praiseworthy and Jack continued along the boardwalk, which was hammered together mostly out of barrel staves, and reached the United States Hotel. Their ship's captain had recommended it.

"A fine room, if you please," Praiseworthy said to the hotel clerk. "And I think a tub bath would be in order."

"Very good, sir," replied the clerk. He was a bald-headed man with thin strands of hair combed sideways, from ear to ear. "That'll be ten dollars extra—each."

"What's that?" Praiseworthy scowled. "We don't want to bathe in champagne. Water will do, sir."

"Champagne'd be almost cheaper, gents. Water's a dollar a bucket. Unless you want to wait until next November. Prices come down when it rains."

"We'll wait," said Praiseworthy with decision. In this part of the world, he thought, a man had to strike it rich just to keep his neck clean. He signed the register and Jack gazed at a bearded miner pacing back and forth across the lobby floor. He wore a floppy hat and chestnut hair tumbled out on all sides like mattress stuffing coming loose. He kept glancing at the loud wall clock as if every advancing second might be his last.

Jack couldn't take his eyes off the man. Tucked in his wide leather belt were a revolver, a horn spoon, and a soft buckskin bag. Gold dust! Jack thought. He must have just got in from the mines!

"Ruination!" the miner began to mutter. "Ruination!"

Praiseworthy blotted the register. "How," he asked the clerk, "does one get to the mines?"

"Riverboat leaves every afternoon at four o'clock from the Long Wharf. Fare to Sacramento City is twenty-five dollars. From there you make your way to the diggings by stage, muleback, or foot."

Jack shot a glance at Praiseworthy. Twenty-five dollars—each! Why, they didn't *have* that much money! But the butler didn't so much as raise an eyebrow. "We'll be taking the boat tomorrow," he told the clerk.

"Ruination!" said the miner.

"Come along, Master Jack," said Praiseworthy.

The walls of their room were lined with blood-red calico and there was China matting on the plank floor. The window looked out on the shipping in the bay, the masts as thick as a pine forest. There were not only gold ships, but Navy frigates and Chinese junks and the going and coming of longboats. But Jack wasn't interested in the view.

"*Fifty* dollars just to get to Sacramento City!" he said. "We'll have to walk."

"Good exercise, no doubt, but we haven't time for it." Praiseworthy gazed out at the distant hills across the bay. Sacramento City was more than a hundred miles up river, he had heard, and the diggings in the foothills beyond that. "Let me see. It took us five months to get this far and it will take us another five months to get home. If we are to keep your Aunt Arabella from being sold out—we have two months left. Two months to fill our pockets with nuggets."

Jack found himself pacing back and forth like the miner in the lobby below. "Ruination!" Jack said. "We've come all this way and now—we're no closer."

"Nonsense," said Praiseworthy. There was a pitcher half filled with water on the chest and he poured a small amount into the washpan. "We'll be on tomorrow's riverboat, I promise you. Now then, I suggest we wash up as best we can, Master Jack."

Wash! Jack thought. There wasn't time to wash! "How will we pay the fare?"

"Let me see. We have thirty-eight dollars left. That's a start, isn't it? Of course, we'll have our room and meals to pay. But if I detect one thing in the air—it's opportunity. The sooner you wash, Master Jack, the sooner we can tend to our financial dilemma. Your Aunt Arabella wouldn't allow you abroad on the streets with dirty ears and sea salt in your eyebrows. And don't forget the soap."

"Ruination," Jack muttered again. He might as well be home in Boston.

They washed and changed into fresh clothes. Then they returned to the lobby. The shaggy miner was still there, pacing and muttering in his dusty beard. He glanced at Jack, a dark sudden glance—and then the butler and the boy went out on the street.

But as they ambled along the boardwalk looking for opportunity, Jack began to realize that the miner was following them. He was still at their heels when the butler and the boy crossed the street. Jack was beginning to feel anxious. Even a little scared. Finally he looked up at Praiseworthy.

"He's following us."

"Who's following us?" asked the butler.

"That miner from the hotel."

"Stuff and nonsense. The streets are free to every-one."

"But he's following us, Praiseworthy."

"Nothing to fear in broad daylight, Master Jack."

They continued along the sandy plaza, still looking for opportunity, and the miner marched right behind them.

"Must be a madman," said Praiseworthy, turning. He stopped and the miner stopped and they stood face to face. "Sir," said the butler. "Are you following us?"

"Ruination! I shore am!"

"I'll thank you to go your way, sir!"

"No offense, gents," the miner said. "Been on the verge of breakin' in on your conversation, but it didn't seem courteous." It was hard to see his mouth for the fullness of his beard. "They call me Quartz Jackson, and I just come in from the diggin's. My fiancée's due in on the stage any minute. Comin' up from the capital at Monterey. We ain't never met, but we writ a lot of letters. And that's just it."

"And that's just what?" said Praiseworthy.

"We're supposed to be gettin' married. But *ruination*—when she takes one look at me, she's goin' to think I'm part grizzly bear." He whipped off his floppy hat and his dusty hair fell out on all sides. "She'll get right back on the stage for Monterey. But shucks, I ain't such a badlookin' gent—leastways, I wasn't when I went to the diggin's. I'm just a mite growed over, you might say. Well, I been trampin' every street in town lookin' for a barber, but they all lit out for the mines. Don't seem to be anyone left here but the auctioneers. Anyway, that's why I couldn't help starin' at the lad here."

"Me?" said Jack.

"Why, that yeller hair of yours looks fresh from the barber shop. All cut and trimmed. I figured you must have flushed out a barber and maybe you'd do Quartz Jackson the favor of leadin' me to him."

If Jack had feared the miner for a moment, he couldn't help smiling at him now. He liked the man. "No, sir," he said. "I haven't been to a barber. Unless you mean Praiseworthy."

"Praiseworthy?"

"At your service," said the butler. "It's true, I've been cutting Master Jack's hair, but only out of necessity."

The miner's face—what could be seen of it—broke into a sunny smile. "I'd be much obliged if you'd barber me up, Mr. Praiseworthy. Name your price."

"But I'm not a barber, sir. I'm a butler."

"A what?"

"I couldn't accept any money for merely—"

"Well, now, that's mighty good of you. Tell you what I'll do. I'll let you have all the hair you cut off."

Praiseworthy and Jack exchanged fresh glances. The man was some sort of lunatic after all. What earthly use did they have for the man's shorn locks? But it seemed wise to humor him, and Praiseworthy said, "I'll be glad to help you in your hour of need, sir. Consider it a modest wedding present."

Twenty minutes later the miner was seated on a nail keg in a corner of the hotel porch, and Praiseworthy was snipping away with the shears. Quartz Jackson insisted that every lock be caught as it fell.

Jack was kept busy holding a washpan under Praiseworthy's busy scissors. It worried him that time
was wasting and they were yet to make their boat
fare. But he knew it would have been impossible
for Praiseworthy to turn his back on a gentleman
in distress—even a peculiar miner like Mr. Quartz
Jackson.

"My, ain't the town growed, though," said the miner. "Must be all of four-five thousand folks in the place. You gents figure on goin' to the diggin's?"

"We do indeed," said Praiseworthy.

"I come from Hangtown. The boys have been locatin' a good lot of color up that way."

"Color?"

"The yeller stuff. Gold. If you get up Hangtown way, tell 'em you're a friend of Quartz Jackson. Tell 'em I'll be comin' home with my bride in a couple of weeks. Shore is nice of you to shear me this way. Would you mind trimmin' the beard while you're at it? Always itchin', and I can hardly find my mouth to spit with. Jack, young Jack, a bit of sideburn is gettin' away in the breeze. Wouldn't want you to lose any."

"Yes, sir," said Jack, catching the lock of hair.

Quartz Jackson's face began to appear, snip by snip, like a statue being chipped out of stone. When Praiseworthy had finished the miner turned to look at himself in the hotel windowpane, and he almost jumped out of his jackboots.

"By the Great Horn Spoon!" he said. "Is that *me?*" Quartz Jackson was obviously pleased. "Why, I'd forgot I was so young!"

Quartz Jackson was a fine-looking gent at that, Jack thought. He had good teeth and an easy smile. Except for his revolver, his horn spoon, and his red flannel shirt, he hardly seemed the same man. But what did he expect them to do with the hair cuttings? Stuff a mattress?

"Your fiancée will be very pleased," smiled Praiseworthy. "Our congratulations on your forthcoming marriage, sir."

"Much obliged, Praiseworthy. You saved me from certain ruination. The least I can do is learn you how to work a gold pan. Water boy! You there! Fetch us a bucket of dew over here."

The miner paid for the water by taking a pinch of fine gold dust from his buckskin pouch. Jack was eager to get the hang of mining and Quartz Jackson, peculiar or not, was clearly an expert.

"Gimme the washpan, Jack, young Jack."

Jack handed over the tin pan, piled high with chestnut whiskers and trimmings. The miner wet them down with fresh water and began to swish the pan around.

"Gold's heavy," he explained. "Nothin' heavier. Even the yeller dust sinks to the bottom if you keep workin' the pan. Like this."

Then he handed the washpan to Jack and taught him the motion. The water turned brown from the dirt and mud that had gathered in Quartz Jackson's whiskers and hair. Finally he poured off everything—everything but a thin residue at the bottom of the pan. Jack's eyes opened like blossoms.

Gold dust!

"Why, look there!" the miner roared with laughter. "The boy's panned himself some color. I figured I scratched enough pay dirt into my beard to assay out at about $14 an ounce. Since I give you the whiskers and all—the gold is yours!"

Jack had never known a more exciting moment in his life. The grains of dust sparkled like yellow fire—and there was even a flake or two.

Half an hour later, while Quartz Jackson was having a $10 tub bath, Praiseworthy and Jack were plucking opportunity from the air. They put up a sign that said, "FREE HAIRCUTS Miners Only."

Questions

1. Praiseworthy said that he detected opportunity in the air. Why did he say that?

2. What opportunity came to Praiseworthy and Jack?

3. Why, at the end of the story, did the sign say "Miners Only"?

4. Do you think that Jack and Praiseworthy struck gold when they got to the foothills? How does the story help you form your opinion?

5. Suppose someone were to say, "Life was very hard for the forty-niners." What would you say as a result of reading "Saved by a Whisker"?

6. Comparisons that use the words *like* or *as* are called *similes* (SIM·uh·leez). Complete these similes with words from the story.
   a. "Sea gulls flocked in the air like _____."
   b. The masts in the harbor were "as thick as _____."
   c. Quartz Jackson's face began to show during the barbering "like a _____."
   d. "Jack's eyes opened like _____. Gold dust!"

Activity   Describe the Story Setting

When you read a story, your mind becomes a camera, showing you a picture of the *setting*—where and when the story takes place. Find a way to describe the *images,* or mental pictures, your mind "photographed" as you read "Saved by a Whisker." Describe the setting in a picture, a diagram, or words.

About SID FLEISCHMAN

Sid Fleischman is a master of the tall tale. His stories are so outlandish, and his characters so funny, that they make us laugh. Many of his stories are about the American frontier. To gather information, Sid Fleischman reads old books, newspapers, and magazines. His characters often speak in *dialects*, which are special ways of speaking that some groups of people share. The dialects help give the flavor of the times and places he writes about.

Sid Fleischman's early ambition was to become a magician. In fact, while he was in high school, he and a friend put on magic shows. After he finished college, he worked as a newspaper reporter. Then he began writing books.

Unlike many authors, Sid Fleischman doesn't outline his stories ahead of time. He usually starts with a background, like the California gold rush in *By the Great Horn Spoon!* Then he just writes. "I rarely know what is going to happen next," Sid Fleischman says, "and I have to sit at the typewriter to find out."

More Books by Sid Fleischman

McBroom & the Big Wind
McBroom's Zoo
The Ghost on Saturday Night
Jim Bridger's Alarm Clock & Other Tall Tales

Oh, My Darling Clementine

A song by P. Montrose

In the mid-1800s gold had been discovered in California. Soon the small village of San Francisco became a city filled with people with gold dust in their pockets, or with golden dreams in their heads. Tales of new gold discoveries, lost fortunes, and wild mining town doings were on everyone's lips. A few of the stories were true, many were lies, and some became songs to be sung over and over again.

1. In a cav-ern in a can-yon, Ex-ca-va-ting for a mine, Dwelt a min-er, for-ty-nin-er, And his daugh-ter Cle-men-tine.

Refrain
Oh, my dar-ling, Oh, my dar-ling, Oh, my dar-ling Cle-men-tine, You are lost and gone for-ev-er, Dread-ful sor-ry, Cle-men-tine.

2. Light she was and like a fairy,
   And her shoes were number nine,
   Herring boxes without topses,
   Sandals were for Clementine.

3. Drove her ducklings to the water,
   Every morning just at nine,
   Hit her foot against a splinter,
   Fell into the foaming brine.

4. Ruby lips above the water,
   Blowing bubbles soft and fine,
   Alas, for me! I was no swimmer,
   So I lost my Clementine.

5. In a churchyard, near the canyon,
   Where the myrtle doth entwine,
   There grow roses and other posies,
   Fertilized by Clementine.

6. Then the miner, forty-niner,
   Soon began to droop and pine,
   Thought he "oughter jine" his daughter,
   Now he's with his Clementine.

Illustrated by Michel Allaire

The Railroad Crosses America

On May 10, 1869, a large, happy crowd gathered at Promontory Point, Utah. The crowd was there to celebrate the end of a long, hard job—the building of a railroad across the United States.

The crowd watched and cheered as railroad workers laid the last two *ties*, the heavy wooden beams that held the rails in place. Then the last spike—one made of gold—was positioned. The spike was attached to a telegraph wire. When the spike was hit, an electric charge would be carried over the telegraph wire to telegraph stations all over the United States. Everyone would know that the railroad was finished.

A railroad worker hammered the gold spike down with a silver hammer. The electric charge traveled over the telegraph wires. In cities such as New York, Boston, Philadelphia, and Washington, the charge touched off bell-ringing and cannon-firing. At Promontory Point, Utah, the crowd gave a rousing cheer. The Pacific Railroad, the first transcontinental railroad in the United States and in the world, was finished.

Building the railroad across the continent had taken two crews of workers more than five years. By

Illustrated by Joanna Adamska Koperska

1850, railroads criss-crossed the eastern part of the
United States from north to south and east to west.
However, no railroad connected the eastern part
with the huge sections of land in the Midwest and
Far West and South. These sections of the United
States were far from transportation and markets.
People believed that if railroads were built to these
areas, more settlers would follow.

In 1862, President Abraham Lincoln and Congress
gave two railroad companies permission to build
different sections of the railroad line. The Union
Pacific Railroad would start its part of the line near
Omaha, Nebraska, and build across the Platte River
Valley and over the Rocky Mountains. The Central
Pacific Railroad would start its section at Sacramento,
California, and build over the Sierra Nevada and
across the desert.

OMAHA
NEBRASKA

GREAT PLAINS

Rocky
Mountains

Promontory
Point

Great
Basin

DESERT

Sierra
Nevada

SACRAMENTO
CALIFORNIA

Work did not begin immediately in 1862, however. It took many months for both railroad companies to hire workers and get supplies. The Union Pacific hired thousands of Irish *immigrants,* people who had come from their native country to live in the United States. The Central Pacific hired thousands of Chinese immigrants.

The Central Pacific crew began laying rails in 1863, the Union Pacific crew in 1865. Both crews faced huge challenges. The men on the Union Pacific crew had to lay tracks across the Great Plains and over the towering Rockies. The Central Pacific crew had to lay tracks over the jagged Sierra Nevada and the desert regions of the country.

Both crews worked in all kinds of weather and under many hardships. They pushed slowly but steadily toward each other, laying tracks at the rate of one to two miles a day. By 1868, however, the work had turned into a race between the two crews. On one day alone, the Union Pacific boasted that its Chinese workers had laid ten miles of railroad tracks!

It is little wonder, then, that there was a noisy and happy celebration when the two crews met at Promontory Point. They had finished a long, hard job. The two coasts of the United States were now connected by rail. The "Iron Horse" that would travel these rails would carry passengers, manufactured goods, farm and ranch products, and mail from coast to coast in seven days or fewer. What an improvement this was over a long, uncomfortable journey by wagon train, stagecoach, or clipper ship. A new period of growth was beginning, and the transcontinental railroad would help it along.

Questions

1. Why might the railroad have been called the "Iron Horse"?

2. What were some problems faced by the railroad crews in building the first transcontinental railroad?

3. Why might the job of laying track have turned into a contest between the crews?

Activities

1. **Plan and Write a Report**

   Read library books or encyclopedia articles about the Irish or Chinese immigrants who worked on the railroad. Find out how they came to the United States, how they were hired by the railroad companies, and what their working conditions were like. Write a short report about what you learn. Share your findings with your classmates.

2. **Write a Journal**

   Pretend you are one of the workers on the transcontinental railroad. Think about your work and the dangers and hardships you might face. Write a page in your journal describing a day "workin' on the railroad." Use library books, encyclopedias, and maps to help you.

John Henry

A ballad

Was John Henry a real flesh and blood man, a steel driver of great strength and grit? To this day people wonder about that. Some say John Henry was an imaginary hero, like Paul Bunyan and his Blue Ox Babe. Others say he really did help build the Big Bend Tunnel for the railroad in West Virginia in the 1870s. But on one thing almost everyone agrees: John Henry is a man worth singing about.

1. When John Hen-ry was a-bout three days old,

Just a - sittin' on his pap - py's knee,

He gave one loud and lone-some cry:

"The___ ham-mer'll be the death of me,

The___ ham-mer'll be the death of me."

2. Well, the captain said to John Henry one day:
   "Gonna bring that steam drill 'round,
   Gonna take that steam drill out on the job,
   Gonna whop that steel on down,
   Gonna whop that steel on down."

3. John Henry said to the captain:
   "Well, the next time you go to town
   Just bring me back a twelve-pound hammer
   And I'll beat your steam drill down," etc.

4. John Henry said to the captain:
   "Well, a man ain't nothin' but a man,
   And before I let a steam drill beat me down
   Gonna die with the hammer in my hand."

5. John Henry went to the tunnel,
   And they put him in the lead to drive,
   The rock so tall and John Henry so small,
   He laid down his hammer and he cried.

6. John Henry said to his shaker:
   "Shaker, why don't you sing?
   For I'm swingin' twelve pounds from the
       hips on down,
   Just listen to that cold steel ring."

7. John Henry told his captain:
   "Look-a yonder what I see—
   Your drill's done broke and your hole's
       done choke',
   And you can't drive steel like me."

8. Well, the man that invented the steam drill,
   He thought he was mighty fine,
   But John Henry drove his fifteen feet,
   And the steam drill only made nine.

9. John Henry looked up at the mountain,
   And his hammer was striking fire,
   Well, he hammered so hard that he broke
       his poor old heart,
   He laid down his hammer and he died.

10. They took John Henry to the graveyard,
    And they laid him in the sand,
    Three men from the east and a woman
        from the west
    Came to see that old steel-drivin' man.

11. They took John Henry to the graveyard,
    And they laid him in the sand,
    And every locomotive comes a-roarin' by
    Says: "There lies a steel-drivin' man."

466   Illustrated by Michel Allaire

BOOKSHELF

Runaway to Freedom by Barbara Smucker. Harper & Row, 1977. Disguised as boys, Julilly and her friend Liza escape from slavery and manage to reach Canada by way of the Underground Railroad.

American Tall Tales by Adrien Stoutenburg. Viking Press, 1966. These are eight tough and bold tales about such American folk heroes as Pecos Bill, Mike Fink, Paul Bunyan, and John Henry.

Caddie Woodlawn by Carol Ryrie Brink. Macmillan, 1935. This story of pioneer life, set on the Wisconsin frontier of the 1860s, features the adventures of a courageous eleven-year-old girl and her two brothers.

Meet the Real Pilgrims by Robert H. Loeb, Jr. Doubleday, 1979. Through photographs and interviews with the town's inhabitants, the author takes the reader on an actual visit to a working replica of the original Plymouth Plantation as it was in 1627.

Sounder by William Armstrong. Harper & Row, 1969. When a sharecropper takes food for his starving family, he is sent to jail. The family's faithful and courageous hound, Sounder, helps them through the difficult years of the father's absence.

The Amazing Voyage of the New Orleans by Judith St. George. G. P. Putnam's, 1980. This true story of the first steamboat trip from Pittsburgh to New Orleans includes dangerous floods and a violent earthquake.

7 America Grows Up

From

Steal Away Home

A novel by Jean Kristof

Illustrated by Phill Renaud

What a powerful—and secret—word freedom *was to the slaves. Many slaves risked their lives trying to reach the North to be free. Amos and Obediah knew that their father had made the dangerous journey and was free. He lived up North in the big city of Philadelphia.*

Amos and Obediah still lived with their mother and sister on a plantation in Searsville, South Carolina. One hot summer day, a minister stopped by their slave shack and spent time talking to the boys' mother. Soon after that talk, the boys finally understood the secret word freedom *and the secret way to get it: "Take the Underground Railroad north."*

On July 4, 1853, Amos and Obediah became passengers on the Underground Railroad. The boys ran barefoot from station to station, almost always at night and always afraid of being caught. Their second station on the Railroad was the home of Mr. and Mrs. Strauss in Raleigh, North Carolina. The Strausses were German immigrants who had come to America to enjoy its freedom. They wanted to share that freedom with all the slaves they could.

This is Amos's account of how the Strauss family helped him and his brother Obie on their way to being free.

Mr. and Mrs. Strauss looked very much alike. They were both small, frail-looking and gray-haired, but they didn't seem old or tired. It's hard to really explain, but their wrinkled faces seemed kind of transparent. In some funny way they made me think of the beat-up hurricane lamp in the Brickers' barn; you hardly noticed the chips and cracks in its chimney when you saw the bright flame inside.

They lived in two small rooms over the pharmacy with little furniture but a lot of books. We had never been in a white person's house before, except once in a while in the Brickers' kitchen, and at first we felt mighty strange and uncomfortable. The Strausses must have understood our feeling, because they did everything they could to make us welcome. Whenever they could get away from their customers one or the other would come up the stairs to us, bringing something nice to eat or some game or trick to entertain us. They even let me look at one of the books with very fancy, exciting pictures in it. I knew they were being kind, but I just kept wishing they would go back to the store and leave us to ourselves.

In the evening when the store was closed Mr. Strauss unfolded a big sheet of paper all covered with lines and markings, and began to pore over it, muttering names like "Searsville," "Richmond," "Washington," and "Philadelphia."

Obie, always curious, asked, "What's that, Master Strauss?"

"That, my boy, is a map. That is a picture of where you have been and where you must go."

Obie and I crowded around him.

"Raleigh is here and there is Philadelphia. There you must go."

"But that isn't very far at all, Master Strauss. We can do that real quick," exclaimed Obie. "Where did we come from?"

"Hm, let me see. This village Searsville, it is here. Just over the line in South Carolina."

Obie's face fell. "But we been gone more than a week. We got to be farther than that."

Mr. Strauss chuckled. "Everything is small on the map. You have come about a hundred miles, more or less. You must go still—let me see—two hundred sixty to Washington, to Philadelphia must be about four hundred miles."

That sounded like a long, long way.

"But now," continued Mr. Strauss, "we shall plot only the next step. We must get you here, to Dr. Culpepper in Henderson. Do you know your letters, my boys?"

"I know *B*," said Obie proudly. "That's the first letter in Bricker and it's on the sign on his driveway. Amos knows more than me, though. Pa started to teach him before they took him away."

"He just taught me a few, and I forgot them pretty well," I admitted.

"That is a great trouble. How to find the way when you cannot read the sign and you cannot ask the people. Well, we must think."

He scratched his head, wrinkled up his forehead and talked for a while to his wife in a foreign language. Then he turned to us and switched back to English.

"We have the plot," he announced. "You must go by day. At night you shall be lost. You were sent to Raleigh by Dr. Culpepper to try if any pharmacy has a certain new medicine. You found it at my store and now you take it back to him. You have lost your pass, but I shall give you a letter to the doctor that you can show if somebody shall stop you. I shall give you a little map also."

"Only one thing," added Mrs. Strauss. "When you come near Henderson, so if anybody ask, you do not belong to Dr. Culpepper. Many there shall know that he has no slaves. Say that you belong to Mr. Strauss and he send you with medicine that the doctor ordered."

"If they ask why we do not use the mail, say we are foreigners—how do you say—eccentric, and you can still show the letter."

473

The rest of the evening was spent in preparations. Mrs. Strauss filled a large medicine jar with red candy and pasted labels and warnings all over it while Mr. Strauss wrote his letter. Then they both went over the route to Henderson with us. It was a distance of about thirty miles, and they expected it to take us two days. They wrote down the names of some of the places we would pass on the way and we tried to memorize them.

Then Mrs. Strauss glanced up at the clock.

"Ach! It is eight and a half. You children shall sleep here on the sofa. I get a blanket."

It was a hot night and we soon kicked off the blanket, but late at night I heard Mrs. Strauss tiptoe in and I felt her tucking the blanket around my shoulders. I almost thought I was back in the cabin with Mama, and all of a sudden I wanted to cry.

The Strausses were up before us in the morning. Mrs. Strauss had made us a big breakfast of eggs and sausages and had stuffed our food sack. Mr. Strauss was once again checking the "pill" jar, the letter and the map. At last all was ready. We said good-by and set off.

That morning I felt for the first time the joy and excitement of the road. The sun was bright and the air warm and soft. The country was green and rolling, and my heart was all grateful and full of hope. Obie whistled as he walked along beside me, and I knew he felt the same.

We were stopped once on the edge of town by a well-dressed young white man. We told him we were buying medicine for our master, and when he had looked at the pills and read Mr. Strauss's letter he shrugged his shoulders and went on his way.

About five miles along the road we were stopped again, this time by a rough-looking man in a farm cart.

"Hey, where d'you think you're going?"

We told the story about the medicine again and showed him the letter. He read it out loud to himself, slowly sounding out the words and following them with a grubby finger:

"Dear Dr. Culpepper, I send the medicine requested by you with these boys. It is already widely used in Europe but difficult to obtain in this country. I would advise a dosage of two pills before breakfast and one before bed. Please inform me of the progress of your patient. Your obedient servant, Joseph Strauss."

He handed back the letter.

"Wonder what that there medicine's for?"

"Sciatica," answered Obie off the top of his head.

"Sciatica, eh? That's what my old lady complains of. Maybe I'll get some of them pills next time I'm in town."

He started up again, then stopped.

"Where'd you say your master lives—Henderson?"

"Yes, sir."

"Well, jump in the back. I'm going up that way about fourteen miles and I'll give you a lift."

The more you got to know our driver the nicer he seemed to get. By the time he let us off in the middle of the afternoon, we had talked over his wife's sciatica, the awful cost of medicine, the cleverness of his horse, and a lot of other things, and we felt pretty friendly. When we separated he gave us each a stick of licorice. Right away Obie dug into his pocket and fished out a handful of candy that Mrs. Strauss had given him to offer in return. To my horror I saw that it was the same round, red candy that was shining out from the medicine jar. Luckily, our friend wasn't a very noticing person. Or what he noticed was the wrong thing—my face.

"Naw," he told Obie. "You're going to be in trouble with your big brother if you give me any of that candy. Thanks anyway." And he turned into a side road and drove off.

We were only about eleven miles from Henderson now and well rested, with several hours of daylight still ahead of us, so we decided to try to walk straight through without stopping for the night. We made it, too, though we had to walk the last few miles in the dark. Those last miles were the hardest and slowest. Every sound frightened us, and even the trees, hills and bushes seemed alive and unfriendly. At last we saw the dim shapes of the town ahead of us. By the time we walked down the main street many of the lights were already in upper windows, and in some houses there was no light at all. We carefully followed the Strausses' directions through the town until we came to a large white frame house with a fence around it. By the light of the full moon we were just able to make out the letters on the gate. They spelled out the name we had memorized the night before: Culpepper.

We went around to the back door and knocked softly. There was no sound from the dark house. We knocked again louder. There was some movement inside, and a sleepy voice called, "Coming." In a minute the door was opened by a pleasant-faced middle-aged gentleman holding a candle. Even in his nightcap he looked dignified.

"What is it, my lads? Who sent you?" he asked.

"Dr. Culpepper?"

"I am he."

"Master Strauss sent us. We're going north."

The doctor looked at us blankly for a moment; then a light dawned.

"Surely you're not alone?" he inquired, peering into the darkness behind us.

"Yes, sir. There's just us."

"Well, come in and welcome," said the doctor.

Once inside he searched about in the larder and soon had two plates of cold meat before us. While we ate he asked us questions and we told him our story. I could see that he was surprised and concerned at our traveling so far alone.

After we had eaten he led us up the back stairs to a small guest room.

"Sleep as late as you wish in the morning," he told us. "You'll have to get used to sleeping during the day and traveling at night."

That night for the first time in our lives we slept between sheets. I can still remember how clean and smooth and rich they felt.

Questions

1. What did Obie and Amos carry with them instead of a pass?

2. Why do you think the Strausses were so kind to Obie and Amos?

3. What mistake did Obie make? What saved Obie and Amos from paying for that mistake?

4. The Strausses thought the trip to Henderson would take the boys two days. How long did the trip actually take? Why didn't it take two days?

5. Amos compared the Strausses to a hurricane lamp. Why did Amos use that comparison?

6. Which words from the story were used in place of the underlined words?
   a. If anyone asks, tell him we are peculiar people. (page 473)
   b. Get cold meat from the food storage room. (page 478)

Activity   Write a Scene for a Radio Play

Suppose that you are planning to present "Steal Away Home" as a radio play. You can use the *dialogue,* or conversation, that is already in the story and also add more. There is little dialogue between Obie and Amos on the road from Raleigh to Henderson. Yet that conversation could tell your listeners about some important events and also what the boys think and feel about their situation. Write that on-the-road scene as it would be read in a radio play.

Ambassador to the Enemy

From the novel *Caddie Woodlawn* by Carol Ryrie Brink

Illustrated by Dan Siculan

Caddie Woodlawn and her family pioneered the Wisconsin wilderness during the 1860s. At the age of eleven, Caddie was one of the strongest and most independent members of her large family. Her parents often allowed her to roam freely through the wilderness with her two brothers. They rarely made her stay at home.

Since she had been four years old, Caddie and her father had had a special friendship with John, one of the Indians who lived nearby. Other settlers, however, were fearful and not so trusting of the Indians. One night Caddie overheard some of the settlers planning an attack on the peaceful Indian village. Afraid for her friend John, Caddie rode her mare, Betsy, through the darkness to warn John of the intended attack.

Clip-clop-clip sounded Betsy's hoofs across the field. There was a treacherous slime of mud on the surface, but underneath it the clods were still frozen as hard as iron. Then the bare branches of the woods were all around them, and Caddie had to duck and dodge to save her eyes and her hair. Here the February thaw had not succeeded in clearing the snow. It stretched gray and dreary underfoot, treacherously rotted about the roots of the big trees. Caddie slowed her mare's pace and guided her carefully now. She did not want to lose precious time in floundering about in melting snow. Straight for the river she went. If the ice still held, she could get across here, and the going would be easier on the other side. Not a squirrel or a bird stirred in the woods. So silent! So silent! Only the clip-clop-clip of Betsy's hoofs.

Then the river stretched out before her, a long expanse of blue-gray ice under the gray sky.

"Carefully now, Betsy. Take it slowly, old girl." Caddie held a tight rein with one hand and stroked the horse's neck with the other. "That's a good girl. Take it slowly." Down the bank they went, delicately onto the ice. Betsy flung up her head, her nostrils distended. Her hind legs slipped on the ice and for a quivering instant she struggled for her balance. Then she found her pace. Slowly, cautiously, she went daintily forward, picking her way, but with a snort of disapproval for the wisdom of her young mistress. The ice creaked, but it was still sound enough to bear their weight. They reached the other side and scrambled up the bank. Well, so much done! Now for more woods.

There was no proper sunset that day, only a sudden lemon-colored rift in the clouds in the west. Then the clouds closed together again and darkness began to fall. The ride was long, but at last it was over.

Blue with cold, Caddie rode into the clearing where the Indians had built their winter huts. Dogs ran at her, barking, and there was a warm smell of smoke in the air. A fire was blazing in the center of the clearing. Dark figures moved about it. Were they preparing for an attack? Caddie's heart pounded as she drew Betsy to a stop. But, no, surely they were only old women bending over cooking pots. The running figures were children, coming now to swarm about her. Surely she and Father had been right! Tears began to trickle down Caddie's cold cheeks.

Now the men were coming out of the bark huts. More and more Indians kept coming toward her. But they were not angry, only full of wonder.

"John," said Caddie, in a strange little voice, which she hardly recognized as hers. "Where is John? I must see John."

"John," repeated the Indians, recognizing the name the white men had given to one of their men. They spoke with strange sounds among themselves, then one of them went running. Caddie sat her horse, half-dazed, cold to the bone, but happy inside. The Indians were not preparing an attack. Whatever the tribes farther west might be plotting, these Indians, whom Father and she trusted, were going about their business peacefully. If they could only get away now in time, before the white men came to kill them! Or, perhaps she could get home again in time to stop the white men from making the attack. Would those men whom she had heard talking by the cellar door believe a little girl when she told them that Indian John's tribe was at peace? She did not know.

Indian John's tall figure came toward her from one of the huts. His step was unhurried and his eyes were unsurprised.

"Are you lost, Miss Red Hair?" he inquired.

"No, no," said Caddie, "I am not lost, John. But I must tell you. Some white men are coming to kill you. You and your people must go away. You must not fight. You must go away. I have told you."

"You are cold," said John. He lifted Caddie off her horse and led her to the fire.

"I don't understand," said John, shaking his head in perplexity. "You speak too quick, Miss Red Hair."

Caddie tried again, speaking more slowly. "I came to tell you. Some bad men wish to kill you and your people. You must go away, John. My father is your friend. I came to warn you."

"Red Beard, he sent you?" asked John.

"No, my father did not send me," said Caddie. "No one knows that I have come. You must take your people and go away."

"Are you hungry?" John asked her and mutely Caddie nodded her head. Tears were running again and her teeth were chattering. John spoke to the women, standing motionless about the fire. Instantly they moved to do his bidding. One spread a buffalo skin for her to sit on. Another ladled something hot and tasty into a cup without a handle, a cup which had doubtless come from some settler's cabin. Caddie grasped the hot cup between her cold hands and drank. A little trickle of warmth seemed to go all over her body. She stretched her hands to the fire. Her tears stopped running and her teeth stopped chattering. She let the Indian children, who had come up behind her, touch her hair without flicking it away from them. John's dog came and lay down near her, wagging his tail.

"Now tell John again," said John, squatting beside her in the firelight.

Caddie began again, slowly. She told how the whites had heard that the Indians were coming to kill. She told how her father and she had not believed. She told how some of the people had become restless and planned to attack the Indians first. She begged John to go away with his tribe while there was still time. When she had finished John grunted and continued to sit on, looking into the fire. She did not know whether he had yet understood her. All about the fire were row on row of dark faces, looking at her steadily with wonder but no understanding. John knew more English than any of them, and yet, it seemed, he did not understand. Patiently she began again to explain.

But now John shook his head. He rose and stood tall in the firelight above the little white girl. "Come with me," he said.

Caddie rose uncertainly. She saw that it was quite dark now outside the ring of firelight, and a fine, sharp sleet was hissing down into the fire. John spoke in his own tongue to the Indians. What he was telling them she could not say, but their faces did not change. One ran to lead Betsy to the fire and another brought a spotted Indian pony that had been tethered at the edge of the clearing.

"Now we will go," said the Indian.

"I will go back alone," said Caddie, speaking distinctly. "You and your people must make ready to travel westward."

"Red Hair has spoken," said John. "John's people will go tomorrow." He lifted her onto her horse's back, and himself sprang onto the pony. Caddie was frightened again, frightened of the dark and cold, and uncertain of what John meant to do.

"I can go alone, John," she said.

"John will go, too," said the Indian.

He turned his pony into the faint woods trail by which she had come. Betsy, her head drooping under a slack rein, followed the spotted pony among the dark trees. Farther and farther behind they left the warm, bright glow of fire. Looking back, Caddie saw it twinkling like a bright star. It was something warm and friendly in a world of darkness and sleet and sudden, icy branches. From the bright star of the

Indian fire, Caddie's mind leaped forward to the bright warmth of home. They would have missed her by now. Would Katie tell where she had gone? Would they be able to understand why she had done as she had?

She bent forward against Betsy's neck, hiding her face from the sharp needles of sleet. It seemed a very long way back. But at last the branches no longer caught at her skirts. Caddie raised her head and saw that they had come out on the open riverbank. She urged Betsy forward beside the Indian pony.

"John, you must go back now. I can find my way home. They would kill you if they saw you."

John only grunted. He set his moccasined heels into the pony's flanks, and led the way onto the ice. Betsy shook herself with a kind of shiver all through her body, as if she were saying, "No! No! No!" But Caddie's stiff fingers pulled the rein tight and made her go. The wind came down the bare sweep of the river with tremendous force, cutting and lashing them with the sleet. Betsy slipped and went to her knees, but she was up again at once and on her way across the ice. Caddie had lost the feeling of her own discomfort in fear for John. If a white man saw him riding toward the farm tonight, he would probably shoot without a moment's warning. Did John understand that? Was it courage or ignorance that kept John's figure so straight, riding erect in the blowing weather?

"John!" she cried. But the wind carried her voice away. "John!" But he did not turn his head.

Up the bank, through the woods, to the edge of the clearing they rode, Indian file. Then the Indian pony stopped.

Caddie drew Betsy in beside him. "Thank you!" she panted. "Thank you, John, for bringing me home. Go now. Go quickly." Her frightened eyes swept the farmstead. It was not dark and silent as it had been the night before. Lanterns were flashing here and there, people were moving about, voices calling.

"They're starting out after the Indians!" thought Caddie. "Father hasn't been able to stop them. They're going to massacre."

She laid her cold hand on the spotted pony's neck. "John!" she cried. "John, you must go quickly now!"

"John will go," said the Indian, turning his horse.

But before the Indian could turn back into the woods, a man had sprung out of the darkness and caught his bridle rein.

"Stop! Who are you? Where are you going?" The
words snapped out like the cracking of a whip, but
Caddie knew the voice.

"Father!" she cried. "Father! It's me. It's Caddie!"

"You, Caddie? Thank goodness!" His voice was
full of warm relief. "Hey, Robert, bring the lantern.
We've found her. Caddie! My little girl!"

Suddenly, Father was holding her close in his
arms, his beard prickling her cheek, and over his
shoulder she could see Robert Ireton, the farm hand,
with a bobbing lantern that threw odd shafts of
moving light among the trees. John, too, had dis-
mounted from his pony, and stood straight and still,
his arms folded across his chest.

"Oh, Father," cried Caddie, remembering again her mission and the last uncomfortable hours. "Father, don't let them kill John! Don't let them do anything bad to the Indians. The Indians are our friends, Father, truly they are. I've been to the camp and seen them. They mean us no harm."

"You went to the Indian camp, Caroline?"

"Yes, Father."

"That was a dangerous thing to do, my child."

"Yes, Father, but Kent and some of the men meant to go and kill them. I heard them say so. They said they wouldn't tell you they were going, and you weren't there. Oh, Father, what else could I do?"

He was silent for a moment, and Caddie stood beside him, shivering, and oppressed by the weight of his disapproval. In the swaying lantern light she searched the faces of the three men—Robert's honest mouth open in astonishment, Father's brows knit in thought, John's dark face impassive and remote with no one knew what thoughts passing behind it.

Caddie could bear the silence no longer. "Father, the Indians are our friends," she repeated.

"Is this true, John?" asked Father.

"Yes, it is true, Red Beard," answered John gravely.

"My people fear yours, John. Many times I have told them that you are our friends. They do not always believe."

"My people are foolish sometimes too," said John. "But not now. They will not kill the white men. Red Beard is my friend."

"He brought me home, Father," said Caddie. "You must not let them kill him."

"No, no, Caddie. There shall be no killing tonight, nor anymore, I hope, forever."

Over her head the white man and the red man clasped hands.

"I keep the peace, John," said Father. "The white men shall be your brothers."

"Red Beard has spoken. John's people will keep the peace."

For a moment they stood silent, their hands clasped in the clasp in friendship, their heads held high like two proud chieftains. Then John turned to his pony. He gathered the slack reins, sprang on the pony's back, and rode away into the darkness.

"Oh, my little girl," said Father. "You have given us a bad four hours. But it was worth it. Yes, it was worth it, for now we have John's word that there will be peace."

"But, Father, what about our own men? They meant to kill the Indians. I heard them."

"Those men are cowards at heart, Caddie. Their plans reached my ears when I got home, and I made short work of such notions. Well, well, you are shivering, my dear. We must get you home to a fire.

I don't know what your mother will have to say to you, Caddie."

But when they reached the farmhouse, the excitement of Caddie's return was overshadowed by another occurrence. Katie, who had sat pale and silent in a corner all during the search, rushed out of the house at the sound of Caddie's return.

"Caddie!" she cried. "Caddie!" Then suddenly she crumpled like a wilted flower, and had to be carried away to bed.

In the excitement of fetching smelling salts and water, Mrs. Woodlawn had only time to cry: "Caddie, my dear. You ought to be spanked. But I haven't time to do it now. There's a bowl of hot soup for you on the back of the stove."

In the kitchen Tom, Warren, Hetty, Maggie, and Silas, all the children, crowded around Caddie as she ate, gazing at her in silent admiration, as at a stranger from a far country.

"Golly, Caddie, what did they do to you?"

"Did they have on their war paint?"

"Did they wave their tomahawks at you?"

Caddie shook her head and smiled. She was so warm, so happy to be at home, so sleepy. . . .

Questions

1. One definition of *ambassador* is "an official messenger." In "Ambassador to the Enemy," does Caddie fit that definition? Why or why not?

2. Why do you think John took so long to respond to Caddie's message?

3. Do you think that Caddie acted wisely or foolishly in risking her life to warn the Indians? Explain your answer.

4. At the end, the other children gazed at Caddie "as at a stranger from a far country." Why did they gaze at Caddie so? What does the author mean?

5. Answer each question with *yes* or *no.* Then explain your answer with a definition of the word.
   a. If a face is *impassive,* does it show feelings?
   b. Is a *remote* place a nearby place?
   c. Is a *rift* in the clouds a split in the clouds?

Activity   Write a Secret Message

Imagine that Caddie is sending a secret message to Indian John, warning him of another attack or some other danger. Write Caddie's message. Then put the message into the number code below. Exchange and decode messages with a classmate.

1–Z	7–T	13–N	19–H	25–B
2–Y	8–S	14–M	20–G	26–A
3–X	9–R	15–L	21–F	
4–W	10–Q	16–K	22–E	
5–V	11–P	17–J	23–D	
6–U	12–O	18–I	24–C	

From *Elizabeth Blackwell*

A poem by Eve Merriam

Illustrated by John Slobodnik

Elizabeth Blackwell was the first woman doctor in the United States. Elizabeth was turned away from the leading medical schools because she was a woman. Elizabeth applied to more than twenty-five medical schools before she entered the Geneva College of Medicine in New York state. After Elizabeth got her medical degree, she opened the first hospital in the United States staffed only by women.

What will you do when you grow up,
nineteenth-century-young-lady?
Will you sew a fine seam and spoon dappled cream
under an apple tree shady?

Or will you be a teacher
in a dames' school
and train the little dears
by the scientific rule
that mental activity
may strain
the delicate female brain;
therefore let
the curriculum stress music, French, and especially
etiquette:
teach how to set
a truly refined banquet.
Question One:
What kind of sauce
for the fish dish,
and pickle or lemon fork?
Quickly, students,
which should it be?

Now Elizabeth Blackwell, how about you?
Seamstress or teacher, which of the two?
You know there's not much else that a girl can do.
Don't mumble, Elizabeth. Learn to raise your head.
"I'm not very nimble with a needle and thread.
"I could teach music—if I had to," she said,
"But I think I'd rather be a doctor instead."

"Is this some kind of joke?"
asked the proper menfolk.
"A woman be a doctor?
Not in our respectable day!
A doctor? An M.D.! Did you hear what she said?
She's clearly and indubitably out of her head!"

"Indeed, indeed, we are thoroughly agreed,"
hissed the ladies of society all laced in and prim,
"it's a scientific fact a doctor has to be a him.
"Yes, sir,
"'twould be against nature
"if a doctor were a her."

Hibble hobble bibble bobble
widdle waddle wag
tsk tsk
   twit twit
     flip flap flutter
       mitter matter mutter
      □

To medical schools she applied.
In vain.
And applied again
and again
and again

Elizabeth refused to hide
her feminine pride.
She drew herself up tall
(all five feet one of her!)

and tried again.
And denied again.
The letters answering no
mounted like winter snow.

Until the day
when her ramrod will
finally had its way.

REJECTION
REJECTION
REJECTION
REJECTION
REJECTION
REJECTION
REJECTION

After the twenty-ninth try,
there came from Geneva, New York
the reply
of a blessed
Yes!

Geneva,
Geneva,
how sweet the sound;
Geneva,
Geneva,
sweet sanctuary found. . . .

. . . . and the ladies of Geneva
passing by her in the street
drew back their hoopskirts
so they wouldn't have to meet.

When Elizabeth came to table,
their talking all would halt;
wouldn't so much as ask her
please to pass the salt.

In between classes
without a kind word,
Elizabeth dwelt
like a pale gray bird.

In a bare attic room
cold as a stone,
far from her family,
huddled alone

studying, studying
throughout the night
warming herself
with an inner light:

don't let it darken,
the spark of fire;
keep it aglow,
that heart's desire:

the will to serve,
to help those in pain—
flickered and flared
and flickered again—

until
like a fairy tale
(except it was true!)
Elizabeth received
her honored due.

The perfect happy ending
came to pass:
Elizabeth graduated . . .
. . . at the head of her class.

And the ladies of Geneva
all rushed forward now to greet
that clever, dear Elizabeth,
so talented, so sweet!

Wasn't it glorious
she'd won first prize?

Elizabeth smiled
with cool gray eyes

and she wrapped her shawl
against the praise:

how soon there might come
more chilling days.

Turned to leave
without hesitating.

She was ready now,
and the world was waiting.

The United States Grows and Changes

New Inventions

In 1876, the United States celebrated its hundredth birthday. One of the biggest events of the year was the world's fair in Philadelphia. This fair, called the Centennial Exposition, showed the world how far the United States had come in one hundred years. The most important exhibit was a giant steam engine. Many other inventions were exhibited by the United States: sewing machines, iron cookstoves, locomotives, knitting machines, and canned foods.

Corliss Steam Engine, 1876

Illustrated by Christa Kieffer

1867

1873

1876

The Exposition had one other item that was not getting much attention. A young inventor named Alexander Graham Bell was showing his latest invention, the telephone. Many people laughed at or did not even look at Mr. Bell's telephone. Little did they know that the telephone would soon be found in many homes.

Between 1865 and 1900, many other new inventions appeared. The typewriter (1867), barbed wire (1873), the phonograph (1877), the electric lightbulb (1879), the gasoline automobile (1885), the diesel engine (1892), the zipper (1893), the X-ray machine (1895), and the radio (1895) were introduced to Americans.

1877

All of these inventions became part of the lives of Americans between 1900 and 1920. At home, many women could use sewing machines, washing machines, and carpet sweepers to reduce the amount of time they spent on housework. Grocery stores offered canned food and fresh vegetables. Many women began to do more things outside their homes.

1879

Machines also changed people's lives in offices and factories. With the coming of the steam engine, steam-powered machines run by workers produced more goods faster than ever before. By 1900, more people in the United States made their living by producing goods and services than by farming. The United States had changed from an agricultural country to the largest manufacturing nation in the world.

1885

The Immigrants

The growth of factories and industry in the United States meant thousands of new jobs. People were needed to work in coal mines, to build railroads, to cut timber, to run machines. The workers came from Europe and Asia to the United States as *immigrants,* people who come to a new country to settle.

Twelve million immigrants came to the United States between 1865 and 1900. These immigrants came from countries such as Great Britain, Ireland, Germany, Sweden, Italy, Russia, and Hungary. They also came from China and Japan.

The immigrants came to the United States for many reasons. They came to look for gold or to find land and build new homes. They came to find work to support their families. They came to get away from poverty or war in their own countries.

Many of the immigrants settled in cities. There they went to work in factories or mills. Many worked long hours for little pay and lived in crowded housing with no conveniences. Often it seemed to the immigrants that their new lives in the United States were not much different from their old lives in the countries they had left.

Many other immigrants became part of the great wave of settlers who were moving over the land. The railroad had opened up the Great Plains and brought the Far West closer. More and more people traveled to these parts of the United States. These new settlers put barbed-wire fences around their land and built farms. By the end of the 1800s, the immigrants had helped settle the country from coast to coast.

Henry Ford and the Assembly Line

New ways of making things began in the early 1900s. Many of these new ideas came from a man named Henry Ford. Henry Ford owned an automobile company that had introduced a car called the *Model T* (1908). Unlike other cars of the time, the Model T was a plain, simple car that many people could afford to buy.

Ford's car was inexpensive mainly because his factories were based on a new way of working. In Ford's automobile factories, Model Ts were made on *assembly lines.* These were long lines of workers, who each had one special job. The parts of each Model T were put on a belt that moved past the different workers. Each worker did one task, such as bolting two pieces of metal together or adding a nut and bolt. The worker did that job over and over as the pieces passed by on the belt.

Henry Ford

Since each worker had only one job to do, the worker learned to do that job very quickly. This assembly-line process allowed large numbers of cars to be made quickly and cheaply. Ford, therefore, could sell the cars for a low price.

Many other companies began to use Ford's assembly-line idea. More products at lower prices became available. Advertisements in popular magazines told people about the products. New department stores or mail-order houses sold these products. Many kinds of products that once only the rich could afford to buy could now be bought by everyone.

Henry Ford wanted to raise workers' pay and improve working conditions. Between 1910 and 1920, many organizations to help workers were started. These organizations worked for more laws guaranteeing shorter work days and better working conditions for workers. They worked for hospital care for workers and their families. Conditions improved for many factory workers during the early 1900s.

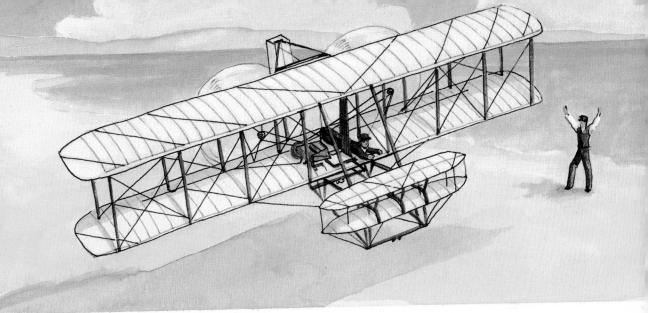

The Wright Brothers and the Airplane

In 1903, the airplane flew into American history at Kitty Hawk, North Carolina. Two brothers, Wilbur and Orville Wright, made four different flights into the air. The longest flight on that day, December 17, 1903, was for 825 feet in 59 seconds.

Only five other people saw the flight. Only three newspapers in the country reported on the flights. The reports were based on hearsay, and were short and inaccurate. Many people laughed at the Wright brothers' invention as they had done with the telephone.

For the next several years, the Wright brothers worked on perfecting their machine of wire, wood, and canvas. They also worked on changing public opinion about their airplane. In 1909, the brothers formed a company to manufacture airplanes. One of the first planes was ordered by the United States government.

By 1918, airplanes were carrying mail across the United States. The pilots on these flights used railroad tracks as landmarks. They flew only during daylight hours. They had to land every few hours to refuel. Airports existed only at major cities. By 1920, however, many of the problems were being solved. Mail flights across the country happened regularly, taking about three-and-a-half days.

Other Changes

By 1920, the United States had changed and grown tremendously. Then it seemed that the country began to "shrink." Bell's telephone, Ford's car, the Wright brothers' airplane—all these inventions brought far parts of the country closer together. People traveled longer distances, more often and more easily than ever before. News also traveled faster. The radio and the telephone brought news from city to city almost at once.

For many people, the early 1920s were years of happiness and excitement. New machines were doing jobs that were once done by people. The same new machines were opening up new areas of work. Many people were learning new skills. More women were working outside the home or going to college. People were using new ways of travel to visit new places and have new experiences. The United States and its people were growing and changing and would continue to do so in the years ahead.

Questions

1. What were some of the inventions that changed Americans' way of living between 1870 and 1920?

2. How did life change for people during these years?

3. Why did immigrants come to the United States?

4. What did Henry Ford contribute to manufacturing? to American society?

5. What does the statement "The United States began to shrink" mean?

Activities

1. **Share What You Learn**

    Below are some of the important events in United States history between 1870 and 1930. Choose one of them and use library books to learn more about the event. Share what you learn with your classmates.
    a. the coming of the immigrants
    b. changes in communication
    c. changes in transportation

2. **Find Out How Life Changed**

    The way Americans lived changed greatly between 1870 and 1930. Choose one of the topics below. Use books, pictures, records, and other library resources to find out how American life changed during those fifty years. Write or give a short report on what you learn.
    a. clothing
    b. houses and furniture
    c. entertainment
    d. music
    e. art
    f. travel

Our First Thanksgiving

From the novel *Call Me Ruth* by Marilyn Sachs

Illustrated by George Suyeoka

Mama and ten-year-old Rifka were finally in America. They had traveled a long way from their small Russian village to the city of New York to join Papa. When Rifka was just a baby, Papa had come to America to find a new and better way of life for himself and his family. Now, almost ten years later, Papa had finally saved enough money to bring them to America.

In Russia, Rifka and her mother had lived with Rifka's grandmother, Bubba, who cooked and cared for them. They had lived according to the "old country" ways. Now, in America, everything changed. Rifka's name became Ruth. Ruth was learning all about America, and she loved it. Ruth loved her new American clothes, the American way of talking, her new teacher, and her new school. When the American holiday of Thanksgiving came, Ruth wanted to celebrate it "the American way."

The week before Thanksgiving, Teacher taught us a song to sing for fun.

Over the river and through the wood,
To Grandfather's house we go;
The horse knows the way
To carry the sleigh
Through the white and drifted snow . . .

We drew pictures of turkeys and horns of plenty, and Teacher told us how she was going to spend the holiday with her parents and brothers and sisters. Her parents lived in the country, and every Thanksgiving all the children and grandchildren gathered at their house for the Thanksgiving feast. She described the menu to us—roast turkey with stuffing, cranberry sauce, mashed potatoes, home-baked rolls, salad, and apple and pumpkin pies. She told us how the dining room table would look, covered with a lovely, clean white cloth, the family china, and sparkling glasses.

"Ever since the Pilgrims came, Americans have always held a feast and thanked God that He brought them here to America," Miss O'Brien said.

I told my father and mother about Thanksgiving and what Miss O'Brien had said. "All Americans are supposed to have a feast and be thankful," I said.

My father said he would be working on Thanksgiving, and my mother said nothing.

"Mama," I asked, "why couldn't we prepare a feast and celebrate when Papa comes home from work?" I described to her the different kinds of food Miss O'Brien and her family would be eating on Thanksgiving.

My mother looked up at me from her sewing. There was a large pile of men's jackets on the kitchen table and she was finishing the buttonholes and collars. More and more now, during the busy season, my father brought home clothes from work to finish at home. He still had not paid off all the debts he had incurred from bringing us over and setting up our own household.

Papa was a tailor and worked on men's suits. Every morning when there was work, he left the house at seven-fifteen to walk to his shop by eight o'clock. Some nights he came home at eight and sometimes even later. Whenever he brought work home, he might stay up until midnight finishing it. Mama worked with him. During the day too, he left a pile of clothes for her to finish and often when I came home from school she would be sitting there, sewing by the kitchen table.

"I don't know," said my mother, helplessly, "what it means—Thanksgiving."

"Mama," I said impatiently, "I told you already. It's a holiday when Americans say thanks to God because He brought them over here to America."

"I don't know," my mother repeated, shaking her head.

"You have to go to school, Fanny," said my father. "I keep telling you. Go over to one of the classes at the Educational Alliance. Take off an hour a day. Learn to speak. I did when I first came. I went for a couple of years and now I can speak as good as anybody and I know all about the American holidays."

"I'll go, I'll go," my mother promised and she bent her head over her sewing again.

My father and I looked at each other, and then he said, "Maybe Sadie is going to make a Thanksgiving dinner. Maybe she'll ask us."

"No," I told him, "Shirley said they're going to Uncle Barney's cousin's house. Papa, why can't we have our own Thanksgiving dinner? I'll help Mama. Please, Papa!"

"Well!" My papa looked doubtfully over at my mother. He didn't say anything but we both knew that my mother was not a balabusta, not a woman who was either a good cook or an accomplished housekeeper. Bubba had been right. My mother tried but managing a household was still difficult for her.

"Please, Papa! Teacher says all Americans are supposed to have a Thanksgiving dinner."

"So what do you say, Fanny?" asked my papa. "It will make Ruthie happy."

"But I don't even know what it is," my mother cried. "Cranberry sauce and pumpkin pie? I don't know."

"I'll help you, Mama," I said. "I'll go shopping with you. We don't need the cranberry sauce and the pumpkin pie. And we don't have to make the rolls either. Please, Mama!"

My mother did not exactly say yes but my father and I began making plans. "Maybe," said my father, "I can go in at six in the morning and get off a little earlier at night. And maybe I can ask Sol Becker to come too. He works next to me in my shop. Poor man, he's all alone here and he has no family. Like I was all those years. But now—I've got my family. I really have something to be thankful about."

I sat in my father's lap while my mother kept sewing and the two of us worked out the details for Thanksgiving. I would come right home from school on the Wednesday before Thanksgiving and go shopping with Mama. Papa said we should buy a chicken instead of a turkey since it would cost less and besides we were only going to be four people. On Thursday, Mama and I would do the cooking, fix up the house, and set the table. Papa said he would buy a cake and some rolls in a bakery on the way home from work.

Mama and I went to the chicken market on Wednesday afternoon. We inspected the live chickens in their crates, all clacking away at the tops of their lungs. Mama couldn't make up her mind. "I don't know," she kept saying, "I don't know." Finally, I picked one out—a noisy one with angry little eyes.

After the butcher had slaughtered it, I helped Mama pluck it. She began laughing as the feathers tickled our noses and made both of us sneeze. It felt good to be laughing again with my mother. We walked back through the crowded streets that day before Thanksgiving, rubbing up against other shoppers. We stood in front of pushcarts and bought our potatoes and our carrots and we argued about the prices and my mother's cheeks turned rosy again and her eyes shone.

On Thursday, I helped Mama clean the house. All the scattered papers and clothes I shoved under my parents' bed or stacked in a corner of their bedroom. Mama sang some of the old Yiddish songs from Europe as she worked.

I've fallen in love with a handsome lad
Who shines like the midday sun,
Oh, Mother dear, it's him that I love,
He's the only possible one.

"You should learn some English songs now that you're an American," I told my mother.

"I will, I will," she promised.

"I'll teach you one for Thanksgiving," I told her and began singing "Over the River and Through the Wood."

"Ofer de river and true de vood," my mother repeated.

"No, no, no," I corrected, just like Miss O'Brien, and showed her how to hold her lips to form the *th* and the *w*. My mother always learned new songs quickly and soon the two of us were singing it together.

When we set the kitchen table for dinner, Mama spread out a tablecloth that she had embroidered for her own trousseau before she was married. It was a very beautiful one with a center design of red and gold flowers. But my mother shook her head sadly when she looked at it. "The one I made for you," she said, "nobody ever saw a tablecloth like that."

I brought out the one napkin that remained and spread it open on the table. Both of us bent over it and studied it. There were blue and white flowers

connected by a delicate silver stem with silver leaves.
My mother's fingers stroked the flowers lovingly.
"At least," she said, "that wicked woman left me this
one so I can remember the pattern. It's a good thing
it got separated from the others and was hidden
under the stockings. Otherwise she would have stolen
it too. For that, at least, I should be thankful."

"See, Mama," I told her. "We all have something to
be thankful for. That's why today is Thanksgiving."

As we set our table, I thought about the Thanksgiving table in Teacher's house, about the fine white
china, the sparkling glasses, and the heavy silver. On
our table, only Mama's tablecloth was beautiful and
festive. Our dishes were cracked and unmatched and
the glasses were dull and of different sizes. But I
knew in the years to come, when my papa became
rich, we could buy a set of dishes and some shining
glasses. Then our table would look just like Teacher's.
I could wait.

By seven o'clock, all was ready. The potatoes and carrots simmered on the stove and the chicken baked and baked inside the oven. Mama and I dressed in our good clothes and waited for Papa in the warm, fragrant kitchen.

He came at seven-thirty with his friend Sol Becker.

"Mmm!" he said as he came through the door. "Something smells wonderful." He smiled as he looked around the tidy kitchen, at the table set for dinner, and at Mama and me, all dressed in our good clothes. Proudly, he introduced us to his friend.

The men washed up at the sink.

"Sit! Sit!" Mama ordered the two of them. She bustled around as if she was an experienced house-wife. My papa was looking with pleasure at Mama and me as we carried the food to the table. There was plenty of it even if the chicken was burned, the stuffing tasted like straw, and the mashed potatoes were dry and lumpy. It didn't matter that my mother still had not mastered the stove. Today was a special day—our first Thanksgiving in America.

Questions

1. What was Ruth learning at school to help her life in the United States?

2. If you had been the teacher, what would you have done to help Ruth?

3. What was difficult for Mama? How did Ruth help her?

4. What did Mama mean when she said, "The one I made for you . . . nobody saw a tablecloth like that"? What did this incident show that Mama could do well?

5. How did Mama have use her sewing ability in the United States?

6. What are two things Papa said or did that show that the family is likely to do well in the United States?

7. Copy the part of a sentence in the story that defines the word *balabusta*. Why is that word important in the story?

Activity   Write a One-paragraph Description

Years have gone by. Ruth has grown up. Now she is telling a group of children about her first Thanksgiving. She wants to tell them what that first Thanksgiving meant to her—not all the details, but the feelings that she had and still has about it. In one good paragraph, summarize what Ruth might say. Write it using *I*, as if Ruth is speaking.

Wilbur Wright and Orville Wright

A poem by Rosemary and Stephen Vincent Benét

Illustrated by George Suyeoka

*"If people were supposed to fly, they would have
been born with wings." That is what many people said
when they heard that Wilbur and Orville Wright were
building the first airplane. Yet Wilbur and Orville did
not pay any attention to the laughter of those around
them. They were determined to get their "aer-o-plane"
up in the sky, and in December of 1903, they did!*

Said Orville Wright to Wilbur Wright,
"These birds are very trying.
I'm sick of hearing them cheep-cheep
About the fun of flying.
A bird has feathers, it is true.
That must I freely grant.
But, must that stop us, W?"
Said Wilbur Wright, "It shan't."

And so they built a glider, first,
And then they built another.
—There never were two brothers more
Devoted to each other.

518

They ran a dusty little shop
For bicycle-repairing,
And bought each other soda-pop
And praised each other's daring.

They glided here, they glided there,
They sometimes skinned their noses,
—For learning how to rule the air
Was not a bed of roses—
But each would murmur, afterward,
While patching up his bro.
"Are we discouraged, W?"
"Of course we are not, O!"

And finally, at Kitty Hawk
In Nineteen-Three (let's cheer it!),
The first real airplane really flew
With Orville there to steer it!
—And kingdoms may forget their kings
And dogs forget their bites,
But, not till Man forgets his wings,
Will men forget the Wrights.

The Homecoming

A television play by Earl Hamner, Jr.

Illustrated by David Cunningham

The Depression years of the 1930s were hard for everyone in America. Money was in short supply and jobs were scarce. John Walton from Walton's Mountain in Virginia was one of the lucky ones. He had a job, but it was fifty miles from his family.

That family, headed by mother Olivia and oldest son John-Boy, worked and tried to stay together on Walton's Mountain. Olivia and the family greatly missed John, for he could not often afford the price of a bus ticket home. Now, however, the family knows that John is coming home because it is Christmas Eve. John has promised his family he will be home for Christmas, no matter what.

CHARACTERS

Narrator

John-Boy, 17

Jason, 14

Elizabeth, 5

Ben, 10

Mary Ellen, 13

Erin, 12

Jim-Bob, 7

Grandma

Grandpa

Olivia Walton

Ike

Sheriff

Announcer's Voice

Charlie Sneed

John Walton

Fade in on Walton's Mountain. Near the foot of the mountains is a small farm. We see the Walton children leading a cow into the barn.

Narrator *(John-Boy as a man):* I grew up in the Blue Ridge Mountains of Virginia. In the winter of 1933, I was trying hard to fill my father's shoes. It was the middle of the Depression. There was no work in our town. My father had to take a job fifty miles away. He could only come home on weekends. It was Christmas Eve, in the afternoon. We were looking forward to his homecoming.

(The children take the cow into the barn. John-Boy begins to milk her. Jason plays "Happy Days Are Here Again" on a harmonica.)

John-Boy: Play something Christmasy, Jason.

Jason: It's not Christmas yet. (*He goes on playing.*)

John-Boy: Well, it's Christmas Eve.

Elizabeth: When will it really be Christmas?

John-Boy: Tonight at midnight. (*To the whole group*) I want you all to listen to me a minute. (*Jason stops playing the harmonica.*) Try not to worry Mama today.

Ben: Something wrong?

John-Boy: She's got a lot on her mind.

Mary Ellen: Like what?

John-Boy: Daddy promised to be home early today. He's not here yet.

Erin: Daddy will get here.

John-Boy: Sure he will. But he's

got to pick up his paycheck and cash it. Then he has to catch a bus to Charlottesville. And another bus to Hickory Creek. Then he's got to hitchhike six miles. Well, let's get this wood in the house. We'll have a warm fire when he gets here.

(They all carry some wood into the house. Then they go into the kitchen. Grandpa Walton is sitting at the table. Grandma is putting bowls of soup on the table.)

Grandma: Come and eat before your soup gets cold.

Jim-Bob: I'm hungry enough to eat a horse.

Grandma: If this Depression gets any worse, you may have to.

Grandpa: Oh, it will never come to that. Franklin D. Roosevelt is going to put this country back on its feet. You watch my words.

John-Boy *(copying President Roosevelt):* My friends, and you are my friends—

Grandma: You hush your disrespect. He's your President!

Grandpa: You get the cow in the barn, son?

John-Boy: Yes, sir.

Grandpa: Storm's going to hit here any time now.

Mary Ellen *(who questions everything)*: How do you know that, Grandpa?

Grandpa: I feel it in my bones.

Mary Ellen: How do you explain that?

Grandpa: It's a science, honey. *(The children hear their mother singing, as she comes up from the cellar.)*

Erin: Mama's got the Christmas spirit.

Olivia *(enters):* Who wants to see something pretty?

Jim-Bob: Me!

Elizabeth: Me!

Olivia *(holding up a Christmas cactus):* I stuck it in the cellar last fall. Now look. It's blooming!

Mary Ellen: How can a plant know it's Christmas?

Ben: Maybe it feels it in its bones, like Grandpa.

Olivia: I rooted this plant from one Mama used to have. It's seventeen years old.

Grandma: Has it been that long?

Olivia: I started it when John and I were married.

Mary Ellen: Why did you marry Daddy, Mama?

Olivia: Same reason as anybody. Love.

Mary Ellen: How did you know you loved him?

Olivia: I just *knew*. He was a handsome thing in those days. Wasn't he, Grandma?

Grandma: All my boys were handsome.

Grandpa: Took after their daddy.

Grandma: Listen to that old man!

Ben *(looking out the window):* You know those bread crumbs you put out, Mama? The red bird ate every speck.

Jim-Bob: That red bird is going to freeze tonight.

Grandpa: He won't freeze. He's got the knack of getting through the winter. Otherwise, he'd have gone south with the other birds.

Elizabeth: I wish Daddy could fly. *(The children laugh at her. Her feelings are hurt.)*

Jim-Bob *(explaining for her):* If he could fly, he wouldn't have to wait for the bus.

Jason: If Daddy goes around flying, somebody might think he's a turkey buzzard. They'd shoot him down.

Olivia *(putting on her coat):* I'm going to get some sugar for my applesauce cake.

Grandpa: I'll go with you. You'll need help carrying the sugar and all the other stuff for Christmas dinner.

Olivia: I wish John would get here with some money. If he doesn't, all we'll have for dinner is applesauce cake. You stay here, Grandpa. I can carry the sugar. *(Cut to the barn. The children are cracking walnuts for the applesauce cake.)*

Elizabeth: I wrote a letter to Santa Claus.

Jason: What did you ask him to bring?

Elizabeth: A whole page of dolls in the Sears Roebuck Catalogue.

John-Boy: I bet I know what you want, Ben.

Ben: A catcher's mitt.

John-Boy: I thought so. How about you, Jim-Bob?

Jim-Bob: A teddy bear. Daddy said he'd talk to Santa Claus about it.

Jason: I was thinking about writing him myself.

John-Boy: What are you asking for, Jason?

Jason *(laughing):* A piano!

Ben: That man can't carry a piano down the chimney.

Mary Ellen: Everybody's so ignorant around here!

Erin: What makes you say that?

Mary Ellen: There's no such thing as Santa Claus!

Jim-Bob: I don't believe you.

Mary Ellen: That's because you're ignorant. *(John-Boy swats her on the seat. She jumps up, ready to box with him.)* Son, you're going to be sorry you did that! *(John-Boy goes on cracking walnuts.)* Stand up and fight like a man!

Erin: I'm going to tell Mama what you just said. I hope she washes your mouth out with soap.

Mary Ellen *(to Erin):* You little mealy-mouth! I hope you get a bad cold and sneeze your eyeballs loose!

John-Boy: You want another swat, Mary Ellen?

Mary Ellen: I'm not having anything to do with any of you. *(She starts walking around in a circle.)*

Jim-Bob: What's the matter with her?

John-Boy: She's just crazy. Everybody goes crazy when they're thirteen.

Ben: Did you go crazy when you were thirteen?

John-Boy: I didn't have to. I was too busy looking after you kids. *(Jason starts playing his harmonica. Mary Ellen joins the group again.)*

Elizabeth: Mary Ellen? There really is a Santa Claus isn't there?

Mary Ellen: Sure there is, honey. *(Daringly to John-Boy)* And my name is Charlie McCarthy! *(Cut to the general store. Olivia enters. Ike, the owner, looks up.)*

Ike: Merry Christmas, Olivia. Where's John?

Olivia: He's not home yet, Ike.

Ike: He'll be along. He wouldn't

stay away from home on Christmas Eve.

Olivia: Oh, he'll get here, if he can. But it's fifty miles on slippery roads. Then that long walk from the bus. I didn't mean to tell you my troubles, Ike. I came to buy two pounds of sugar.

Ike *(getting the sugar):* Did you notice the new toys we've got? Your little one has had her eye on that doll over there.

Olivia *(looking at the doll):* It's hard to explain the Depression to children.

Ike: The price tag says ninety-eight cents. I can let you have it for sixty-five cents.

Olivia: Thank you just the same, Ike.

Ike: If cash is the problem, I can give you credit.

Olivia: Don't tempt me, Ike. You know John and I have never bought anything on credit in our lives.

Ike: Just thought I'd make an offer.

Olivia: And I appreciate it. *(She takes the sugar.)* Merry Christmas, Ike.

(Olivia leaves the store. A man comes in.)

Ike: What are you doing out this way, Sheriff? Looking for somebody?

Sheriff: Maybe.

Ike: You wouldn't put a man in jail on Christmas Eve, would you?

Sheriff: I would if I could catch him.

Ike: What man you looking for? *(The Sheriff gives him a newspaper clipping. As Ike reads it aloud, he begins to smile.)* "Robin Hood Bandit strikes again. Many local citizens are enjoying Christmas this year due to the Robin Hood Bandit. Every Christmas since 1929, needy people have found food at their back doors. At the same time, food has been missing from local markets. This year, it is the J and M Produce Company. All their hams and turkeys were robbed last night."

Sheriff: He's making me the laughing stock of the whole county. You know, it's funny he's never robbed you. Maybe you know who he is. *(Ike doesn't say anything.)*

(Cut to the Walton living room. Grandpa is trying to tune in the radio. All he gets is static.)

Grandma: I don't think you know how to work a radio.

Grandpa: Don't tell me I don't know how to work a radio. *(He hits the radio. The static gets worse.)*

Grandma: You're only going to break it again. *(She turns the dials. Then a voice is heard clearly.)*

Announcer's Voice: The snow has caused a number of accidents. *(Olivia enters.)* A bus overturned on Route 29. No deaths have been reported. But two men are still trapped inside the bus. The injured have been taken to the University Hospital in Charlottesville.

Olivia *(turns off radio):* I wish it were spring.

Grandpa: Daughter, we don't know if John was on that bus.

Olivia: Don't tell the children about this. Has anybody seen John-Boy?

Grandma: He went up to his room. And I heard him lock the door again.

Olivia: What does he do up there? *(She goes to the stairway.)* John-Boy!

(Inside his room, John-Boy stuffs a pad and pencil under his mattress. Then he goes downstairs.)

John-Boy: Yes, Mama?

Olivia: What were you doing up there?

John-Boy: Nothing, Mama.

Olivia: Then why was the door locked?

John-Boy: I guess it just got locked.

Olivia: A door doesn't get locked by itself.

John-Boy: Sometimes I like a little privacy, Mama.

Olivia *(to Grandpa):* John usually gets the tree. But maybe you and John-Boy better get one this year.

Grandpa: I know where there's a real pretty one.

(Cut to a field of pines. John-Boy follows Grandpa.)

John-Boy: Grandpa, have you ever been away from here?

Grandpa: Not if I could help it. I've lived here all my life.

John-Boy: How did we get Walton's Mountain?

Grandpa: My granddaddy came here in 1789. He had nothing but an ax, a plow, a mule, and a rifle. He built a log cabin. Then he planted a garden, and started raising a family. The Waltons have been here ever since.

John-Boy: Have we got a deed? Something to show that we own Walton's Mountain?

Grandpa: You can't own a mountain, son. No more than you can own the ocean or a piece of sky. You live on it. You take life from it. And once you're dead, you rest in it *(He stops walking.)* There's your tree, boy.

(Cut to the Walton living room. The children are decorating the tree. Mary Ellen brings in a bird's nest.)

Jason: What's that?

Mary Ellen: A blue jay's nest.

Jason: You can't put that dirty thing on the tree.

Mary Ellen: It's not dirty.

Erin: You're such a crazy!

Mary Ellen: Turn blue, Erin. *(She puts the nest on a tree branch.)*

Erin: Look what she's done, John-Boy!

John-Boy: Santa Claus will take one look at that thing—and go right back up the chimney.

Elizabeth: And I won't get my doll! *(She starts to cry.)*

Olivia *(enters):* What's the matter now?

Erin: Mary Ellen made Elizabeth cry. And she ruined the tree with a smelly old bird's nest!

Olivia *(looks at the nest):* That's nice there. It looks real natural.
(They hear a sound at the back door.)

Ben: There's Daddy!
(They rush into the kitchen. John-Boy opens the door.)

John-Boy *(disappointed):* It's Charlie Sneed.

Olivia: Come on in, Charlie.
(Charlie comes in with a package. The children go back to the living room.)

Charlie: I usually get a bigger welcome around here.

Olivia: We're glad to see you, Charlie. But we thought maybe you were John.

Charlie: Ain't that rascal home yet?

Olivia: We're right worried. Would you like a cup of coffee or something?

Charlie: I can't stay, Olivia. I knew John wouldn't have a chance to go hunting. And I thought he'd like a little meat on the table. *(He gives her the package. Olivia unwraps it. It's a large turkey.)*

Olivia: Charlie, I don't know how to thank you.

Charlie: I shot him over on Wales Mountain.

Grandma: That don't look like a wild turkey to me. Never saw one wrapped up so fancy.

Charlie: I wrapped it to look Christmasy. Well, I've got some more stops to make. Merry Christmas, everybody.

Olivia: Much obliged to you, Charlie. Stop by tomorrow.

Charlie: I'll do that. Good night.
(He goes out.)

Grandma: I never saw a wild turkey with a price tag still on it.
(Later, the children are in bed. Olivia, Grandma, and Grandpa are listening to the radio. There have been more highway accidents. And no more buses are running.)

Grandpa: There's nothing to do but sit and wait.

Olivia: I cannot wait another minute! *(She goes up to John-Boy's room. The door is locked.)* John-Boy, unlock this door! *(After a pause, the door opens. Olivia enters the room.)* Are you smoking cigarettes up here?

John-Boy: No, Mama.

Olivia *(sees a lump under the bedcovers):* Are you hiding something in that bed?

John-Boy: Yes.

Olivia: What is it?

John-Boy: A writing pad.

Olivia: Why would you want to hide a writing pad?

John-Boy: Mama, I've got a right to some privacy!

Olivia: Is it something you're ashamed of?

John-Boy (*pulls out the pad*)*:* You know what's on this pad, Mama? All my secret thoughts. How I feel and what I think about. I have to write them down. If things had been different, I might have become something different. I would have liked to—to be a writer.

Olivia (*after a pause*)*:* If that's what you want, couldn't you still try?

John-Boy: Not in these times. You have to go to college to be a writer. And we haven't got the money. Besides, Daddy wants me to learn a trade.

Olivia: He just wants you to know how to make a living.

John-Boy: Well, I could never do that by scribbling things on paper.

Olivia: We'll talk about this some more. Right now, there's something else to think about. There are no more buses tonight.

John-Boy: Daddy won't get home, will he?

Olivia: Not unless somebody goes after him. Try to find Charlie Sneed. He's probably at Ike's store. Ask him to drive you to Charlottesville. Here's a dollar for the gas. You might meet your father on the way. If not, go to the bus station. If he's not there, try the hospital.

John-Boy: Hospital?

Olivia: A bus went off the road today. One man is dead. Some others are hurt.

John-Boy: I better get moving.
(*Cut to the general store. John-Boy finds Charlie Sneed in handcuffs. The Sheriff has arrested him for stealing the hams and turkeys. Charlie gives John-Boy the keys to his truck. We see John-Boy driving through the night. And we hear his thoughts. He remembers a talk he had with his father.*)

John's Voice: A man should learn a trade.

John-Boy's Voice: There are things I can't tell you, Daddy.

John's Voice: It worries me when you sit up there in your room all the time.

John-Boy's Voice: I want to be like you, Daddy. I'm trying.

John's Voice: You'll find your way. Mine is my own.

A sputtering automobile engine recalls John-Boy to reality. The car has run out of gas, and John-Boy leaves the auto, heading for the nearest building, the Baptist church. The minister, Mr. Hawthorne, has no gasoline, and sends John-Boy to the Baldwin house, where the elderly Baldwin sisters invite John-Boy to come in and dry off. The sisters have no gasoline, either, but help John-Boy continue his search in their sleigh. A fallen tree across the road stops their search, and the sisters take John-Boy home. John-Boy thanks the sisters and goes into the house.

(Cut to the Walton living room. The children have heard sleigh bells, and come downstairs. The younger children think it's Santa Claus. They are disappointed when John-Boy comes inside.)

Olivia *(upset):* What am I going to do with you, boy? You go to look for your father. And you end up joyriding with two crazy ladies!

John-Boy: They took me to look for Daddy, Mama. But a tree was down in the road. So they brought me home.

Olivia *(sorry she has yelled at him):* That was real thoughtful of them. Well, you children better go along to bed now.

Mary Ellen: I want to wait up for Daddy.

Erin: Me, too.

Olivia: Tomorrow's Christmas. If you're sleepy, you won't enjoy it.

Jason: Where do you think Daddy is, Mama?

Olivia: I wish I knew. *(There is a loud thud on the roof.)* What's that?

Elizabeth: Santa Claus!

John-Boy: Something's on the roof. *(He opens the door. John Walton stands there, smiling. He holds a lot of packages.)* Daddy!

(John comes in. The children run to him. He hugs them, dropping his packages. Then he looks over at his wife. He knows what she's been through.)

Olivia: You'll want some coffee. *(She goes to the stove. Suddenly, she covers her face with her hands.)*

Mary Ellen: Don't cry now, Mama. He's home!

John *(goes over to Olivia):* What a woman I married! *(He picks her up and whirls her around.)*

Olivia: Put me down, you crazy thing. I set a good example for these children. And you act like a crazy man.

John *(puts her down and hugs her):* I'll have my coffee now. I'm frozen through and through.

Olivia: I was sure you were in a bus accident.

John: No. But the buses stopped running. So I started hitchhiking. I spent half the day with my thumb in the air. I got as far as Hickory Creek. Then I walked the rest of the way.

Ben: What's in those bundles, Daddy?

John: Be doggoned if I know. Something came flying across the sky when I came up. Landed on the roof.

Jim-Bob: We heard it, Daddy!

John: I looked up and saw a team of animals. They had something pointy on their heads.

Elizabeth: Reindeer!

John: I don't know. I never saw one before. But this old man in a red suit got out. I thought he was somebody trying to break into the house. So I picked up the biggest rock I could find.

Ben *(horrified):* You hit him with a rock?

John: Not exactly. But I scared him off. And he left these packages. *(He picks one up and gives it to Elizabeth.)* I think this one is for you.

Elizabeth *(finds a doll inside):* I never in all my life saw anything so pretty.
(John gives a present to each child. They tear into them.)

Jim-Bob: A teddy bear!

Ben *(holding up a catcher's mitt):* Anybody want to play ball?

Erin *(holding a dress):* Mama, look!

Mary Ellen *(also holding a dress):* It's too pretty to wear.
(Jason starts playing an expensive harmonica he has gotten. John-Boy watches his brothers and sisters.)

John *(to John-Boy):* Open yours, son. *(John-Boy finds five notebooks and a pen. He looks up surprised.)* I wonder how the news got all the way to the North Pole that you wanted to be a writer?

John-Boy: I guess he's a smart man.

John: I don't know a thing about the writing trade, boy. But you give it the best you've got.

John-Boy: Yes, sir.

John *(giving a package to Olivia):* This one must be for you.

Olivia *(unwraps a pot of flowers in bloom):* In the dead of winter. It's a miracle!

Ben *(points to two more presents):* There's two more.

John: Grandma and Grandpa.

Elizabeth: Everybody got a present but you, Daddy.

John: I've got Christmas every day in you kids and your mama.

Olivia: All right, everybody to bed now. You can play in the morning. *(Everybody goes upstairs and gets into bed. As the lights go out, we hear everyone call "good night" to everyone else.)*

Narrator *(John-Boy as a man):* I became the writer I promised my father I'd be. My work took me far from Walton's Mountain. My mother still lives there. My father died in 1969. My brothers and sisters, now with children of their own, live nearby. We are still a close family. We see each other when we can. And we will never forget that Christmas Eve in 1933.

Questions

1. What was the *homecoming* in this television play? Why was it such an important event?

2. Why do you think Ike smiled as he read about the Robin Hood Bandit?

3. Be John Walton. Answer these questions.
   a. What made the loud thud on the roof? (page 536)
   b. What did you give John-Boy? Why did you select that gift?

4. The Walton family members argued with each other in the play. Does this mean that they were angry and did not like each other? Explain.

Activity   Prepare to Write Details of Setting

Authors use *local color*—details about a specific time and place—to help us imagine what it was like to be in a setting such as the Blue Ridge Mountains during the Depression in 1933. In "The Homecoming" local color includes a song sung and played during the Depression. It also includes several names famous during that time: President Franklin D. Roosevelt, Charlie McCarthy, and the Sears Roebuck Catalogue.

If you were writing a play about your own time and place, you could make the play more believable by including local color. List at least four names or items for local color to be included under each of these topics: names of well-known people, famous events, and things that people use that will help give the feeling of your own time and place.

CONNECTIONS

Many Faces of America

People whose ancestors came from all parts of the world have helped make this country great. These are some of those people and their contributions to American life and history.

Jane Addams (1860–1935). English and German ancestry. Jane Addams set up a "settlement house" called Hull House in Chicago in 1889. Her immigrant neighbors came there for education, social life, and help. She also fought for laws to improve these people's living and working conditions.

Ruth Asawa (1926–   ). Japanese ancestry. Ruth Asawa's sculptures and fountains brighten many public places in her home city, San Francisco. Others are in art museums across the country. In 1968, she started an art program for schoolchildren, bringing artists to the public schools.

Henry Bergh (1813–1888). German ancestry. Henry Bergh founded the American Society for Prevention of Cruelty to Animals in 1866. He fought for laws to keep people from mistreating horses, dogs, cats, and other animals. In 1874, he started a society for prevention of cruelty to children.

Illustrated by Mike Muir

Shirley Chisholm (1924–   ). African/Caribbean ancestry. Independent Shirley Chisholm called herself "unbought and unbossed" when she became the first black Congresswoman in 1968. She worked for laws to help women, blacks, and poor people. She was the first black woman to run for President (1972).

Samuel Clemens (1835–1910). English and Irish ancestry. Writing under the name Mark Twain, Samuel Clemens praised the best of American life and made fun of the worst. His best-known books, such as *Huckleberry Finn* (1885), were about boyhood adventures and the everyday life of small towns.

Thomas A. Edison (1847–1931). Dutch and Scottish ancestry. Thomas Edison received patents for 1099 different inventions. Among the best known are the electric light, the phonograph, and the movie camera. He also improved the telegraph, the typewriter, and the telephone.

Amadeo Peter Giannini (1870–1949). Italian ancestry. A. P. Giannini started the Bank of Italy in San Francisco, California, in 1904. Unlike other banks, it made loans to ordinary working people. Loans from Giannini helped people rebuild the city after the 1906 earthquake. His bank became the Bank of America.

Woody Guthrie (1912–1967). Scottish and Irish ancestry. In the Great Depression of the 1930s, Woody Guthrie wrote and sang songs about people who had lost their jobs or farms but were bravely trying to "get by." Other Woody Guthrie songs, such as "This Land Is Your Land," describe America's beauty.

Dolores Huerta (1930–   ). American Indian and Spanish ancestry. Dolores Huerta has worked for better pay and working conditions for people who work on large farms in the Southwest.

Belva Lockwood (1830–1917). Scottish ancestry. In 1879, Belva Lockwood became the first woman lawyer allowed to practice before the United States Supreme Court. She ran for President of the United States in 1884. She wanted equal rights for all Americans, including women and blacks.

Maria Mitchell (1818–1889). English ancestry. In 1847, Maria Mitchell discovered an unknown comet through a telescope, the first person to do so. The King of Denmark sent her a gold medal for her discovery. She taught astronomy for 23 years at Vassar, an American women's college.

Garrett Morgan (1877–1963). African ancestry. In 1912, Garrett Morgan invented a device called the Safety Hood. It protected fire fighters against poison gases in burning buildings. His other inventions include the three-color electric traffic signal, patented in 1923.

John Muir (1838–1914). Scottish ancestry. John Muir wrote many books about the beauty of America's wild lands, especially the southwestern mountains. He became friends with President Theodore Roosevelt. They worked together to preserve wilderness lands as national parks and national monuments.

Maria Tallchief (1925–   ). American Indian (Osage) and Scottish/Irish ancestry. Maria Tallchief became one of America's most famous ballerinas. She danced important roles in many ballets such as *The Firebird* and *Swan Lake*. In *The Nutcracker,* she danced the role of the Sugar Plum Fairy.

Activities

1. **Prepare a Report**

   Choose one of the people described in this article. Use books in the library to find out more about that person and what he or she did. Report to your classmates about what you learn.

2. **Research Information**

   People from many countries and *cultures,* or ethnic groups, have helped to make America great. Use books in the library to find out when most people belonging to a particular culture came to the United States, what work they did, and what problems (if any) they had. Find out about at least two famous Americans who belong to this group, other than those named in this article. Take notes that you could use in preparing a written oral report.

The Fourth

Light them up, America,
Your sizzling candles.
Shoot them sky high—

Let the blue air
Of this birthday night
Explode them into billions
    of dizzying stars,
Then, blow them out with a wish

    for everyone
    who stands
    below

    watching,
    waiting,
    shouting,
    singing

Happy Birthday to You!

—Myra Cohn Livingston

BOOKSHELF

An Orphan for Nebraska by Charlene Talbot.
Atheneum, 1979. Orphaned Kevin comes from
Ireland in 1872 to find that his only relative is in jail.
Kevin is then placed in the home of a Nebraska
newspaper editor and becomes his assistant.

The Year of the Flying Machine, 1903 by Genevieve
Foster. Charles Scribner's Sons, 1977. Many
inventions were created from 1900 to 1909. Some
of these included the Wright brothers' airplane and
Henry Ford's Model T.

Children's Plays for Creative Actors by Claire Boiko.
Plays, 1981. Included within are thirty-five one-act
plays to be used for productions in the classroom
or assemblies.

Franklin D. Roosevelt, Gallant President by Barbara
Feinberg. Lothrop, Lee & Shepard, 1981. This
biography follows Franklin D. Roosevelt from his
childhood through his political career and his fight
with polio.

The Journey of the Shadow Bairns by Margaret J.
Anderson. Alfred A. Knopf, 1980. In the early 1900s
a young Scottish orphan and her brother take what
little money they have to start a new life in Canada.

A Matter of Pride by Emily Crofford. Carolrhoda
Books, 1981. Meg and her family live in Arkansas
where her father works on a cotton plantation.
When the cow runs away, Meg's mother goes after
it and shows a courageous side that Meg has never
seen before.

LITERARY TERMS

BIOGRAPHY   *A history of a person's life written by another person.*
A successful biography combines facts with an interesting story. Facts make a biography seem truthful and real. The facts about a person in a biography must be accurate. Historical details must be *authentic,* or genuine. Famous people are often the subjects of biographies. For example, Patrick Henry is the subject of Jean Fritz's biography *Where Was Patrick Henry on the 29th of May?*

CHARACTERS   *The people (or animals) in a story, poem, or play.*
Sometimes authors are concerned mainly with bringing their story characters to life. How the characters think, feel, act, and change are more important than the story's main action or plot. For example, in "Something for Davy," author Barbara Cohen gives us much information about Sam Greene. We learn what he thinks and feels, and how he acts. The story is *about Sam,* not just about a baseball game. Other stories, such as "Emergency in Space," by Robert A. Heinlein, are built around the plot.

CHARACTERIZATION   *The ways in which writers present and develop characters to make the characters seem real.* Here are several ways in which writers develop their characters:

1. *By describing how the character looks:* "He had a strange, but pleasant face with a short pointed beard and curly hair. . . ."

2. *By showing the character's words and actions and letting the character speak:* "'Ohhhhh,' I said, touching my lips to his warm head. 'You are a beautiful baby brother.'"

3. *By telling the character's thoughts and feelings:* "How could I yell and tell everyone what a fool I was to be falling that second into the bag which was for the wool?"

4. *By telling what others think of the character:* "The mean knights who were jealous of Sir Launcelot began to laugh. . . ."

5. *By stating something about the character:* "And he was young and strong, alone—and determined."

DIALOGUE   *Conversations between or among characters.* Dialogue is used in almost all forms of literature to move the **plot,** or main action, forward and to tell the reader something about the characters. In the story "Lucy's Adventure," author C. S. Lewis uses dialogue to introduce Lucy to Mr. Tumnus:

"My name's Lucy," said she, not quite understanding him.

"But you are—forgive me—you are what they call a girl?" asked the Faun.

"Of course I'm a girl," said Lucy.

In these few lines of dialogue, the reader knows that Mr. Tumnus has never met a girl before.

Dialogue is especially important in plays, where conversation is the main way to tell the story and to show each character's personality. In the play *The Great Quillow,* the villagers grumble about Quillow:

Town Crier: Where is Quillow?
   Where is that foolish little fellow?
Lamplighter: He was in his shop
   at midnight, making toys.
Villagers (*Together*): Toys!
Locksmith: He could have helped
   with the key.
Baker: The pie.
Butcher: The sheep.
Cobbler: The shoes.

Through this conversation, the reader learns that the villagers think Quillow is foolish and are angry he did not help them with their tasks.

FICTION *A story invented by the writer.* A work of fiction may be *based* on real events, but it always includes made-up (fictional) characters and experiences. A work of fiction may be brief, like a fable, a folk tale, or a short story, or it may be a book-length story called a **novel**.

FIGURATIVE LANGUAGE *Words used in unusual, rather than literal (exact) ways.* Whenever you feel "free as a bird" or think that a task is "a piece of cake," you are using figurative language.

The most common forms of figurative language in literature are **simile** and **metaphor**. A **simile** uses the words *like* or *as* to compare two very different things: "That cat is **as** stubborn **as** a mule" or "She runs **as** fast **as** the wind." A **metaphor** *suggests* a comparison by saying one thing *is* another: "This car **is** a lemon" or "Morning **is** a new sheet of paper for you to write on."

FOLK TALE *A fiction story made up long ago and handed down in written or spoken form.* Many folk tales have no known authors. Though folk tales come from different parts of the world, many characters, plots, and ideas in them are similar. *Fairy tales* such as the story "Cinderella" are a kind of folk tale.

METAPHOR *A way of comparing how two different things are alike.* A metaphor *suggests* a comparison by saying that one thing *is* another: "This car **is** a lemon" or "The sun **is** a bright, new penny." Writers use metaphors to help us picture things in new ways.

See also **Figurative Language.**

NONFICTION *A true (factual) story; any writing that describes things as they actually happened, or that presents information or opinions about something.* One type of nonfiction is the written history of a person's life. When a person writes his or her own life story, it is called an **autobiography**. When someone else writes a person's life story, it is called a **biography**. Other common forms of nonfiction include news reports, travel stories, personal journals and diaries, and articles on science or history.

PLAY   *A story that is acted out, usually on a stage, by actors.* In its written form, a play begins with a **cast of characters**, or a list of the people (or sometimes animals) in the play. A play has a **plot**, or action, just like a story. However, a play is meant to be acted out. The characters in a play tell the story through their words, or **dialogue**.

During a play, the actors follow **stage directions**, which tell them how to act and speak. Stage directions may also describe the **setting**, where the action takes place. Stage directions are usually not read aloud when a play is acted out.

See also **Dialogue**.

PLOT   *The action in a story.* When you tell *what happens* in a story, you are talking about the plot. For instance, in the story "The Megrimum" by Natalie Babbitt, the plot tells how a boy climbs a mountain to find a monster, then discovers the monster is only wind whistling through a cave.

The plot is also the writer's overall *plan* of the action—how, when, and why things happen. The writer uses this plan to arrange the action in an inter-esting and reasonable order. Each happening becomes a link in a chain of events that makes sense and holds the reader's attention.

The most important part of the plot is **conflict**, a character's struggle with opposing forces. Sometimes the conflict is from an outside force: a character struggles with nature (as in Scott O'Dell's story "Dangerous Voyage") or with another character (as in "A Hero's Promise"). At other times the conflict is *internal*: it is within the character's own mind (as in Bette Greene's "An Allergy Is a Bothersome Thing," where Beth learns to accept the fact that she cannot have a dog).

PUN   *A "play on words"—that is, a joke based on the different uses of a word or on words that sound alike but have different meanings.* Riddles often use puns made on two meanings of a word. The pun in the following riddle is based on two meanings of the word *chicken:*

Why did the rooster refuse to fight?

Because it was chicken.

Other puns are based on **homonyms**, words that sound the same or nearly the same. In the next riddle, the word *scenter* sounds like *center*.

Why is your nose in the middle of your face?

Because it's a scenter.

Puns can also be made when one word sounds like several words strung together.

Why should people never suffer from hunger in the Sahara desert?

Because of the sand which is there.

QUATRAIN *A four-line verse, usually rhymed.* Quatrains can have many different rhyming patterns. The usual patterns are *abab, abba,* or *abcb.* Quatrains can be funny or serious. One quatrain can make up a whole poem, or a poem can have several quatrains, all with different rhyming patterns, as in Ted Hughes's poem "My Aunt Dora."

SETTING *When and where a story takes place.* If you say, "Today at school Susan won a race," you've given the setting (when and where) before describing the action. Authors can choose any time or any place as a setting for a story. In the story "The Megrimum," author Natalie Babbitt gives us a clear picture of the setting as Egan is climbing Kneeknock Rise.

> Looking up, he saw the moon as a shapeless radiance, like a candle seen through steamy glass. Each drop of moisture in the mist had become a tiny prism, filtering and fanning the dim light into a million pale rainbows of softest color. From a shrouded tree-top nearby came the soft, clear notes of a bird's call . . . .

The writer does not always give us the setting so directly. Sometimes we figure it out as the story goes along. Most stories include several different types of information about where and when the story takes place. For instance, at the beginning of the story "Old Ben" by Jesse Stuart, the action is set on a July morning in a clover field. As the story continues, we see that the main characters live on a farm and that the events take place over a year's time.

When the setting is essential to understanding the characters and their conflicts, it is called an *integral* (or essential) setting. In Edward Eager's story "The Tournament," the setting is essential: without the characters going back in time to a tournament at Camelot, there would be no story.

SIMILE *A way of comparing how two different things are alike.* Writers use similes to surprise us or to make us look at our world in a new way. Similes are different from metaphors because they use the words *like* or *as.* "Over the mountains there were clouds looking **like** a flock of sheep grazing around up there," said Miguel in "The Worst Morning."

GLOSSARY

This glossary gives the meanings of unfamiliar words used in the text of this book. The meanings given here define words only the way they are used in the book. You can find other meanings for these words in a dictionary.

The correct pronunciation of each glossary word is given in the special spelling after that word. The sounds used in these spellings are explained in the following Pronunciation Key. Each symbol, or letter, stands for a sound, a sound you can recognize in the words following it. In addition to these sounds, each glossary pronunciation includes marks to show the kind of force, or stress, with which certain syllables are pronounced. A heavy mark, ′, shows that the syllable it follows is given the strongest, or primary, stress, as in **sis·ter** (sis′·ter). A lighter mark, ′, shows that the syllable it follows is given a secondary, or lighter, stress, as in **tax·i·cab** (tak′·sē·kab′).

Several abbreviations are used in the glossary: *v.,* verb; *adv.,* adverb; *n.,* noun; *adj.,* adjective; *pl.,* plural.

Pronunciation Key

a	add, map	m	move, seem	u	up, done
ā	ace, rate	n	nice, tin	û(r)	urn, term
â(r)	care, air	ng	ring, song	yōo	use, few
ä	palm, father	o	odd, hot	v	vain, eve
b	bat, rub	ō	open, so	w	win, away
ch	check, catch	ô	order, jaw	y	yet, yearn
d	dog, rod	oi	oil, boy	z	zest, muse
e	end, pet	ou	out, now	zh	vision, pleasure
ē	even, tree	ōō	pool, food	ə	the schwa,
f	fit, half	ŏŏ	took, full		an unstressed
g	go, log	p	pit, stop		vowel representing
h	hope, hate	r	run, poor		the sound spelled
i	it, give	s	see, pass		a in above
ī	ice, write	sh	sure, rush		e in sicken
j	joy, ledge	t	talk, sit		i in possible
k	cook, take	th	thin, both		o in melon
l	look, rule	th	this, bathe		u in circus

ac·com·plice (ə·kom′·plis) *n.* A helper or partner, especially in a wrongdoing.

al·ler·gy (al′·ər·jē) *n.* A disease marked by sensitivity to one or more substances.

am·bas·sa·dor (am·bas′·əd·ər) *n.* An important messenger.

am·ble (am′·bəl) *v.* To walk at a slow and easy pace.

an·ces·tor (an′·ses·ter) *n.* A person from whom one is descended, especially a person further back than a grandparent.

arch ri·val (ärch rī′·vəl) *n.* The main person with whom one competes.

at·ten·dant (ə·ten′·dənt) *adj.* Serving or attending.

at·tor·ney (ə·tûr′·nē) *n.* A lawyer.

au·burn (ô′·bûrn) *adj.* Reddish brown.

auc·tion (ôk′·shən) *n.* A public sale at which each item is sold to the person offering the highest price for it.

au·to·graph (ô′·tə·graf) [1]*v.* To write one's name on something.   [2]*n.* A person's name in his or her own handwriting.

ax·is (ak′·səs) *n.* The straight line around which an object turns.

ba·la·bus·ta (bal·ə·bus′·tə) *n.* An efficient or competent Jewish housewife.

bi·fo·cals (bī·fō′·kəlz) *n.* Eyeglasses having two kinds of lenses, one kind for seeing close objects, the other kind for seeing distant objects.

bil·low (bil′·ō) *n.* A large wave.

bis·cuit (bis′·kit) *n.* A small quick bread made from dough that is rolled and cut or dropped from a spoon into a pan.

bleach·ers (blē′·chərz) *n., pl.* A grandstand without a roof in a stadium or ball park.

blue·bot·tle (bloo′·bot·əl) *n.* A large fly with a metallic-blue body.

bond·age (bon′·dij) *n.* Slavery.

boon (boon) *n.* A blessing.

brine (brīn) *n.* Salty water.

broach (brōch) *v.* To break into or puncture.

cal·dron (kôl′·drən) *n.* A large kettle used for boiling.

cat·a·pult (kat′·ə·pult) *n.* An ancient device for throwing or shooting stones.

ce·leb·ri·ty (sə·leb′·rət·ē) *n.* A famous person.

cen·ten·ni·al (sen·ten′·ē·əl) *adj.* The celebration of a 100th anniversary.

cer·e·bral pal·sy (ser′·ə·brəl pöl′·zē) *n.* A type of brain damage that affects a person's ability to control movements.

chaf·ing (chāf′·ing) *v.* Rubbing.

chief·tain (chēf′·tən) *n.* The head of a group of people.

chiv·al·rous (shiv′·əl·rəs) *adj.* Having to do with the code of life of knights in the Middle Ages—the qualities of gallantry, courtesy, bravery, and kindness.

claim (klām) *n.* A tract of land staked out.

clar·i·on (klar′·ē·ən) *adj.* Clear and piercing.

cli·ent (klī′·ənt) *n.* A customer.

co·hort (kō′·hôrt) *n.* A companion or follower.

com·bat (kom′·bat) *n.* A fight between two people or groups, usually with weapons.

com·et (kom′·ət) *n.* A mass of frozen gases, water, and rock that orbits the sun and appears to have a long, fiery tail.

com·mut·er (ko·myoo′·tər) *n.* A person who travels a route regularly to get to work.

com·ply (kəm·plī′) *v.* To do as asked; to obey.

con·cer·to (kən·cher′·tō) *n.* A piece of classical music written for an orchestra and solo instruments. Most concertos have three parts, or *movements.*

con·spir·a·to·ri·al·ly (kən·spir′·ə·tôr′·ē·əl·lē) *adv.* Acting in a way that suggests a secret plan.

con·trive (kən·trīv′) *v.* To figure out; to design or invent.

cop·per·head (kop′·ər·hed′) *n.* A poisonous snake with a copper-colored head.

corn·crib (kôrn′·krib) *n.* A building for drying and storing corn.

court (kôrt) *v.* To seek the affections of for the purpose of marriage.

cow·er (kou′·ər) *v.* To crouch quivering in fear of something.

crit·i·cal (krit′·i·kəl) *adj.* Most important; being a turning point.

crum·pet (krum′·pit) *n.* A flat, unsweetened cake baked on a griddle.

cu·po·la (kyōō′·pə·lə) *n.* A small tower built on a roof, usually having a dome-shaped top.

cur·ric·u·lum (kə·rik′·yə·ləm) *n.* The courses or subjects taught in a school.

curt·sy (kûrt′·sē) *n.* A bow made by bending the knees with one foot forward, used by women and girls.

cut to (kut tōō) *v.* A television term meaning that the play moves from one scene to the next without interruption.

dagger (dag′·ər) *n.* A small weapon for stabbing.

dames' school (dāmz skōōl) *n.* A school in which reading and writing were taught by a woman in her own home.

dazed (dāzd) *adj.* Stunned or confused.

de·ci·phered (di·sī′·fərd) *v.* Figured out the meaning of.

deign (dān) *v.* To think fit; lower oneself.

del·i·ca·cy (del′·i·kə·sē) *n.* A choice food.

dep·o·si·tion (dep·ə·zish′·ən) *n.* A testimony given by witnesses under oath, especially a written testimony.

de·pot (dē′·pō) *n.* A train station.

de·pres·sion (di·presh′·ən) *n.* A time when money and jobs are scarce.

de·vi·ous (dē′·vē·əs) *adj.* Not direct or straight.

dig·gings (dig′·ings) *n.* The place where precious metals, such as gold, are mined or dug out.

dig·ni·fied (dig′·nə·fīd) *adj.* Showing formal, reserved manners or speech.

di·lem·ma (di·lem′·ə) *n.* A situation in which the choices are unpleasant.

dis·a·bled (dis·ā′·bəld) *adj.* Having lost certain abilities due to illness or injury.

dis·cred·it (dis·kred′·it) *v.* To disgrace; to bring dishonor to.

dis·em·bark (dis′·em·bärk′) *v.* To go ashore from a ship.

dis·re·spect (dis′·ri·spekt) *v.* To have a lack of respect or high regard for.

dis·taff (dis′·taf) *n.* A stick holding unspun flax or wool used in spinning.

do·sage (dō′·sij) *n.* An amount of medicine.

doubt·less (dout′·ləs) *adv.* Probably or without a doubt.

dredg·er (drej′·ər) *n.* A barge or ship with a machine that scoops earth from underwater to deepen a waterway.

droll (drōl) *adj.* Amusing in an odd or strange way.

dug·out (dug′·out) *n.* A shelter for a baseball team at the edge of the baseball field.

ec·cen·tric (ik·sen′·trik) *adj.* Not display-ing the usual accepted conduct.

em·bers (em′·bərz) *n., pl.* The glowing remains of a fire.

en·chan·tress (in·chan′·tris) *n.* A woman who practices magic; a sorceress.

en·core (än′·kôr) *n.* Pieces played after the regular performance in response to a demand for more.

en·twine (in·twīn′) *v.* To twist together or around.

e·rupt (i·rupt′) *v.* To explode or release material violently.

et·i·quette (et′·i·kət) *n.* A code of behav-ior to be observed in social life.

ex·am·ine (ig·zam′·ən) *v.* To test to deter-mine knowledge.

ex·ca·vate (eks′·kə·vāt) *v.* To dig out.

ex·panse (ik·spans′) *n.* Land spread out over a wide area.

ex·ploit (eks′·ploit) *n.* A heroic act or adventure.

ex·po·si·tion (eks′·pə·zish′·ən) *n.* A large display for the public.

fade-in (fād-in) *n.* A television term mean-ing to show gradually the next scene for the audience to see.

fan·fare (fan′·fâr) *n.* Music played on trumpets to attract attention.

fault (fôlt) *n.* A break in the earth.

fend·er (fen′·dər) *n.* A metal guard or frame set in front of a fireplace to keep in sparks or hot coals.

fi·an·cée (fē·än·sā′) *n.* A woman engaged to be married.

fiend (fēnd) *n.* A cruel or wicked person.

fi·es·ta (fē·es′·tə) *n.* A festival.

flail·ing (flāl′·ing) *adj.* Waving wildly.

fleece (flēs) *n.* The coat of wool covering a sheep or similar animal.

floun·der (floun′·dər) *v.* To move about clumsily or awkwardly.

flushed (flushd) *adj.* Turned red; blushed.

fly·wheel (flī′·hwēl′) *n.* A heavy wheel that helps maintain constant speed.

fol·ly (fol′·ē) *n.* Foolishness.

for·ma·tion (fôr·mā′·shən) *n.* Something that has taken a particular form.

for·ty ni·ner (fort′·ē nī′·nər) *n.* A person who went to California to look for gold during the Gold Rush.

foun·da·tion (foun·dā′·shən) *n.* The base or support of a building.

foy·er (foi′·ər) *n.* The entrance hallway of a house.

frail (frāl) *adj.* Having a slim or delicate build; lacking strength.

frig·ate (frig′·ət) *n.* A warship fitted with rectangular sails and 30 to 50 guns.

fund (fənd) *n.* A sum of money available for a certain purpose.

gal·lant (gal′·ənt) *adj.* Bold and coura-geous; brave.

gas·ket (gas′·kət) *n.* A piece of rubber, metal, or other material that is placed around a joint to prevent leakage.

gli·der (glīd′·ər) *n.* A small engineless aircraft, like an airplane, that flies sup-ported only by air currents.

grim·ly (grim′·lē) *adv.* Sternly.

guise (gīz) *n.* A false appearance; a costume.

hai·ku (hī′·kōō) *n.* A traditional form of Japanese poetry that has nature as its subject and that follows a strict pattern.

hand (hand) *n.* A worker doing general physical labor.

hand·i·capped (han′·di·kapd) *adj.* Having a physical problem that makes move-ment difficult.

hawk·er (hô′·kər) *n.* One who sells goods.

haz·ard (haz′·ərd) *n.* A danger.

head·land (hed′·lənd′) *n.* A point of high land sticking out into a body of water.

her·ring (her′·ing) *n.* A kind of fish.

hi·er·o·glyph·ics (hī′·rə·glif′·iks) *n.* A system of picture writing used by ancient Egyptians.

hilt (hilt) *n.* A handle of a sword or dagger.

hitch·hike (hich′·hīk′) *v.* To travel by getting free rides from passing automobiles or trucks.

hith·er (hith′·ər) *adv.* To this place; here.

home·com·ing (hōm′·kum·ing) *n.* A return to home, especially for a special occasion.

horn spoon (hôrn spo͞on) *n.* A scoop that was used to test gold washings.

i·de·al (ī·dē·əl) *n.* A goal; an idea of what would be perfect.

ig·no·rance (ig′·nə·rəns) *n.* The state of being without knowledge or uninformed.

im·mi·grant (im′·i·grənt) *n.* A person who moves from his or her original home to settle in another land.

im·plore (im·plôr′) *v.* To plead; to call or ask for sincerely.

im·pu·dence (im′·pyə·dəns) *n.* Boldness; disrespect.

in·cin·er·a·tor (in·sin′·ə·rā′·tər) *n.* A furnace for burning rubbish or waste.

in·cred·i·ble (in·kred′·ə·bəl) *adj.* Amazing; hard to believe.

in·fec·tious (in·fek′·shəs) *adj.* Likely to spread to other people; catching.

in·stru·ment (in′·strə·mənt) *n.* Something used to achieve a purpose.

in·su·la·tion (in·sə·lā′·shən) *n.* Material used to prevent heat or cold from entering.

in·ter·lock (in′·tər·lok′) *n.* A device designed to seal off a section.

in·ter·mis·sion (in′·tər·mish′·ən) *n.* The interval between parts of an entertainment.

in·trep·id (in·trep′·id) *adj.* Brave; fearless.

in·trigu·ing (in·trēg′·ing) *adj.* Causing one to be curious or interested.

joust·ing (jous′·ting) *n.* A formal combat between two knights armed with lances.

junk (jəngk) *n.* A Chinese sailing ship.

kay·ak (kī′·ak) *n.* An Eskimo canoe made of animal skins stretched over a wood frame with a hole in the center where the paddler sits.

kelp (kelp) *n.* Large brown seaweed.

ken·nel (ken′·əl) *n.* A place that raises or keeps dogs.

lab·y·rinth (lab′·ə·rinth′) *n.* A place built with confusing passages that turn suddenly or lead to dead ends.

lance (lans) *n.* A weapon with a sharp steel point mounted on a long handle carried by knights on horseback.

lar·der (lär′·dər) *n.* A pantry; a place where food is kept.

lass·ie (las′·ē) *n.* A young girl.

league (lēg) *n.* An old measure of distance. A league was usually equal to three miles on land or sea.

leg·end (lej′·ənd) *n.* A story, usually having some historical basis, telling a hero's exploits.

len·tils (len′·təlz) *n.* A type of edible seed.

lim·ber (lim′·bər) *v.* To cause to become nimble.

lime·stone (līm′·stōn) *n.* A rock formed by layers of fossil remains such as shells.

lin·tel (lin′·təl) *n.* The beam across the top of a door frame or window frame.

lo·cal (lō′·kəl) *adj.* Relating to nearby areas only.

locks (loks) *n.* Ringlets of hair.

long·boat (lông′·bōt) *n.* A large boat carried aboard a huge sailing ship.

make·shift (māk′·shift) *adj.* Serving as a temporary substitute.

mal·a·dy (mal′·ə·dē) *n.* A disease, sickness, or illness.

man·sard roof (man′·särd ro͞of) *n.* A roof with two slopes on all sides, the lower slope steeper than the upper one.

mas·sa·cre (mas′·i·kər) *v.* To kill helpless people.

maze (māz) *n.* A confusing system of paths that crisscross or lead down blind alleys.

meal·y mouth (mē′·lē mouth′) *adj.* An insincere person.

me·an·der (mē·an′·dər) *v.* To wander.

mem·o·rize (mem′·ə·rīz) *v.* To learn by heart; to commit to memory.

met·a·phor (met′·ə·fôr) *n.* A form of figurative language that suggests a comparison by saying one thing is another.

me·te·ors (mēt′·ē·ərz) *n.* Bits of rock traveling through space.

min·gle (ming′·gəl) *v.* To mix together.

mi·rage (mə·räzh′) *n.* Optical illusions often seen in deserts, caused by the bending of light rays.

mire (mīər) *n.* Heavy, deep mud or slush.

mirth (mûrth) *n.* Great merriment, usually expressed by laughter.

mo·men·tum (mō·men′·tum) *n.* Force or strength that keeps growing.

mon·u·ment (mon′·yə·ment) *n.* A building or an object erected in memory of someone or something.

mu·si·col·o·gist (myo͞o′·zi·kol′·ə·jəst) *n.* A person who studies the history and science of music.

myr·tle (mərt′·əl) *n.* An evergreen bush or tree with shiny leaves, white or rosy flowers, and black berries.

nug·get (nug′·it) *n.* A lump of anything, especially gold.

ob·sta·cles (ob′·stə·kəlz) *n.* Things that get in the way of achieving a goal.

o·dom·e·ter (ō·dom′·ə·tər) *n.* A device that measures how far a vehicle travels.

o·men (ō′·mən) *n.* A sign that something is going to happen.

om·ni·bus (om′·ni·bəs) *n.* A bus.

op·er·at·ic (op·ə·rat′·ik) *adj.* Of or like a musical play called an *opera*.

op·por·tu·ni·ty (op·ər·to͞o′·nə·tē) *n.* A right time or occasion.

op·po·si·tion (op′·ə·zish′·ən) *n.* Feelings or actions against something.

op·ti·cal il·lu·sion (op′·ti·kəl i·lo͞o′·zhən) *n.* A false or distorted impression of a sight.

op·tic nerve (op′·tik nerv) *n.* The nerve that carries messages from the eye to the brain.

or·a·tor (ôr′·ə·tər) *n.* A person who is skilled in delivering public speeches.

pass (pas) *n.* A moving of an object over or along something; a wave.

par·a·lyzed (par′·ə·līzd) *adj.* Unable to move all or part of one's body.

pa·te·rol·ler, usually **patroller** (pə·trō′·lər) *n.* During Harriet Tubman's time, patrollers were armed men who hunted runaway slaves, often using bloodhounds.

ped·i·gree (ped′·ə·grē) *n.* The recorded purity of an animal's ancestors or breed.

pen·non (pen′·ən) *n.* A small flag ending in a point carried by a knight on a lance.

per·son·i·fi·ca·tion (pər·son′·ə·fə·kā′·shən) *n.* Giving nonliving things the attributes of living things.

phar·aoh (fâr′·ō) *n.* Any one of the kings of ancient Egypt.

phar·ma·cy (fär′·mə·sē) *n.* A drugstore.

Phil·har·mon·ic (fil′·här·mon′·ik) *n.* A symphony orchestra.

pine (pīn) *v.* To lose strength and health through grief.

plun·der (plun′·dər) *v.* To take by force.

pov·er·ty (pov′·ər·tē) *n.* The state of being poor.

preen (prēn) *v.* To smooth or clean (feathers) with a beak.

pre·vail·ing (pri·vā′·ling) *adj.* Frequent; common over a wide area.

pre·vi·ous (prē′·vē·əs) *adj.* Going before in time.

pri·va·cy (prī′·və·sē) *n.* The state of being alone and unobserved.

prom·i·nent (prom′·ə·nənt) *adj.* Well-known; distinguished.

pro·vi·sion (prə·vizh′·ən) *n.* The act of providing something.

prow (prou) *n.* The forward part of a ship; the bow.

quartz (kwôrts) *n.* A crystal mineral.

quatre·foil (ka′·trə·foil) *n.* A design of a flower with four petals.

quest (kwest) *n.* An expedition, as by a knight seeking adventure.

ram·rod (ram′·rod) *adj.* Stiff; severe; strong.

rec·om·men·da·tion (rek′·ə·men·dā′·shən) *n.* A favorable statement concerning someone's character or qualifications.

reg·u·la·tion (reg·yə·lā′·shən) *n.* Made according to certain requirements or rules.

rel·a·tive (rel′·ə·tiv) *adj.* Pertaining to the theory of relativity.

re·mote (ri·mōt′) *adj.* Distant; far away.

re·peal (ri·pēl′) *v.* Officially withdrawn or cancelled.

rep·tile (rep′·təl) *n.* A cold-blooded animal with lungs, a backbone, and a body covered with scales.

res·i·due (rez′·ə·doo) *n.* What is left after part is taken away; remainder.

res·o·lu·tion (rez′·ə·loo′·shən) *n.* A formal statement of opinion adopted by a governing body.

re·tri·al (rē·trī′·əl) *n.* A second trial.

ri·val (rī′·vəl) *n.* A person who is equal to another in certain ways.

row (rouw) *n.* A noisy quarrel.

rus·set (rus′·it) *n.* Reddish brown.

sanc·tu·ary (sangk′·chə·wer′·ē) *n.* A place of refuge and protection.

sand·spit (sand′·spit) *n.* A finger of sandy land that juts into the ocean.

sci·at·i·ca (sī·at′·i·kə) *n.* Pain along a certain large nerve located at the back of the thigh.

scorched (skôrcht) *adj.* Burned slightly on the surface.

scribe (scrīb) *n.* A person who copies manuscripts; an official writer.

scruff (skruf) *n.* The back of the neck.

seam·stress (sēm′·strəs) *n.* A woman whose occupation is sewing.

seem·ly (sēm′·lē) *adj.* Decent or proper; suitable.

shak·er (shāk′·ər) *n.* A person who holds a steel spike in place while the steel driver hammers it.

shan·ty (shan′·tē) *n.* A small rough building, usually of wood.

shear·ing (shir′·ing) *v.* Cutting the wool from sheep, usually with electric clippers.

shell (shel) *v.* To remove kernels from corn cobs.

shel·lack (shə·lak′) *v.* To coat a surface so that it is smooth.

shorn (shôrn) *v.* Cut.

side·wheel·er (sīd′·hwēl′·ər) *n.* A steamboat with its paddle wheel on the side.

sig·net ring (sig′·nət ring) *n.* A finger ring adorned with a seal for stamping important papers or documents.

skirt (skərt) *v.* To run along the edge of.

slough (slōō) *n.* A marshy place of deep mud; swamp.

slump (slump) *n.* A period when a baseball player is not hitting or playing as well as usual.

smote (smōt) *v.* To hit very hard.

sneer (snēr) *v.* To show contempt or dislike for in speech or facial expression.

sol·emn (sol′·əm) *adj.* Very serious; earnest.

so·pra·no (sə·pran′·ō) *n.* A singer with a high-pitched voice.

sor·cer·ess (sôr′·sər·is) *n.* A woman who practices magic, especially with the assistance or control of evil spirits.

spe·cial·ist (spesh′·ə·ləst) *n.* A person who is an expert in a particular job.

spec·ta·cles (spek′·tə·kəls) *n.* Eyeglasses.

spec·ta·tor (spek′·tā·tər) *n.* A person who watches an event.

spell (spel) *n.* A word or words that, when spoken, are believed to have magic power.

spell·bind·ing (spel′·bīnd·ing) *adj.* Holding one's attention as if casting a spell.

spin·dle (spin′·dəl) *n.* A stick or rod used in spinning for winding thread.

stat·ic (stat′·ik) *n.* A cracking noise that interrupts sounds heard on the radio.

staves (stāvz) *n., pl.* Narrow strips of wood that form sides of a barrel.

stile (stīl) *n.* Steps for climbing over a fence or wall.

stow·a·way (stō′·ə·wā′) *n.* A person who hides aboard a ship or other form of transportation to obtain free passage.

strains (strānz) *n., pl.* Musical sounds.

sub·lime (sə·blīm′) *adj.* Noble, supreme.

sub·scrip·tion (səb·skrip′·shən) *n.* An arrangement to pay ahead of time to receive or use something on a regular basis.

sub·way (sub′·wā) *n.* An underground railroad.

suf·fo·cate (suf′·ə·kāt) *v.* To kill from lack of air.

sus·pend (sə·spend′) *v.* Stop or put off until a later time.

sym·bol (sim′·bəl) *n.* Something that stands for something else.

sym·phon·ic (sim·fän′·ik) *adj.* Having a similarity to classical music as played by an orchestra.

symp·tom (sim′·təm) *n.* A sign or indication of something, especially of a disease.

tar·pau·lin (tär′·pə·lin) *n.* Waterproofed material used to protect objects.

tax·a·tion (tak·sā′·shən) *n.* Collection of money or goods by a government.

ter·ri·er (ter′·ē·ər) *n.* A small, active dog once used for hunting animals underground.

ther·a·pist (ther′·ə·pəst) *n.* A person trained in ways to apply treatments in cures of diseases.

throng (thrông) *n.* A crowd of people.

tim·id (tim′·id) *adj.* Afraid; shy.

tit·ter (tit′·ər) *v.* To laugh as if making fun; to snicker.

tour·na·ment (toor′·nə·ment) *n.* A contest in which knights on horseback tried to unseat one another with lances.

trans·con·ti·nen·tal (trans′·kon′·tə·nen′·təl) *adj.* Across a continent.

trans·fixed (trans·fikst′) *adj.* Motionless, as with horror, fear, or admiration.

trans·por·ta·tion (trans′·pər·tā′·shən) *n.* A means of moving something from one place to another.

treach·er·ous (trech′·ər·əs) *adj.* Not as good or safe as it appears; dangerous.

trea·son (trēz′·ən) *n.* The offense of being disloyal to the government of one's country.

trem·or (trem′·ər) *n.* 1. A quick shaking movement. 2. A nervous or trembling feeling of excitement.

trice (trīs) *n.* A short time.

troll (trōl) *n.* In Scandinavian folklore, a troublesome dwarf or giant who lives in caves or under bridges.

trous·seau (trōō′·sō) *n.* A bride's personal possessions such as clothes, household linens, and kitchenware.

truce (trōōs) *n.* A temporary relief or rest.

tu·ber (tōō′·bər) *n.* A short fleshy stem.

tu·nic (tōō·nik) *n.* A loose, sleeveless garment worn by the ancient Greeks and Romans.

tu·tor (tōō′·tər) 1. *n.* A person who teaches another, usually privately. 2. *v.* To give or receive private instruction.

un·chart·ed (un·chär′·tid) *adj.* Having no maps or written plan.

un·furl (un·fûrl′) *v.* To open or unroll.

vac·u·um (vak′·yōōm) *n.* An empty space where no air or matter exists.

val·iant (val′·yənt) *adj.* Brave; courageous.

val·or (val′·ər) *n.* Great courage or bravery.

ven·i·son (ven′·ə·sən) *n.* The flesh of the deer, used for food.

ve·ran·da (və·ran′·də) *n.* A roofed porch on a house.

verge (vûrj) *n.* 1. The edge of something. 2. The point at which some action or condition is likely to occur.

ve·to (vē′·tō) *v.* To use authority to forbid.

vin·dic·tive (vin·dik′·tiv) *adj.* Revengeful; unforgiving.

vi·per (vī′·pər) *n.* Any of a family of various poisonous snakes.

vi·tal (vīt′·əl) *adj.* 1. Necessary or essential to life. 2. Important.

ward·robe (wôr′·drōb) *n.* A closet or piece of furniture in which clothes are hung.

weld (weld) *v.* To join two metals by heating them and allowing them to flow together.

wharf (hwôrf) *n.* A structure built along or out from a shore at which boats may tie up and load or unload; a pier.

whim (hwim) *n.* A sudden desire, notion, or idea; an impulse.

wire·less (wīər′·ləs) *n.* A British term for radio.

wretch·ed (rech′·id) *adj.* Very unhappy; miserable.

Yid·dish (yid′·ish) *n.* A language formerly spoken by many eastern European Jews.

Words and Word Parts: PREFIXES

A **prefix** is a word part added to the beginning of a root word. A prefix changes the meaning of a root.

prefix + root = new word
in + hale = **in**hale
ex + hale = **ex**hale

Some roots are words by themselves: **approve, lock, nation.** Other roots must be attached to other word parts: in + **spect** = inspect.

Below are some prefixes that are commonly added to roots. Look at the meaning of each and see how it changes the meaning of the roots.

ex-   **inter-**

ex means "out" **ex** + claim = **ex**claim **ex**claim means "to shout out"	**inter** means "between or among" **inter** + national = **inter**national **inter**national means "involving more than one nation or among nations"

Words from the Selections

excited p. 51	intermission p. 136	interplanetary p. 254
interrupted p. 114	explain p. 145	expression p. 277

con-   **com-**

con means "together or with" **con** + nect = **con**nect **con**nect means "to join together"	**com** means "together or with" **com** + bine = **com**bine **com**bine means "to put or mix together"

Words from the Selections

contain p. 61	continued p. 449	companion p. 145
confined p. 428	complete p. 100	compared p. 319

in-, im-

in or **im** often means "not" **im** + possible = **im**possible **im**possible means "not possible"	**in** or **im** also means "in or into" **in** + spect = **in**spect **in**spect means "to look into"

Words from the Selections

insecurely p. 64	incredible p. 16	including p. 299
impatient p. 140	infectious p. 115	intricate p. 77

Which roots in the examples above are words that can stand alone?

Words and Word Parts: SUFFIXES

A **suffix** is a word part added to the end of a root. A **suffix** changes the meaning of a root.

$$\text{root} + \textbf{suffix} = \text{new word}$$
$$\text{fool} + \textbf{ish} = \text{foolish}$$

Below are some suffixes that are commonly added to words. Look at the meaning of each suffix and see how it changes the meaning of the root. Also notice that sometimes adding a suffix changes the spelling of a root.

-y

-ic
-y means "characterized by or inclined to" curl + **y** = curly curly means "tending to curl or inclined to curl"	-ic also means "characterized by or the nature of" angel + **ic** = angelic angelic means "having the nature of an angel"

Words from the Selections

trusty p. 26
symphonic p. 130

allergic p. 214
stormy p. 299

gloomy p. 358
weary p. 358

-ous

-al
-ous means "possessing the quality of" monster + **ous** = monstrous monstrous means "having the qualities of a monster"	-al means "relating to" magic + **al** = magical magical means "relating to magic"

Words from the Selections

mysterious p. 67
infectious p. 115
glorious p. 130

musical p. 131
traditional p. 277
luminous p. 304

practical p. 312
occasional p. 406

When a suffix beginning with a vowel is added to a word that ends in *y*, the *y* is changed to *i* and the suffix is added.

Which words in the examples above change the *y* to *i* before adding a suffix?